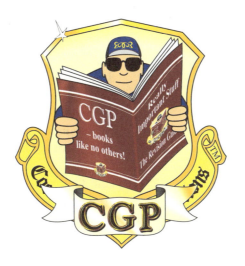

It's another Quality Book from CGP

This book is for anyone doing Edexcel Modular GCSE Mathematics
at Higher Level.

Whatever subject you're doing it's the same
old story — there are lots of facts and you've just got
to learn them. KS4 Maths is no different.

Happily this CGP book gives you all that important
information as clearly and concisely as possible.

It's also got some daft bits in to try and make the whole
experience at least vaguely entertaining for you.

What CGP is all about

Our sole aim here at CGP is to produce the highest quality books
— carefully written, immaculately presented and dangerously
close to being funny.

Then we work our socks off to get them out to you
— at the cheapest possible prices.

Contents

Published by Coordination Group Publications Ltd.
Written by Richard Parsons
Updated by: Alison Chisholm, Phillipa Falshaw, Sharon Keeley, Simon Little, Sam Norman,
Alison Palin, Claire Thompson, Mark Turner, Sharon Watson

ISBN 1 84146 093 1
Groovy website: www.cgpbooks.co.uk
With thanks to Frances Knight, Glenn Rogers and Sam Norman for the proofreading.
Printed by Elanders Hindson, Newcastle upon Tyne.
Text, design, layout and original illustrations © Richard Parsons

Squares, Cubes, Roots and Negative Numbers

1) SQUARE NUMBERS:

They're called SQUARE NUMBERS because they're like the areas of this pattern of squares:

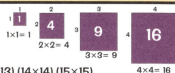

$1 \times 1 = 1$
$2 \times 2 = 4$
$3 \times 3 = 9$
$4 \times 4 = 16$

(1×1) (2×2) (3×3) (4×4) (5×5) (6×6) (7×7) (8×8) (9×9) (10×10) (11×11) (12×12) (13×13) (14×14) (15×15)

| 1 | 4 | 9 | 16 | 25 | 36 | 49 | 64 | 81 | 100 | 121 | 144 | 169 | 196 | 225... |

3 5 7 9 11 13 15 17 19 21 23 25 27 29

Note that the DIFFERENCES between the square numbers are all the ODD numbers.

2) CUBE NUMBERS:

They're called CUBE NUMBERS because they're like the volumes of this pattern of cubes.

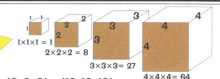

$1 \times 1 \times 1 = 1$
$2 \times 2 \times 2 = 8$
$3 \times 3 \times 3 = 27$
$4 \times 4 \times 4 = 64$

(1x1x1) (2x2x2) (3x3x3) (4x4x4) (5x5x5) (6x6x6) (7x7x7) (8x8x8) (9x9x9) (10x10x10)...

| 1 | 8 | 27 | 64 | 125 | 216 | 343 | 512 | 729 | 1000... |

3) SQUARE ROOTS:

"Squared" means "times by itself" : $P^2 = P \times P$
— SQUARE ROOT is the reverse process.

> **"Square Root" means**
> **"What Number Times by Itself gives...?"**

Example: *"Find the square root of 49"* (i.e. "Find $\sqrt{49}$" or "Find $49^{\frac{1}{2}}$")
To do this you should say it as: *"What number TIMES BY ITSELF gives... 49?"*
Now, if you just look at the square numbers in section 1 above, you can instantly see that the answer is 7.

> On your calculator, *it's easy to find any positive square root*
> using the SQUARE ROOT BUTTON: Press $\sqrt{}$ 49 = = 7

Square Roots can be Positive or Negative

If you multiply a negative number by itself, you get a positive one (see section 4 below):

$(-2)^2 = (-2) \times (-2) = 4$ But $2^2 = 4$ as well. (What's going on...)

It's actually quite simple: $\sqrt{4} = +2$ or -2

... and that goes for all square roots —
whenever you get a positive square root, you also get a negative one.

4) NEGATIVE NUMBERS:

Negative numbers crop up everywhere, so you
need to learn this rule for how to deal with them.

+	+	makes	+
+	−	makes	−
−	+	makes	−
−	−	makes	+

1) Multiplying or dividing: e.g. $-2 \times 3 = \underline{-6}$, $-8 \div -2 = \underline{+4}$ $-4p \times -2 = \underline{+8p}$

2) Two signs are together: e.g. $5 - -4 = 5 + 4 = \underline{9}$ $4 + -6 - -7 = 4 - 6 + 7 = \underline{5}$

The Acid Test:

LEARN the sequences of squares and cubes, and the rule for negative numbers. Then turn the page and write it all down.

1) From this list of numbers: 8, 81, 27, 25, 125, 36, 1, 64, 1000, 225
   write down a) all the square numbers   b) all the cube numbers

2) Calculate the following: a) $\sqrt{200}$ b) If $4 \times r^2 = 36$, find r   c) $120 \div -40$

Prime Numbers

1) Basically, _PRIME_ Numbers _don't divide_ by anything

And that's the <u>best way to think of them</u>.   (Strictly, they divide by themselves and 1)

So <u>Prime Numbers</u> are all the numbers that <u>DON'T come up in Times Tables</u>:

2   3   5   7   11   13   17   19   23   29   31   37   ...

As you can see, they're an <u>awkward-looking bunch</u> (that's because they don't divide by anything!).   For example:

> <u>The only numbers</u> that multiply to give 7 are   1 × 7
> <u>The only numbers</u> that multiply to give 31 are   1 × 31

In fact the <u>only way</u> to get <u>ANY PRIME NUMBER</u> is   1 × ITSELF

2) _They_ _All End_ in _1, 3, 7_ or _9_

1) <u>1 is NOT a prime number</u>

2) The first four prime numbers are <u>2, 3, 5 and 7</u>

3) <u>2 and 5 are the EXCEPTIONS</u> because <u>all the rest</u> end in 1, 3, 7 or 9

4) But <u>NOT ALL</u> numbers ending in 1, 3, 7 or 9 are primes, as shown here:
(Only the <u>circled ones</u> are <u>primes</u>)

```
 2    3    5    7
11   13   17   19
21   23   27   29
31   33   37   39
41   43   47   49
51   53   57   59
61   63   67   69
```

3) _How to Find_ Prime Numbers — _a very simple method_

For a chosen number to be a <u>prime</u>:

1) It must <u>end</u> in either <u>1, 3, 7 or 9</u>.

2) It <u>WON'T DIVIDE</u> by any of the <u>primes</u> below the value of its own <u>square root</u>.

If something like this comes up on the non-calculator paper, you'll have to start by estimating the square root — see P. 7.

Example   "Decide whether or not 233 is a prime number."

1) Does it end in either <u>1, 3, 7 or 9</u>?   **Yes**

2) Find its <u>square root</u>: $\sqrt{233} = 15.264...$

3) List <u>all primes (apart from 2 and 5)</u> which are <u>less</u> than this square root: **3, 7, 11 and 13**

4) <u>Divide</u> all of these primes into the number under test:

233 ÷ 3 = 77.6667   233 ÷ 7 = 33.2857

233 ÷ 11 = 21.181818   233 ÷ 13 = 17.923077

5) Since <u>none</u> of these divide <u>cleanly</u> into 233 then it <u>IS</u> a <u>prime number</u>.   Easy Peasy.

The Acid Test: <u>LEARN the main points in ALL 3 SECTIONS above.</u>

Now <u>cover the page and write down</u> everything you've just learned.

1) Write down the first 15 prime numbers (*without* looking them up).

2) Find all the prime numbers between a) 100 and 110   b) 200 and 210   c) 500 and 510

Multiples, Factors and Prime Factors

Multiples

The **MULTIPLES** of a number are simply its **TIMES TABLE**:

E.g. the multiples of 13 are   13   26   39   52   65   78   91   104 ...

Factors

The **FACTORS** of a number are all the numbers that **DIVIDE INTO IT EXACTLY**. There is a special way to find them:

Example 1:   "Find ALL the factors of 24"

Start off with 1 x the number itself, then try 2 x, then 3 x and so on, listing the pairs in rows like this. Try each one in turn and put a dash if it doesn't divide exactly. Eventually, when you get a number *repeated*, you *stop*.

> So the **FACTORS OF 24** are 1,2,3,4,6,8,12,24

$$1 \times 24$$
$$2 \times 12$$
$$3 \times 8$$
$$4 \times 6$$
$$5 \times -$$
$$6 \times 4$$

Increasing by 1 each time

This method guarantees you find them **ALL**. And don't forget 1 and 24!

Example 2:   "Find the factors of 64"

$$1 \times 64$$
$$2 \times 32$$
$$3 \times -$$
$$4 \times 16$$
$$5 \times -$$
$$6 \times -$$
$$7 \times -$$
$$8 \times 8$$

Check each one in turn, to see if it divides or not. Use your calculator if you are not totally confident.

> So the **FACTORS of 64** are 1,2,4,8,16,32,64

The 8 has *repeated* so *stop here*.

Finding Prime Factors — The Factor Tree

Any number can be broken down into *a string of PRIME NUMBERS all multiplied together* – this is called *"Expressing it as a product of prime factors"*, and to be honest it's pretty tedious – but it's in the Exam, *and it's not difficult so long as you know what it is.*

   The mildly entertaining *"Factor Tree" method* is best, where you start at the top and split your number off into factors as shown. Each time you get a prime you ring it and you finally end up with all the prime factors, which you can then arrange in order.

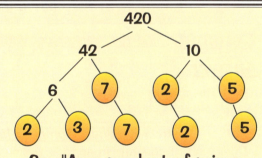

So, "As a product of prime factors", 420 = 2x2x3x5x7 or $2^2 \times 3 \times 5 \times 7$

The Acid Test:

LEARN what Multiples, Factors and Prime Factors are, AND HOW TO FIND THEM. Turn over and write it down.

Then try these *without the notes*:
1) List the first 10 multiples of 7 and of 9.
2) List *all* the factors of 36 and 84.
3) Express as a product of prime factors: a) 990   b) 160.

LCM and HCF

Two big fancy names, but don't be put off — they're both _really easy_.

LCM — _"Least Common Multiple"_

"Least Common Multiple" — sure, it sounds kind of complicated but _all it means is this_:

> The _SMALLEST_ number that will _DIVIDE BY_ _ALL_ the numbers in question.

Method
1) _LIST_ the _MULTIPLES_ of _ALL_ the numbers.
2) Find the _SMALLEST_ one that's in _ALL the lists_.
3) Easy peasy, innit.

Example _Find the least common multiple (LCM) of 6 and 9_

Answer Multiples of 6 are: 6, 12, 18, 24, 30, 36, 42, 48, 54, 60, 66, ...
Multiples of 9 are: 9, 18, 27, 36, 45, 54, 63, 72, 81, 90, 99, ...

So the _least common multiple_ (LCM) of 6 and 9 is _18_.
Told you it was easy.

HCF — _"Highest Common Factor"_

"Highest Common Factor" — all it means is _this_:

> The _BIGGEST_ number that will _DIVIDE INTO_ _ALL_ the numbers in question.

Method
1) _LIST_ the _FACTORS_ of _ALL_ the numbers.
2) Find the _BIGGEST_ one that's in _ALL the lists_.
3) Easy peasy innit.

Example _Find the highest common factor (HCF) of 36, 54 and 72_

Answer Factors of 36 are: 1, 2, 3, 4, 6, 9, 12, 18, 36
Factors of 54 are: 1, 2, 3, 6, 9, 18, 27, 54
Factors of 72 are: 1, 2, 3, 4, 6, 8, 9, 12, 18, 24, 36, 72

So the _highest common factor_ (HCF) of 36, 54 and 72 is _18_.
Told you it was easy.

Just _take care_ listing the factors — make sure you use the _proper method_ (as shown on the previous page) or you'll miss one and blow the whole thing out of the water.

The Acid Test:
LEARN what LCM and HCF are, AND HOW TO FIND THEM. _Turn over and write it all down._

1) List the first 10 multiples of 8, and the first 10 multiples of 9. What's their LCM?
2) List _all_ the factors of 56 and _all_ the factors of 104. What's their HCF?
3) What's the Least Common Multiple of 7 and 9?
4) What's the Highest Common Factor of 36 and 84?

Rounding Off

There are *two different ways* of specifying *where* a number should be *rounded off*.
They are: "Decimal Places" and "Significant Figures". Doing "Decimal Places" is easier.

The question might say "... to 5 DECIMAL PLACES", or "... to 4 SIGNIFICANT FIGURES".
Don't worry — these are just different ways of *setting the position* of the *LAST DIGIT*.
Whichever way is used, the *basic method* is *always the same*, and is *shown below*:

The Basic Method has Three Steps

1) Identify the position of the LAST DIGIT.

2) Then look at the next digit to the RIGHT – called the DECIDER.

3) If the DECIDER is 5 or more, then ROUND UP the LAST DIGIT.
If the DECIDER is 4 or less, then leave the LAST DIGIT as it is.

EXAMPLE: *"What is 7.45839 to 2 Decimal Places?"*

7.45839   = 7.46

LAST DIGIT to be written
(2nd decimal place because
we're rounding to 2 d.p.)   DECIDER

The *LAST DIGIT* rounds *UP* because the *DECIDER* is 5 or more

Decimal Places   (d.p.)

This is pretty easy:
1) To round off to, say, 4 decimal places, the *LAST DIGIT* will be the *4th one after the decimal point*.
2) There must be *no more digits* after the LAST DIGIT (not even zeros).

DECIMAL PLACES EXAMPLES

Original number: 45.319461

Rounded to 5 decimal places (5 d.p.) 45.31946   (DECIDER was 1, so don't round up)
Rounded to 4 decimal places (4 d.p.) 45.3195   (DECIDER was 6, so do round up)
Rounded to 3 decimal places (3 d.p.) 45.319   (DECIDER was 4, so don't round up)
Rounded to 2 decimal places (2 d.p.) 45.32   (DECIDER was 9, so do round up)

The Acid Test: LEARN the 3 Steps of the Basic Method and the 2 Extra Points for Decimal Places.

Now turn over and write down what you've learned. Then try again till you know it.
1) Round 3.5743 to 2 decimal places
2) Give 0.0481 to 2 decimal places
3) Express 12.9096 to 3 d.p.
4) Express 3546.054 to 1 d.p.

Rounding Off

Significant Figures (sig. fig.)

The method for sig. fig. is _identical_ to that for DP except that finding the _position_ of the LAST DIGIT is more difficult — it wouldn't be so bad, but for the ZEROS ...

> **1) The 1st significant figure of any number is simply THE FIRST DIGIT WHICH ISN'T A ZERO.**

> **2) The 2nd, 3rd, 4th, etc. significant figures follow on immediately after the 1st, REGARDLESS OF WHETHER THEY'RE ZEROS OR NOT ZEROS.**

e.g **0.002309**   **2.03070**

SIG FIGS: 1st 2nd 3rd 4th   1st 2nd 3rd 4th

(If we're rounding to, say, 3 sig. fig. then the LAST DIGIT is simply the 3rd sig. fig.)

> **3) After _Rounding Off_ the LAST DIGIT, end ZEROS must be filled in up to, BUT NOT BEYOND, the decimal point.**

No _extra zeros_ must ever be put in _after_ the decimal point.

Examples	to 4 s.f.	to 3 s.f.	to 2 s.f.	to 1 s.f.
1) 54.7651	54.77	54.8	55	50
2) 17.0067	17.01	17.0	17	20
3) 0.0045902	0.004590	0.00459	0.0046	0.005
4) 30895.4	30900	30900	31000	30000

POSSIBLE ERROR OF HALF A UNIT WHEN ROUNDING

> Whenever a measurement is _rounded off_ to a _given UNIT_ the _actual measurement_ can be anything up to HALF A UNIT bigger or smaller.

Examples:

1) A room is given as being _"9m long to the nearest METRE"_ — its actual length could be anything from _8.5m to just under 9.5m_ — i.e. HALF A METRE either side of 9m.

2) If it was given as _"9.4m, to the nearest 0.2m"_, then it could be anything from _9.3m to almost 9.5m_ — i.e. _0.1m either side_ of 9.4m.

3) _"A school has 460 pupils to 2 sig. fig."_ (i.e. to the nearest 10) — the actual figure could be anything _from 455 to 464_. — (Why isn't it 465?)

The Acid Test:
LEARN the whole of this page, then turn over and write down everything you've learned. It's all good clean fun.

1) Round these to 2 d.p.:   a) 3.408   b) 1.051   c) 0.068   d) 3.596
2) Round these to 3 s.f., and for each one say which of the 3 rules about ZEROS applies: a) 567.78   b) 23445   c) 0.04563   d) 0.90876
3) A car is described as 17 feet long to the nearest foot. What is the longest and shortest it could be, in feet and inches? (e.g. 14 feet 4 inches)

Also in stage 2:

Accuracy and Estimating

Appropriate *Accuracy*

To decide what is appropriate accuracy, you need only remember these three rules:

1) For fairly <u>casual measurements</u>, <u>2 SIGNIFICANT FIGURES</u> is most appropriate.

<u>EXAMPLES</u>: Cooking – 250g (2 sig. fig.) of sugar, not 253g (3 s.f.), or 300g (1 s.f.)

Distance of a journey – 450 miles or 25 miles or 3500 miles (All 2 s.f.)

Area of a garden or floor — 330m² or 15m²

2) For <u>more important or technical things</u>, <u>3 SIGNIFICANT FIGURES</u> is essential.

<u>EXAMPLES</u>: <u>A technical figure</u> like <u>34.2</u> miles per gallon, rather than 34 mpg.

A length that will be <u>cut to fit</u>, e.g. measure a shelf <u>25.6cm</u> long, not just 26cm.

Any <u>accurate</u> measurement with a ruler: <u>67.5cm</u>, not 70cm or 67.54cm

3) Only for <u>really scientific work</u> would you have <u>more than 3 SIG. FIG.</u>

Also in stage 2:

Estimating

This is <u>VERY EASY</u>, so long as you don't <u>over-complicate it</u>.

1) ROUND EVERYTHING OFF to nice easy CONVENIENT NUMBERS
2) Then WORK OUT THE ANSWER using these nice easy numbers — that's it!

In the Exam you'll need to <u>show all the steps</u>, to prove you didn't just use a calculator.

<u>EXAMPLE</u>:   Estimate the value of $\dfrac{127.8 + 41.9}{56.5 \times 3.2}$, showing all your working.

Ans: $\dfrac{127.8 + 41.9}{56.5 \times 3.2} \approx \dfrac{130 + 40}{60 \times 3} \approx \dfrac{170}{180} \approx 1$ (" $\approx$ " means "<u>roughly equal to</u>")

Estimating *Areas* and *Volumes*

1) Draw or imagine a <u>RECTANGLE OR CUBOID</u> of similar size to the object in question
2) <u>Round off all lengths</u> to the <u>NEAREST WHOLE</u>, and work it out — easy.

<u>EXAMPLES</u>:   *"<u>Estimate</u> the <u>area of this shape</u> and the <u>volume of the bottle</u>:"*

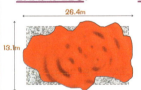

Area ≈ rectangle
26m x 13m = <u>338m²</u>
(or without a calculator:
         30 x 10 = 300m²)

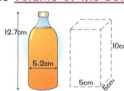

Volume ≈ cuboid
=5 x 5 x 10
=<u>250cm³</u>

Estimating *Square Roots*

Looks horrible — but it's OK if you know your square numbers (P.1).

1) Find the TWO SQUARE NUMBERS EITHER SIDE of the number in question.
2) Find the SQUARE ROOTS and pick a SENSIBLE NUMBER IN BETWEEN.

<u>EXAMPLE</u>: *"<u>Estimate</u> $\sqrt{85}$ without using a calculator."*

① The square numbers either side of 85 are <u>81</u> and <u>100</u>.

② The square roots are 9 and 10, so $\sqrt{85}$ must be *<u>between 9 and 10</u>*. But 85 is much nearer 81 than 100, so $\sqrt{85}$ must be much *<u>nearer 9 than 10</u>*. So pick *<u>9.1, 9.2 or 9.3</u>*.

(The answer's actually 9.2195... if you're interested.)

The Acid Test:

LEARN the <u>3 Rules</u> for Appropriate Accuracy and <u>6 Rules</u> for Estimating. Then <u>turn over and write them all down</u>.

1) Decide which category of accuracy these *should* belong in and round them off accordingly:
a) A jar of jam weighs 34.56g   b) A car's max speed is 134.25mph   c) A cake needs 852.3g of flour
2) Estimate the area of Great Britain in square miles, and the volume of <u>a milk bottle</u> in cm³.
3) Without your calculator, estimate: a) $\sqrt{12}$, b) $\sqrt{104}$, c) $\sqrt{52}$, d) $\sqrt{30}$.

Fractions

The Fraction Button:

Use this as much as possible in the calculator paper. It's very easy, so make sure you know how to use it — you'll lose a lot of marks if you don't:

1) To enter ¼ press ⬛1 ⬛a$\frac{b}{c}$ ⬛4

2) To enter $1\frac{3}{5}$ press ⬛1 ⬛a$\frac{b}{c}$ ⬛3 ⬛a$\frac{b}{c}$ ⬛5

3) To work out $\frac{1}{5} \times \frac{3}{4}$ press ⬛1 ⬛a$\frac{b}{c}$ ⬛5 ⬛X ⬛3 ⬛a$\frac{b}{c}$ ⬛4 ⬛=

4) To _reduce a fraction to its lowest terms_ enter it and then press ⬛=

    e.g. $\frac{9}{12}$, ⬛9 ⬛a$\frac{b}{c}$ ⬛12 ⬛=   ⬜3⌐4 = $\frac{3}{4}$

5) To convert between _mixed_ and _top-heavy_ fractions press ⬛SHIFT ⬛a$\frac{b}{c}$

    e.g. $2\frac{3}{8}$ ⬛2 ⬛a$\frac{b}{c}$ ⬛3 ⬛a$\frac{b}{c}$ ⬛8 ⬛= ⬛SHIFT ⬛a$\frac{b}{c}$ which gives $\frac{19}{8}$

Doing Fractions By Hand

You're not allowed to use your calculator in the Non-Calculator Exam (unsurprisingly). Frighteningly, you'll have to _do them "by hand"_ instead, so learn these 5 basic rules:

1) Multiplying — easy.

Multiply top and bottom separately: $\frac{3}{5} \times \frac{4}{7} = \frac{3 \times 4}{5 \times 7} = \frac{12}{35}$

2) Dividing — quite easy.

Turn the _2nd fraction upside down_ and then _multiply_: $\frac{3}{4} \div \frac{1}{3} = \frac{3}{4} \times \frac{3}{1} = \frac{3 \times 3}{4 \times 1} = \frac{9}{4}$

3) Cancelling down — easy.

Divide top and bottom by the same number, till they won't go any further: $\frac{12}{16} = \frac{6}{8} = \frac{3}{4}$

4) Adding/subtracting — fraught.

i) First get the bottom lines the same (get a "common denominator")

    E.g. $\frac{2}{3} + \frac{1}{5} = \frac{2 \times 5}{3 \times 5} + \frac{1 \times 3}{5 \times 3} = \frac{10}{15} + \frac{3}{15}$

ii) _Add or subtract TOP LINES ONLY_ but _only if the bottom numbers are the same._

    E.g. $\frac{10}{15} + \frac{3}{15} = \frac{13}{15}$ or $\frac{2}{6} + \frac{1}{6} = \frac{3}{6}$, $\frac{5}{7} - \frac{3}{7} = \frac{2}{7}$

5) Finding A FRACTION OF something — just multiply.

Multiply by the top, divide by the bottom: $\frac{9}{20}$ of £360 $= \frac{9}{20} \times £360 = \frac{£3240}{20} = £162$

Finally — Checking.

ALWAYS check your answer.

The Acid Test:

LEARN the 5 features of the Fraction Button and the 5 Manual Methods, then _turn over and write it all down._

1) _With your calculator_:
  a) 1/2 x 3/4 b) 3/5 ÷ 2/9 c) 1/3 + 2/5 d) Find x: $2\frac{3}{5} = \frac{x}{5}$ e) Find y: $\frac{14}{98} = \frac{y}{7}$

2) _By hand_: a) 2/3 x 4/5 b) 4/5 ÷ 3/10 c) 5/8 – 2/6 d) Express 36/84 in its simplest form.   e) $3\frac{1}{2} - 2\frac{3}{4}$ f) $2\frac{1}{3} \times 3\frac{1}{5}$ g) $2\frac{3}{5} \div 1\frac{1}{10}$

Fractions and Decimals

Converting *Fractions to Decimals* — Just DIVIDE

Just remember that " / " means " ÷ ",   so ¼ means $1 \div 4 = 0.25$

The *denominator* (bottom number) of a fraction, tells you if it'll be a *recurring* or *terminating decimal* when you convert it. *Recurring* decimals have a *pattern* of numbers which repeats itself forever, e.g. $\frac{1}{3}$ is the decimal 0.333... . *Terminating* decimals are *finite*, e.g. $\frac{1}{20}$ is the decimal 0.05.

only *prime* factors: **2 & 5**

also *other* prime factors

For prime factors see p.2

Fraction	$\frac{1}{5}$	$\frac{1}{125}$	$\frac{1}{2}$	$\frac{1}{20}$
Equivalent Decimal	0.2	0.008	0.5	0.05

$\frac{1}{7}$	$\frac{1}{35}$	$\frac{1}{3}$	$\frac{1}{6}$
0.142857	0.0285714	0.3333	0.16666

Fractions where the denominator has *prime factors* of *only 2 or 5* will give *terminating decimals*. All *other fractions* will give *recurring decimals*.

Converting *Decimals to Fractions*

— It's a simple rule, so work it out for yourself!

$0.6 = \frac{6}{10}$, $0.3 = \frac{3}{10}$, $0.7 = \frac{7}{10}$, $0.X = \frac{X}{10}$, etc.

$0.12 = \frac{12}{100}$, $0.78 = \frac{78}{100}$, $0.45 = \frac{45}{100}$, $0.05 = \frac{5}{100}$, etc.

$0.345 = \frac{345}{1000}$, $0.908 = \frac{908}{1000}$, $0.024 = \frac{24}{1000}$, $0.XYZ = \frac{XYZ}{1000}$, etc.

These can then be *cancelled down*.

The above method is all well and good for converting terminating decimals into fractions, but what about recurring ones? All you need is the lovely method below.

Turning Recurring *Decimals into Fractions*

There's two ways you can do it:
 1) by UNDERSTANDING   2) by just LEARNING THE RESULT.   Both ways are cool.

The *Understanding* Method:

1) Find the *length* of the *repeating sequence* and *multiply* by 10, 100, 1000, 10 000 or whatever to move it all up past the decimal point by *one full repeated lump*:

E.g. $0.234234234... \times 1000 = 234.234234..$

2) *Subtract the original number*, r, from the new one (which in this case is 1000r)
i.e. 1000r − r = 234.234234... − 0.234234...
giving: 999r = 234

3) Then just DIVIDE to leave r: $r = \frac{234}{999}$,   and cancel if possible: $r = \frac{26}{111}$

The "*Just Learning The Result*" Method:

The fraction always has the repeating unit on the top and the same number of nines on the bottom — easy as that. Look at these and marvel at the elegant simplicity of it.

0.4444444 = 4/9   0.34343434 = 34/99
0.124124124 = 124/999   0.14561456 = 1456/9999

Always check if it will CANCEL DOWN of course, e.g. 0.363636.... = 36/99 = 4/11.

The Acid Test:
LEARN how to tell whether a *fraction* will be a *terminating* or *recurring* decimal, and *all* the *methods* above. Then *turn over* and *write it all down*.

1) Express 0.142857142857.... as a fraction. 2) Convert 0.035 into a fraction, and cancel it down.

Calculator Buttons

The next few pages are full of lovely calculator tricks to save you a lot of button-bashing.

1) Entering Negative Numbers

Some calculators have a [+/-] button which you press after you've entered the number.
Others just have a minus button [(-)] which you press before entering the number.

So to work out – 5 × – 6 you'd either press... [(-)] [5] [×] [(-)] [6] [=]

or... [5] [+/-] [×] [6] [+/-] [=]

Why can't they all just be the same... (The examples in this book will use the [(-)] button.)

2) The MEMORY BUTTONS [STO], [RCL] (Store and Recall)

(On some calculators the memory buttons are called [Min] (memory in) and [MR] (memory recall).)

Contrary to popular belief, the memory function isn't intended for storing your favourite phone number, but in fact is a mighty useful feature for keeping a number you've just calculated, so you can use it again shortly afterwards.

For something like $\dfrac{16}{15 + 12\text{SIN}40}$, you could just work out the <u>bottom line</u> first and <u>stick it in the memory</u>. Press [15] [+] [12] [SIN] [40] [=] and then [STO] (Or [STO] [M] or [STO] [1] or [Min]) to keep the result of the bottom line in the memory.

Then you simply press [16] [÷] [RCL] [=], and the answer is 0.7044 (4 d.p.).

(Instead of [RCL], you might need to type [RCL] [M] or [RCL] [1] or [MR] on yours.) Once you've practised with the memory buttons a bit, you'll soon find them very useful. They speed things up no end.

3) BODMAS and the BRACKETS BUTTONS [(] and [)]

One of the biggest problems many people have with their calculator is not realising that it always works things out <u>in a certain order</u>, which is summarised by the word <u>BODMAS</u>, which stands for: **Brackets, Other, Division, Multiplication, Addition, Subtraction.**

This becomes of very pressing importance when you want to work out a simple thing like $\dfrac{23 + 45}{64 \times 3}$ — it's no good just pressing [23] [+] [45] [÷] [64] [×] [3] [=] — it will be completely wrong. The calculator will think you mean $23 + \dfrac{45}{64} \times 3$ because the calculator will do the <u>division and multiplication</u> BEFORE it does the <u>addition</u>.

The secret is to *OVERRIDE the automatic BODMAS order of operations* using the *BRACKETS BUTTONS*. *Brackets are the ultimate priority in BODMAS, which means anything in brackets is worked out before anything else happens to it.* So all you have to do is:

1) Write a couple of pairs of brackets into the expression: $\dfrac{(23 + 45)}{(64 \times 3)}$

2) Then just type it as it's written: [(] [23] [+] [45] [)] [÷] [(] [64] [×] [3] [)] [=]

It's not too difficult to decide where to put the brackets in — just put them in pairs around each group of numbers. It's OK to have brackets within other brackets too, <u>e.g. (4 ÷ (5+2))</u>. As a rule you can't cause trouble by putting too many brackets in, so long as they always go in pairs.

Calculator Buttons

4) The POWERS BUTTON x^y

The powers button is used for working out powers of numbers <u>quickly</u>.

1) For example to find 7^5, instead of pressing $7×7×7×7×7$ you can just press [7] [x^y] [5] [=] [16807]

2) And it's a <u>vital</u> button for working out expressions involving <u>fractional powers</u>.

e.g. $80^{-3/4}$ ANS: press [80] [x^y] [(] [(−)] [3] [a^b/c] [4] [)] [=] [0.037383719]

See p.20 for fractional powers.

3) The powers button can also be used <u>instead</u> of the square, square root and cube root buttons.

e.g. $\sqrt{6\frac{2}{5}} = (6\frac{2}{5})^{1/2}$ ANS: press [(] [6] [a^b/c] [2] [a^b/c] [5] [)] [x^y] [(] [1] [a^b/c] [2] [)] [=] [2.529822128]

(If you didn't use brackets here, your calculator would probably have given the wrong answer. That's because it doesn't know how much of the expression to apply the x^y to unless you make it clear with brackets. Try it. Get in the habit of using brackets and you'll save yourself a lot of headaches.)

5) Converting Time to Hrs, Mins and Secs with [° ' ''']

Here's a tricky detail that comes up when you're doing speed, distance and time: <u>converting an answer like 2.35 hours into hours and minutes</u>. What it <u>definitely ISN'T</u> is 2 hours and 35 mins — remember your calculator <u>does not</u> work in hours and minutes <u>unless you tell it to</u>, as shown below. You'll need to practise with this button, but you'll be glad you did.

1) <u>To ENTER a time in hours, mins and secs</u>

E.g. 5 hrs 34 mins and 23 secs, press 5 [° ' '''] 34 [° ' '''] 23 [° ' '''] [=] to get [5°34°23].

2) <u>Converting hours, mins and secs to a decimal time</u>:

Enter the number in hours, mins and secs as above.

Then just press [° ' '''] and it should convert it to a decimal like this [5.573055556].

(Though some older calculators will automatically convert it to decimal when you enter a time in hours, minutes and secs.)

3) <u>To convert a decimal time (as you always get from a formula) into hrs, mins and secs</u>:

E.g. To convert 2.35 hours into hrs, mins and secs.

Simply press 2.35 [=] to enter the decimal, then press [° ' '''] .

The display should become [2°21°0] , which means <u>2 hours, 21 mins</u> (and 0 secs).

SEE P8 FOR THE FRACTION BUTTON, P19 FOR THE STANDARD FORM BUTTON AND P52 FOR THE 1/X BUTTON.

The Acid test:

LEARN your calculator buttons. Practise until you can answer all of these without having to refer back:

1) Explain what [STO] and [RCL] do and give an example of using them.

2) How do you enter a) 6^8 b) $6 × 10^8$ c) $50^{-4/5}$ d) $\sqrt[6]{4\frac{3}{5}}$ $(= (4\frac{3}{5})^{1/6})$

3) Write down what buttons you would press to work this out in one go: $\dfrac{23.3 + 35.8}{36 × 26.5}$

4) a) Convert 4.57 hrs into hrs and mins.
   b) Convert 5 hrs 32 mins and 23 secs into decimal hrs.

Conversion Factors

Conversion Factors are a mighty powerful tool for dealing with a wide variety of questions. And what's more the method is really easy. Learn it now. It's ace.

Method

1) Find the <u>Conversion Factor</u>
2) <u>Multiply by it AND divide by it</u>
3) Choose the <u>common sense answer</u>

Four Important *Examples*

1) *"Convert 2.55 hours into minutes."* — (N.B. This is NOT 2 hrs 55 mins)

1) Conversion factor = <u>60</u>   — (simply because 1 hour = <u>60</u> mins)
2) 2.55 hrs × 60 = 153 mins (makes sense)
   2.55 hrs ÷ 60 = 0.0425 mins (ridiculous answer)
3) So plainly the answer is that 2.55 hrs = <u>153 mins</u>

2) *"If £1 = 1.5 euros, how much is 47.30 euros in £ and p?"*

1) Obviously, Conversion Factor = <u>1.5</u>   (The "exchange rate")
2) 47.30 × 1.5 = £70.95
   47.30 ÷ 1.5 = £31.53
3) Not quite so obvious this time, but if 1.5 euros = £1, then the answer must be less than 47.30, so the answer must be <u>£31.53</u>

3) *"A map has a scale of 1:20,000. How big in real life is a distance of 3 cm on the map?"*

1) Conversion Factor = 20 000
2) 3 cm × 20 000 = 60 000 cm (looks OK)
   3 cm ÷ 20 000 = 0.00015 cm (not good)
3) So <u>60,000 cm</u> is the answer.
   How do we convert to metres? →

→ To Convert 60,000 cm to m:

1) C.F. = 100   (cm ⟷ m)
2) 60,000 × 100 = 6,000,000 m
                                    (hmm)
   60,000 ÷ 100 = <u>600 m</u>
                          (more like it)
3) So answer = <u>600 m</u>

4) Eeek, it's easy to get confused here —

4 m² looks like this 2m[1m²|1m²/1m²|1m²] not 4m[16m²] which is (4 m)²

a) *"Convert 4 m² into cm²."*
1) Conversion Factor = 10,000
   (1 m² = 100 cm × 100 cm =10,000 cm²)
2) 4 × 10,000 = 40,000 cm² (looks OK)
   4 ÷ 10,000 = 0.0004 cm² (silly answer)
3) So <u>40,000 cm²</u> is the answer.

b) *"Convert 2 m³ into cm³."*
1) Conversion Factor = 1,000,000
   (1 m³ = 100 cm × 100 cm × 100 cm = 1,000,000 cm³)
2) 2 × 1,000,000 = 2,000,000 cm³ (looks OK)
   2 ÷ 1,000,000 = 0.000002 cm³ (silly answer)
3) So <u>2,000,000 cm³</u> is the answer.

The Acid Test:

LEARN the <u>3 steps</u> of the <u>Conversion Factor</u> method. Then turn over and <u>write them down</u>.

1) Convert 2.3 km into m.   2) Which is more, £174 or 260 euros? (Exchange rate = 1.5)
3) A map is drawn to a scale of 2 cm = 5 km. A road is 8 km long. How many cm will this be on the map? (Hint, C.F. = 5 ÷ 2, i.e. 1 cm = 2.5 km)

Metric and Imperial Units

Make sure you learn all these easy facts:

Metric Units

1) <u>Length</u>   mm, cm, m, km
2) <u>Area</u> mm^2, cm^2, m^2, km^2
3) <u>Volume</u> mm^3, cm^3, m^3,
                  litres, ml
4) <u>Weight</u>   g, kg, tonnes
5) <u>Speed</u>   km/h, m/s

MEMORISE THESE KEY FACTS:

1 cm = 10 mm	1 tonne = 1000 kg
1 m = 100 cm	1 litre = 1000 ml
1 km = 1000 m	1 litre = 1000 cm^3
1 kg = 1000 g	1 cm^3 = 1 ml

Imperial Units

1) <u>Length</u>   Inches, feet, yards, miles
2) <u>Area</u>   Square inches, square feet,
              square yards, square miles
3) <u>Volume</u>   Cubic inches, cubic feet,
                  gallons, pints
4) <u>Weight</u>   Ounces, pounds, stones, tons
5) <u>Speed</u>   mph

LEARN THESE TOO!

1 Foot = 12 Inches
1 Yard = 3 Feet
1 Gallon = 8 Pints
1 Stone = 14 Pounds (lb)
1 Pound = 16 Ounces (oz)

Metric-Imperial Conversions

<u>YOU NEED TO LEARN THESE</u> — they DON'T promise to give you these in the Exam and if they're feeling mean (as they often are), they won't.

APPROXIMATE CONVERSIONS

1 kg = 2.2 lbs	1 gallon = 4.5 litres
1 m = 1 yard (+ 10%)	1 foot = 30 cm
1 litre = 1¾ pints	1 metric <u>tonne</u> = 1 imperial <u>ton</u>
1 inch = 2.5 cm	1 mile = 1.6 km
	or 5 miles = 8 km

Using Metric-Imperial Conversion Factors

1) Convert 45mm into cm.   CF = 10, so × and ÷ by 10, to get 450cm or <u>4.5cm</u>. (Sensible)
2) Convert 37 inches into cm.   CF = 2.5, so × and ÷ by 2.5, to get 14.8cm or <u>92.5cm</u>.
3) Convert 5.45 litres into pints   CF = 1¾, so × and ÷ by 1.75, to get 3.11 or <u>9.54 pints</u>.

The Acid Test:

LEARN the <u>21 Conversion factors</u> in the shaded boxes above. Then <u>turn over and write them down</u>.

1) How many litres is 3½ gallons?   2) Roughly how many yards is 200m?
3) A rod is 46 inches long. What is this in cm?
4) Petrol costs £2.83 per gallon. What should it cost per litre?
5) A car travels at 65 mph. What is its speed in km/h?

Ratios

The whole grisly subject of <u>RATIOS</u> gets a whole lot easier when you do this:

Treat RATIOS *like* FRACTIONS

So for the <u>RATIO</u> 3:4, you'd treat it as the <u>FRACTION</u> 3/4, which is 0.75 as a <u>DECIMAL</u>.

What the *fraction* form of the ratio *actually means*

Suppose in a class there's <u>girls and boys</u> in the ratio 3 : 4.
This means there's 3/4 as many girls as boys.
So if there were 20 boys, there would be 3/4 × 20 = 15 girls.
You've got to be careful — it <u>doesn't mean</u> 3/4 of the <u>people</u> in the class are girls.

Reducing *Ratios* to their *simplest form*

You reduce ratios just like you'd reduce fractions to their simplest form.
For the ratio 15 : 18, both numbers have a <u>factor</u> of 3, so <u>divide them by 3</u>:
That gives 5 : 6. We can't reduce this any further. So the simplest form of 15 : 18 is 5 : 6.

Treat them just like *fractions* — use your *calculator* if you can

Now this is really sneaky. If you stick in a fraction using the [a b/c] button, your calculator
automatically cancels it down when you press [=].
So for the ratio 8 : 12, just press 8 [a b/c] 12 [=] , and you'll get the reduced fraction 2/3.
Now you just change it back to ratio form, i.e. <u>2 : 3</u>. Ace.

The More Awkward Cases:

1) The [a b/c] button will *only* accept *whole numbers*

So <u>IF THE RATIO IS AWKWARD</u> (like "2.4 : 3.6" or "1¼ : 3½") then you must:
<u>MULTIPLY BOTH SIDES</u> by the <u>SAME NUMBER</u> until they are both <u>WHOLE NUMBERS</u>
and then you can use the [a b/c] button as before to simplify them down.
e.g. with "<u>1¼ : 3½</u>", × both sides by 4 gives "<u>5 : 14</u>" (Try [a b/c], but it won't cancel further)

2) If the ratio is *MIXED UNITS*

then you must <u>CONVERT BOTH SIDES</u> into the *SMALLER UNITS* using the
relevant <u>CONVERSION FACTOR</u> (see P.12), and then carry on as normal.
e.g. "24mm : 7.2cm" (× 7.2cm by 10) ⇒   24mm : 72mm = 1 : 3 (using [a b/c])

3) To *reduce a ratio* to the form 1 : n   (n can be *any number at all*)

Simply <u>DIVIDE BOTH SIDES BY THE *SMALLEST SIDE*</u>.
e.g. take "<u>3 : 56</u>" — dividing both sides by 3 gives: <u>1 : 18.7</u> (56÷3) (i.e. 1 : n)
The 1 : n form is often the <u>most useful</u>, since it shows the ratio very clearly.

Ratios

Using the Formula Triangle in Ratio Questions

"Mortar is made from sand and cement in the ratio 7:2.
If 9 buckets of sand are used, how much cement is needed?"

This is a fairly common type of Exam question and it's pretty tricky for most people
— but once you start using the formula triangle method, it's all a bit of a breeze really.

This is the basic **FORMULA TRIANGLE** for **RATIOS**, <u>but NOTE</u>:

1) **THE RATIO MUST BE THE RIGHT WAY ROUND**,
with the **FIRST NUMBER IN THE RATIO** relating to
the item **ON TOP** in the triangle.

2) You'll always need to **CONVERT THE RATIO** into its
EQUIVALENT FRACTION or Decimal to work out the answer.

The formula triangle for the mortar question is shown below and the trick is to replace
the <u>RATIO</u> 7:2 by its <u>EQUIVALENT FRACTION</u>: 7/2, or 3.5 as a decimal (7÷2).

So, *covering up cement in the triangle*, gives us "cement = sand / (7:2)"
i.e. "9 / 3.5" = 9 ÷ 3.5 = 2.57 or about <u>2½ buckets of cement</u>.

Proportional Division

In a *proportional division question* a <u>TOTAL AMOUNT</u> is to be *split in a certain ratio*.

For example: *"£9100 is to be split in the ratio 2:4:7. Find the 3 amounts"*.

The key word here is **PARTS**. — concentrate on "parts" and it all becomes quite painless:

Method

1) <u>ADD UP THE PARTS</u>:
The ratio 2:4:7 means there will be a total of 13 *parts* i.e. 2+4+7 = <u>13 PARTS</u>

2) <u>FIND THE AMOUNT FOR ONE *"PART"*</u>
Just *divide* the *total amount* by the number of *parts*: £9100 ÷ 13 = <u>£700</u> (= 1 PART)

3) <u>HENCE FIND THE THREE AMOUNTS</u>:
2 parts = 2×700 = <u>£1400</u>,   4 parts = 4×700 = <u>£2800</u>,   7 parts = 7×700 = <u>£4900</u>

(N.B. It's always a good idea to *check the total*: 1400 + 2800 + 4900 = 9100)

The Acid Test:

LEARN the <u>RULES for SIMPLIFYING</u>, the
FORMULA TRIANGLE for Ratios (plus 2 points),
and the *3 Steps for* PROPORTIONAL DIVISION.

Now *turn over* and *write down what you've learned*. Try again *until you can do it*.

1) Simplify: a) 25:35   b) 3.4 : 5.1   c) 2¼ : 3¾
2) Porridge and ice-cream are mixed in the ratio 7:4. How much porridge should go with
10 bowls of ice-cream?   3) Divide £8400 in the ratio 5:3:4

Percentages

You shouldn't have any trouble with most percentage questions, especially types 1 and 2. However watch out for type 3 questions and make sure you know the proper method for doing them. "Percentage change" can also catch you out if you don't watch all the details – using the ORIGINAL value for example.

Type 1 | *"Find x% of y"* — e.g. Find 15% of £46 $\Rightarrow$ 0.15 × 46 = £6.90

Type 2 | *"Express x as a percentage of y"*
e.g. Give 40p as a percentage of £3.34 $\Rightarrow$ (40 ÷ 334) × 100 = 12%

Type 3 — REVERSE PERCENTAGES *(IDENTIFIED BY NOT GIVING THE "ORIGINAL VALUE")*

These are the type most people get wrong – but only because they don't recognise them as a type 3 and don't apply this simple method:

Example: A house increases in value by 20% to £72,000. Find what it was worth before the rise.

Method

	£72,000	=	120%
÷120	£600	=	1%
×100	£60,000	=	100%

So the original price was £60,000

An **INCREASE** of 20% means that £72,000 represents *120% of the original* value. If it was a **DROP** of 20%, then we would put "£72,000 = 80%" instead, and then divide by 80 on the LHS, instead of 120.

Always set them out exactly like this example. The trickiest bit is deciding the top % figure on the RHS — the 2nd and 3rd rows are always 1% and 100%.

Percentage Change

It is common to give a *change in value* as a *percentage*. This is the formula for doing so — LEARN IT, AND USE IT:

$$\text{PERCENTAGE CHANGE} = \frac{\text{CHANGE}}{\text{ORIGINAL}} \times 100$$

By "change", we could mean all sorts of things such as: "Profit", "loss", "appreciation", "depreciation", "increase", "decrease", "error", "discount", etc. For example,

$$\text{percentage profit} = \frac{\text{profit}}{\text{original}} \times 100$$

Note the great importance of using the ORIGINAL VALUE in this formula.

The Acid Test:

LEARN the details for TYPE 3 QUESTIONS and PERCENTAGE CHANGE, then turn over and write it all down.

1) A trader buys watches for £5 and sells them for £7. Find his profit as a percentage.
2) A car depreciates by 30% to £14,350. What was it worth before?
3) Find the percentage error in rounding 3.452 to 3.5. Give your answer to 2 d.p.

Compound Growth and Decay

This can also be called "Exponential" Growth or Decay. But you don't want to know that. You want to know this:

The Formula

This topic is simple if you <u>LEARN THIS FORMULA</u>. If you don't, it's pretty well impossible:

$$N = N_0\left(1 + \frac{r}{100}\right)^n$$

Existing amount at this time

Initial amount

Percentage change per day/hour/year

Number of days/hrs/yrs

Percentage *Increase* and *Decrease*

The $(1 + r/100)$ bit might look a bit confusing in the formula but in practice it's really easy:

E.g   5% increase will be 1.05   5% decrease will be 0.95 $(= 1 - 0.05)$
      26% increase will be 1.26   26% decrease will be 0.74 $(= 1 - 0.26)$

You can also <u>combine</u> increases and decreases:

E.g. A 20% increase in a value a followed by a 20% decrease will be $1.2 \times 0.8 \times a$.
They <u>don't</u> cancel each other out.

3 Examples to show you how EASY it is:

1) *"A man invests £1000 in a savings account which pays 8% per annum. How much will there be after 6 years?"* *(This is known as compound interest.)*

<u>ANSWER</u>: Usual formula (as above):   Amount $= 1000 \times (1.08)^6 = $ **£1586.87**

                                      Initial amount   8% increase   6 years

2) *"The activity of a radio-isotope falls by 12% every hour. If the initial activity is 800 counts per minute, what will it be after 7 hours?"*

<u>ANSWER</u>: Same old formula:

$$\text{Activity} = \text{Initial value}\left(1 - \frac{12}{100}\right)^n$$

$$\text{Activity} = 800(1 - 0.12)^7 = 800 \times (0.88)^7 = \underline{327 \text{ cpm}}$$

3) *"In a sample of bacteria, there are initially 500 cells and they increase in number by 15% each day. Find the formula relating the number of cells, n, and the number of days, d."*

<u>ANSWER</u>: Well stone me, it's the same old easy-peasy compound increase formula <u>again</u>:
$$n = n_0(1 + 0.15)^d \quad \text{or finished off:} \quad \underline{n = 500 \times (1.15)^d}$$

The Acid Test:

<u>LEARN THE FORMULA</u>. Also learn the <u>3 Examples</u>.
Then <u>turn over and write it all down</u>.

1) A colony of stick insects increases in number by 4% per week. Initially there are 30. How many will there be after 12 weeks?

2) The speed of a tennis ball rolled along a smooth floor falls by 16% every second. If the initial speed was 5 m/s, find the speed after 20 seconds. How long will it take to stop?

Also in stage 2:

Standard Index Form

Also in stage 2:

Standard Form and Standard Index Form are the SAME THING.
So remember both of these names as well as what it actually is:

Ordinary Number: 4,300,000   In Standard Form: 4.3×10^6

Standard form is only really useful for writing VERY BIG or VERY SMALL numbers in a more convenient way, e.g.

$56,000,000,000$ would be 5.6×10^{10} in standard form.
$0.000\,000\,003\,45$ would be 3.45×10^{-9} in standard form.

but ANY NUMBER can be written in standard form and *you need to know how to do it*:

What it Actually is:

A number written in standard form must ALWAYS be in EXACTLY this form:

$$A \times 10^{n}$$

This *number* must *always* be BETWEEN 1 AND 10.
(The fancy way of saying this is:

"$1 \leqslant A < 10$" — they sometimes write that in Exam questions — don't let it put you off, just remember what it means.)

This number is just the NUMBER OF PLACES *the Decimal Point moves*.

Learn The Three Rules:

1) The front number must always be BETWEEN 1 AND 10.

2) The power of 10, n, is purely: HOW FAR THE D.P. MOVES.

3) n is +ve for BIG numbers,   n is −ve for SMALL numbers.
(This is much better than rules based on which way the D.P. moves.)

Examples:

1) "*Express 35 600 in standard form*".

METHOD:
1) Move the D.P. until 35 600 becomes 3.56 ("$1 \leq A < 10$")
2) The D.P. has moved 4 places so n=4, giving: 10^4
3) 35600 is a BIG number so n is +4, not −4

ANSWER:
$3.5600. = 3.56 \times 10^4$

2) "*Express 8.14 × 10^{-3} as an ordinary number*".

METHOD:
1) 10^{-3} , tells us that the D.P. must move 3 places...
2) ...and the "−" sign tells us to move the D.P. to make it a SMALL number. (i.e. 0.00814, rather than 8140)

ANSWER:
$8.14 = 0.00814$

Standard Index Form

Standard Form and The Calculator

People usually manage all that stuff about moving the decimal point OK *(apart from always forgetting that <u>FOR A BIG NUMBER</u> it's "<u>ten to the power +ve something</u>" and <u>FOR A SMALL NUMBER</u> it's "<u>ten to the power –ve something</u>")*, but when it comes to doing standard form on a *calculator* it's invariably a sorry saga of confusion and ineptitude.

But it's not so bad really — you just have to learn it, that's all.....

1) Entering Standard Form Numbers EXP

The button you <u>MUST USE</u> to put standard form numbers into the calculator is the EXP

(or EE) button — but <u>DON'T</u> go pressing   X   10   as well, like a lot of people do,

because that makes it <u>WRONG</u>.

Example: "*Enter 2.67 × 10¹⁵ into the calculator.*"

Just press: 2.67 EXP 15 =   and the display will be   2.67   15

Note that you <u>ONLY PRESS</u> the EXP (or EE) button — you <u>DON'T</u> press   X   or   10   <u>at all</u>.

2) *Reading* Standard Form Numbers:

The big thing you have to remember when you write any standard form number from the calculator display is to put the "×10" in yourself. <u>DON'T</u> just write down what it says on the display.

Example: "*Write down the number*   7.986   05   *as a finished answer*."

As a finished answer this must be written as <u>7.986 × 10⁵</u>.

It is <u>NOT</u> 7.986⁵ so <u>DON'T</u> write it down like that — <u>YOU</u> have to put the $\times 10^n$ in yourself, even though it isn't shown in the display at all. *That's the bit people forget.*

Calculating with Standard Form

Once you've mastered <u>expressing</u> numbers in standard form, you need to make sure you can <u>calculate</u> with them, <u>without</u> using your calculator. Just follow this simple method.

Example: "*Calculate (2.5 × 10⁷) × (6 × 10³). Write your answer in standard form.*"

METHOD:
1) Multiply the front number from the first expression by the front number from the second.
2) Multiply the first power of 10 by the second.
3) Make sure your answer is in standard form (the front number is between 1 and 10).

(To divide expressions, use the same method but replace "<u>multiply</u>" with "<u>divide</u>".)

Answer: *For a reminder about dealing with powers see p.20*

$2.5 \times 6 = 15$ ✓
$10^7 \times 10^3 = 10^{10}$
15×10^{10} isn't in standard form since $15 > 10$
$15 \times 10^{10} = \underline{1.5 \times 10^{11}}$

The Acid Test: LEARN everything from these two pages.

1) Express 958,000 in standard index form.   2) And the same for 0.00018
3) Express 4.56×10^3 as an ordinary number.
4) Write the answer to the following in standard form: $(3.2 \times 10^{12}) \div (1.6 \times 10^{-9})$

Powers (or "Indices")

Powers are a very useful shorthand: $2 \times 2 \times 2 \times 2 \times 2 \times 2 \times 2 = 2^7$ ("two to the power 7")

That bit is easy to remember. Unfortunately, there are NINE SPECIAL RULES for Powers that are not tremendously exciting, but you do need to know them for the Exam:

The Seven Easy Rules:

1) When **MULTIPLYING**, you **ADD THE POWERS**. e.g. $3^4 \times 3^6 = 3^{4+6} = 3^{10}$

2) When **DIVIDING**, you **SUBTRACT THE POWERS**. e.g. $5^6 \div 5^2 = 5^{6-2} = 5^4$

3) When **RAISING one power to another**, you **MULTIPLY THEM**. e.g. $(3^2)^4 = 3^{2 \times 4} = 3^8$

4) $n^1 = n$, **ANYTHING** to the **POWER 1** is just **ITSELF**. e.g. $3^1 = 3$, $6 \times 6^3 = 6^4$

5) $n^0 = 1$, **ANYTHING** to the **POWER 0** is just **1**. e.g. $5^0 = 1$ $67^0 = 1$

6) $1^n = 1$, **1 TO ANY POWER** is **STILL JUST 1**. e.g. $1^{23} = 1$ $1^{89} = 1$ $1^2 = 1$

7) **FRACTIONS** — Apply Power to both TOP and BOTTOM. e.g. $\left(1\tfrac{3}{5}\right)^3 = \left(\tfrac{8}{5}\right)^3 = \tfrac{8^3}{5^3} = \tfrac{512}{125}$

The Two Tricky Rules:

8) NEGATIVE Powers — Turn it UPSIDE DOWN

People do have quite a bit of difficulty remembering this.
Whenever you see a negative power you're supposed to immediately think:
"Aha, that means turn it the other way up and make the power positive"
LIKE THIS:

e.g. $7^{-2} = \dfrac{1}{7^2} = \dfrac{1}{49}$ $(-2)^{-3} = \dfrac{1}{(-2)^3} = -\dfrac{1}{8}$

9) FRACTIONAL POWERS mean one thing: ROOTS

The Power $\tfrac{1}{2}$ means Square Root, e.g. $25^{\frac{1}{2}} = \sqrt{25} = 5$
The Power $\tfrac{1}{3}$ means Cube Root, $64^{\frac{1}{3}} = \sqrt[3]{64} = 4$
The Power $\tfrac{1}{4}$ means Fourth Root etc. $81^{\frac{1}{4}} = \sqrt[4]{81} = 3$ etc.

The one to really watch is when you get a negative fraction like $49^{-\frac{1}{2}}$. This is $\dfrac{1}{\sqrt{49}} = \dfrac{1}{7}$. (People get mixed up and think that the minus is the square root, and forget to turn it upside down as well.)

Raising to the power $\tfrac{1}{n}$ is the inverse operation of raising to the power n.

e.g. $7^2 = 49$. To get back to 7 you just apply the inverse operation $49^{\frac{1}{2}} = \sqrt{49} = 7$.

e.g. $8^{\frac{1}{3}} = \sqrt[3]{8} = 2$. To get back to 8 you just apply the inverse operation $2^3 = 8$.

Clever eh?

The Acid Test:

LEARN ALL NINE Exciting Rules on this page. Then TURN OVER and write them all down with examples. Keep trying till you can.

1) Simplify: a) $3^2 \times 3^6$ b) $4^3/4^2$ c) $(8^3)^4$ d) $(3^2 \times 3^3 \times 1^6)/3^5$ e) $7^3 \times 7 \times 7^2$

2) Evaluate: a) 17^0 b) $(\tfrac{1}{4})^{-3}$ c) 25^{-2} d) $25^{-\frac{1}{2}}$ e) $\left(\tfrac{27}{216}\right)^{-\frac{1}{3}}$

3) Use your Calculator buttons (P.11) to find: a) 5.2^{24} b) $40^{\frac{3}{4}}$ c) $\sqrt[5]{200}$

Also in stage 2:

Basic Algebra

Negative Numbers:

This is the second rule for negative numbers (see p.1 for the first). Make sure you use the number line when adding and subtracting.

Use this when
ADDING OR SUBTRACTING.

THE NUMBER LINE

+6X   +4X

-10 -9 -8 -7 -6 -5 -4 -3 -2 -1 0 1 2 3 4 5 6 7 8 9 10

-3X   -8X

Example:
"Simplify: 4X - 8X - 3X + 6X"   So   4X - 8X - 3X + 6X = -1X (= −X)

Letters Multiplied Together

Watch out for these combinations of letters in algebra that regularly catch people out:

1) abc means a×b×c.   The ×'s are often left out to make it clearer.
2) gn^2 means g×n×n.   Note that only the n is squared, not the g as well. E.g. πr^2
3) $(gn)^2$ means g×g×n×n.   The brackets mean that __BOTH__ letters are squared.
4) $p(q - r)^3$ means $p \times (q - r) \times (q - r) \times (q - r)$.   Only the brackets get cubed.
5) -3^2 is a bit ambiguous. It should either be written $(-3)^2 = 9$, or $-(3^2) = -9$

Terms

Before you can do anything else, you **MUST** understand what a **TERM** is:

1)   **A TERM IS A COLLECTION OF NUMBERS, LETTERS AND BRACKETS,
      ALL MULTIPLIED/DIVIDED TOGETHER.**

2)   **TERMS are SEPARATED BY + AND − SIGNS**   E.g. $4x^2 - 3py - 5 + 3p$

3) **TERMS** always have a   + or −   **ATTACHED TO THE FRONT OF THEM**

4) E.g.

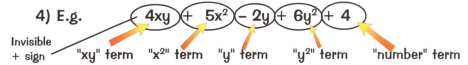

Invisible
+ sign   "xy" term   "x²" term   "y" term   "y²" term   "number" term

Simplifying — or "Collecting Like Terms"

EXAMPLE: Simplify $2x - 4 + 5x + 6$

Invisible
+ sign

x-terms   number terms

= $+2x$ $+5x$ -4 $+6$
=   7x   +2   = $\underline{7x + 2}$

1) Put bubbles round each term — be sure you capture the +/− sign IN FRONT of each.
2) Then you can move the bubbles into the best order so that LIKE TERMS are together.
3) "LIKE TERMS" have exactly the same combination of letters, e.g. x-terms or xy-terms.
4) Combine LIKE TERMS using the NUMBER LINE.

Basic Algebra

Multiplying out Brackets

1) The thing outside the brackets multiplies each separate term inside the brackets.
2) When letters are multiplied together, they are just written next to each other, e.g. pq.
3) Remember, R x R = R², and TY² means TxYxY, whilst (TY)² means TxTxYxY.
4) Remember a minus outside the bracket REVERSES ALL THE SIGNS when you multiply.

1) $3(2x + 5) = 6x + 15$ 2) $4p(3r - 2t) = 12pr - 8pt$

3) $-4(3p^2 - 7q^3) = -12p^2 + 28q^3$ (note both signs have been reversed)

5) DOUBLE BRACKETS — you get 4 terms, and usually 2 of them combine to leave 3 terms.

$$(2P - 4)(3P + 1) = (2P \times 3P) + (2P \times 1) + (-4 \times 3P) + (-4 \times 1)$$
$$= 6P^2 + 2P - 12P - 4$$
$$= 6P^2 - 10P - 4$$

(these 2 combine together)

6) SQUARED BRACKETS — ALWAYS write these out as TWO BRACKETS:

E.g. $(3d + 5)^2$ should be written out as $(3d + 5)(3d + 5)$ and then worked out as above. YOU SHOULD ALWAYS GET FOUR TERMS from a pair of brackets.
The usual WRONG ANSWER is $(3d + 5)^2 = 9d^2 + 25$ (eeek)
It should be: $(3d + 5)^2 = (3d + 5)(3d + 5) = 9d^2 + 15d + 15d + 25 = 9d^2 + 30d + 25$

Factorising — putting brackets in

This is the exact reverse of multiplying out brackets. Here's the method to follow:

1) Take out the biggest number that goes into all the terms.
2) Take each letter in turn and take out the highest power (e.g. x, x² etc) that will go into EVERY term.
3) Open the brackets and fill in all the bits needed to reproduce each term.

EXAMPLE: "Factorise $15x^4y + 20x^2y^3z - 35x^3yz^2$"
Answer: $5x^2y(3x^2 + 4y^2z - 7xz^2)$

Biggest number that'll divide into 15, 20 and 35.

Highest powers of x and y that will go into all three terms.

z was not in ALL terms so it can't come out as a common factor.

REMEMBER: 1) The bits taken out and put at the front are the common factors.
2) The bits inside the brackets are what's needed to get back to the original terms if you multiplied the brackets out again.

The Acid Test: LEARN ALL THE DETAILS, then turn over and write down what you've learned.

1) Calculate these: a) -2 + (3 – 1)   b) -4 + -5 + 3   c) (3X + -2X – 4X) ÷ (2+-5)
2) If m=2 and n=-3 work out: a) mn² b) (mn)³ c) m(4+n)² d) n³ e) 3m²n³ + 2mn
3) Simplify 5x + 3y – 4 – 2y – x   4) Expand 2pq(3p – 4q²)
5) Expand (2g + 5)(4g – 2)   6) Factorise 14x²y³ + 21xy² – 35x³y⁴

Substituting Values into Formulas

This topic is a lot easier than you think! $C = \dfrac{5}{9}(F - 32)$

Generally speaking, algebra is a pretty grim subject, but you should realise that some bits of it are VERY easy, and this is definitely the easiest bit of all, so whatever you do, don't pass up on these easy Exam marks.

Example: Find F when C = 15 in the formula above.

Method

If you don't follow this STRICT METHOD you'll just keep getting them wrong — it's as simple as that.

1) Write out the Formula. e.g $F = \frac{9}{5}C + 32$

2) Write it again, directly underneath, $F = \frac{9}{5}15 + 32$
   but substituting numbers for letters on the RHS. (Right Hand Side)

3) Work it out IN STAGES. $F = 27 + 32$
   Use BODMAS to work things out IN THE RIGHT ORDER. $= 59$
   WRITE DOWN values for each bit as you go along. $\underline{F = 59}$

4) DO NOT attempt to do it all in one go on your calculator.
   That ridiculous method fails at least 50% of the time!

BODMAS

Brackets, Other, Division, Multiplication, Addition, Subtraction

BODMAS tells you the ORDER in which these operations should be done: Work out brackets first, then Other things like squaring, then multiply / divide groups of numbers before adding or subtracting them. This set of rules works really well for simple cases, so remember the word: BODMAS   (See P.10)

Example

A mysterious quantity T is given by: $T = (P - 7)^2 + 4R/Q$
Find the value of T when P = 4, Q = -2 and R = 3.

ANSWER:

1) Write down the formula: $T = (P - 7)^2 + 4R/Q$
2) Put the numbers in: $T = (4 - 7)^2 + 4 \times 3/\text{-}2$
3) Then work it out in stages : $= (-3)^2 + 12/\text{-}2$
   $= 9 + \text{-}6$
   $= 9 - 6 = \underline{3}$

Note BODMAS in operation:

Brackets worked out first, then *squared*. *Multiplications* and *divisions* done before finally *adding* and *subtracting*.

The Acid Test:

LEARN the 4 Steps of the Substitution Method and the full meaning of BODMAS. Then turn over.....

... and write it all down from memory.   1) Practise the above example until you can do it easily without help.   2) If $C = \frac{5}{9}(F - 32)$, find the value of C when F = 77.

Solving Equations

Solving Equations means finding the value of x from something like: $3x + 5 = 4 - 5x$.
Now, not a lot of people know this, but exactly the same method applies to both
solving equations and rearranging formulas (see p.56).

> 1) EXACTLY THE SAME METHOD APPLIES TO BOTH FORMULAS AND EQUATIONS.
> 2) THE SAME SEQUENCE OF STEPS APPLIES EVERY TIME.

To illustrate the sequence of steps we'll use this equation: $\sqrt{2 - \dfrac{x+4}{2x+5}} = 3$

The Six Steps Applied to Equations

1) Get rid of any square root signs by squaring both sides: $2 - \dfrac{x+4}{2x+5} = 9$

2) Get everything off the bottom by cross-multiplying up to EVERY OTHER TERM:

$$2 - \frac{x+4}{2x+5} = 9 \qquad \Rightarrow \qquad 2(2x+5) - (x+4) = 9(2x+5)$$

3) Multiply out any brackets: $4x + 10 - x - 4 = 18x + 45$

4) Collect all subject terms on one side of the "=" and all non-subject terms on
the other. Remember to reverse the +/- sign of any term that crosses the "=".

  +18x moves across the "=" and becomes -18x
  +10 moves across the "=" and becomes -10
  -4 moves across the "=" and becomes +4

$$4x - x - 18x = 45 - 10 + 4$$

5) Combine together like terms on each side of the equation,
and reduce it to the form "Ax = B", where A and B are just
numbers (or bunches of letters, in the case of formulas):

$-15x = 39$
("Ax = B":
A = -15, B = 39,
x is the subject)

6) Finally slide the A underneath the B to give "X = $^B/_A$",
divide, and that's your answer.

$x = \dfrac{39}{-15} = -2.6$

So $\underline{x = -2.6}$

The Seventh Step (if You Need It)

If the term you're trying to find is squared, don't panic.

Follow steps 1) to 6) like normal, but solve it for x^2 instead of x: $x^2 = 9$

$x = \pm 3$

7) Take the square root of both sides and stick a
± sign in front of the expression on the right:

Don't forget the ± sign...
(P.1 if you don't know what I mean).

The Acid Test: LEARN the 7 STEPS for solving equations.
Turn over and write them down.

1) Solve these equations: a) $5(x + 2) = 8 + 4(5 - x)$ b) $\dfrac{4}{x+3} = \dfrac{6}{4-x}$ c) $x^2 - 21 = 5(3 - x^2)$

Trial and Improvement

In principle, this is an easy way to find approximate answers to quite complicated equations, especially "cubics" (ones with x^3 in).   BUT... you have to make an effort to LEARN THE FINER DETAILS of this method, otherwise you'll never get the hang of it.

Method

1) SUBSTITUTE TWO INITIAL VALUES into the equation that give OPPOSITE CASES. These are usually suggested in the question. If not, you'll have to think of your own. Opposite cases means one answer too big, one too small, or one +ve, one –ve, for example. If they don't give opposite cases, try again.

2) Now CHOOSE YOUR NEXT VALUE IN BETWEEN THE PREVIOUS TWO, and SUBSTITUTE it into the equation.
   Continue this process, always choosing a new value between the two closest opposite cases, (and preferably nearer to the one which is closest to the answer you want).

3) AFTER ONLY 3 OR 4 STEPS you should have 2 numbers which are to the right degree of accuracy but DIFFER BY 1 IN THE LAST DIGIT.
   For example if you had to get your answer to 2 d.p. then you'd eventually end up with say 5.43 and 5.44, with these giving OPPOSITE results of course.

4) At this point you ALWAYS take the Exact Middle Value to decide which is the answer you want. E.g. for 5.43 and 5.44, you'd try 5.435 to see if the real answer was between 5.43 and 5.435 or between 5.435 and 5.44 (see below).

Example

"The equation $X^3 + X = 40$ has a solution between 3 and 3.5. Find this solution to 1 d.p."

Try X = 3	$3^3 + 3 = 30$	(Too small)	← (2 opposite cases)
Try X = 3.5	$3.5^3 + 3.5 = 46.375$	(Too big)	

40 is what we want and it's closer to 46.375 than it is to 30 so we'll choose our next value for X closer to 3.5 than 3

Try X = 3.3	$3.3^3 + 3.3 = 39.237$	(Too small)

Good, this is very close, but we need to see if 3.4 is still too big or too small:

Try X = 3.4	$3.4^3 + 3.4 = 42.704$	(Too big)

Good, now we know that the answer must be between 3.3 and 3.4. To find out which one it's nearest to, we have to try the EXACT MIDDLE VALUE: 3.35

Try X = 3.35	$3.35^3 + 3.35 = 40.945$ (Too big)

This tells us with certainty that the solution must be between 3.3 (too small) and 3.35 (too big), and so to 1 d.p. it must round down to 3.3. ANSWER = 3.3

The Acid Test:
"LEARN and TURN" — if you don't actually commit it to memory, then you've wasted your time even reading it.

To succeed with this method you must LEARN the 4 steps above. Do it now, and practise until you can write them down without having to look back at them.
It's not as difficult as you think.
   1) The equation $X^3 - 2X = 1$ has a solution between 1 and 2. Find it to 1 d.p.

Number Patterns

This is an easy topic, but make sure you know **ALL EIGHT** types of sequence, not just the first few. The *main secret* is to *write the differences in the gaps* between each pair of numbers. That way you can usually see what's happening whichever type it is.

1) "COMMON DIFFERENCE" Type — dead easy

e.g.
7 → 11 → 15 → 19 → 23   112 → 105 → 98 → 91 → 84 → 77
  4   4   4   4   7   7   7   7   7

2) "INCREASING DIFFERENCE" Type

Here the differences <u>increase</u> by the <u>same amount</u> each time:

e.g.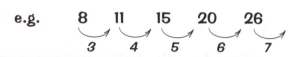
8 → 11 → 15 → 20 → 26
  3   4   5   6   7

3) "DECREASING DIFFERENCE" Type

Here the differences <u>decrease</u> by the <u>same amount</u> each time:

e.g.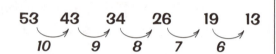
53 → 43 → 34 → 26 → 19 → 13
  10   9   8   7   6

4) "MULTIPLYING FACTOR" Type

This type has a common **MULTIPLIER** linking each pair of numbers:

e.g.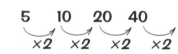
5 → 10 → 20 → 40
  ×2   ×2   ×2   ×2

5) "DIVIDING FACTOR" Type

This type has a common **DIVIDER** linking each pair of numbers:

e.g.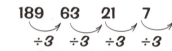
189 → 63 → 21 → 7
   ÷3   ÷3   ÷3   ÷3

6) "ADDING PREVIOUS TERMS" Type

Add the <u>first two terms</u> to get the <u>3rd</u>, then add the <u>2nd and 3rd</u> to get the <u>4th</u>, etc.

e.g.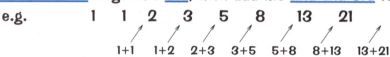
1   1   2   3   5   8   13   21
1+1 1+2 2+3 3+5 5+8 8+13 13+21

7) "TRIANGLE NUMBERS"

To remember the triangle numbers you have to picture in your mind this *increasing pattern of triangles*, where each new row has <u>one more blob</u> than the previous row.

1	3	6	10	15	21	28	36	45	55...
2	3	4	5	6	7	8	9	10	11	12

It's definitely worth learning this simple *pattern of differences*, as well as the formula for the *nth term* (see P.27) which is:

$$\text{nth term} = \tfrac{1}{2}\, n\,(n + 1)$$

8) "POWERS"

Powers are "numbers *multiplied by themselves* so many times".

"Two to the power three" $= 2^3 = 2 \times 2 \times 2 = 8$

Here's the first few *POWERS OF 2*:   ... and the first *POWERS OF 10* (even easier):

2	4	8	16	32...

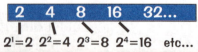
$2^1 = 2$ $2^2 = 4$ $2^3 = 8$ $2^4 = 16$ etc...

10	100	1000	10 000	100 000...

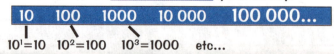
$10^1 = 10$ $10^2 = 100$ $10^3 = 1000$ etc...

The Acid Test:

LEARN the <u>8 types of number pattern</u>.
Then cover the page and answer these:

Find the next two terms in these sequences:
a) 2,6,18,54...   b) 1,3,4,7,11....   c) 3,5,8,12,17,...   d) 128,64,32,...

Finding the nᵗʰ Term

"The nᵗʰ term" is a formula with "n" in it which gives you every term in a sequence when you put different values for n in. There are two different types of sequence (for "nth term" questions) which have to be done in different ways:

Common Difference Type: "dn + (a − d)"

For any sequence such as 3, 7, 11, 15, where there's a COMMON DIFFERENCE,

you can always find "the nᵗʰ term" using the FORMULA: **nᵗʰ Term = dn+(a−d)**

Don't forget:

1) "a" is simply the value of THE FIRST TERM in the sequence.
2) "d" is simply the value of THE COMMON DIFFERENCE between the terms.
3) To get the nth term, you just find the values of "a" and "d" from the sequence and stick them in the formula.
    You don't replace n though — that wants to stay as n
4) Of course YOU HAVE TO LEARN THE FORMULA, but life is like that.

Example:

"Find the nᵗʰ term of this sequence: 5, 8, 11, 14, ..."

ANSWER: 1) The formula is dn + (a−d)
2) The first term is 5, so a = 5   The common difference is 3 so d = 3
3) Putting these in the formula gives: nᵗʰ term = 3n + (5−3)
    so nᵗʰ term = 3n + 2

Changing Difference Type:

"a + (n−1)d + ½(n−1)(n−2)C"

If the number sequence is one where the *difference* between the terms is *increasing or decreasing* then it gets a whole lot more complicated (as you'll have spotted from the above formula — which you'll have to *learn!*). This time there are *THREE* letters you have to fill in:

"a" is the FIRST TERM,
"d" is the FIRST DIFFERENCE (between the first two numbers),
"C" is the CHANGE BETWEEN ONE DIFFERENCE AND THE NEXT.

Example:

"Find the nᵗʰ term of this sequence: 2, 5, 9, 14, ..."
3 4 5

ANSWER: 1) The formula is "a + (n−1)d + ½(n−1)(n−2)C"
2) The first term is 2, so a = 2   The first difference is 3 so d = 3
3) The differences increase by 1 each time so C = +1
Putting these in the formula gives: "2 + (n−1)3 + ½(n−1)(n−2)×1"
Which becomes: 2 + 3n − 3 + ½n² − 1½n + 1
Which simplifies to: ½n² + 1½n = ½n(n+3)
    so the nᵗʰ term = ½n(n+3)   (Easy peasy, huh!)

The Acid Test:

LEARN the definition of the nᵗʰ term and the 4 steps for finding it, and LEARN THE FORMULA.

1) Find the nth term of the following sequences:
a) 4, 7, 10, 13.... b) 3, 8, 13, 18,.... c) 1, 3, 6, 10, 15,.... d) 3, 4, 7, 12,...

D/T Graphs and V/T Graphs

Distance-time graphs and *Velocity-time graphs* are so common in Exams that they deserve a page all to themselves *just to make sure you know all the vital details* about them. The best thing about them is that they don't vary much and they're always easy.

1) Distance-Time Graphs

Just remember these 4 important points:

1) At any point, GRADIENT = SPEED, but watch out for the UNITS.

2) For a CURVED GRAPH you'll need to draw a TANGENT to work out the SPEED (gradient) at any particular point.

3) The STEEPER the graph, the FASTER it's going.

4) FLAT SECTIONS are where it is STOPPED.

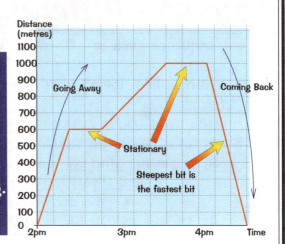

EXAMPLE: *"What is the speed of the return section on the graph shown?"*

Speed = gradient = 1000 m / 30 mins = **33.33** m/min. But m/min are naff units so it's better to do it like this: 1km ÷ 0.5 hrs = 2 km/h

2) Velocity-Time Graphs

A *Velocity-Time graph* can LOOK just the same as a *Distance-Time graph* but means something *completely different*. The graph shown here is exactly the same SHAPE as the one above, *but the actual motions are completely different*.

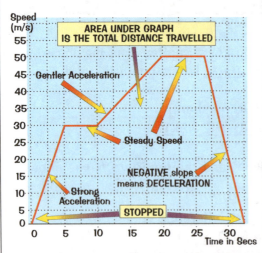

Remember these 5 important points:

1) At any point, GRADIENT = ACCELERATION, (The UNITS are m/s² don't forget).

2) For a CURVED GRAPH you'll need to draw a TANGENT to work out the ACCELERATION (gradient) at any particular point.

3) NEGATIVE SLOPE is DECELERATION.

4) FLAT SECTIONS are STEADY SPEED.

5) AREA UNDER GRAPH = DISTANCE TRAVELLED.

The *D/T graph* shows something *moving away and then back again* with *steady speeds* and *long stops*, rather like a DONKEY ON BLACKPOOL BEACH. The *V/T graph* on the other hand shows something that *sets off from rest*, *accelerates strongly*, *holds its speed*, then *accelerates again up to a maximum speed* which it holds for a while and then *comes to a dramatic halt at the end*. MORE LIKE A FERRARI! THAN A DONKEY!

The Acid Test:

LEARN the 9 IMPORTANT POINTS and the TWO DIAGRAMS then turn over and write them all down.

1) For the D/T graph shown above, work out the speed of the middle section in km/h.
2) For the V/T graph, work out the three different accelerations and the two steady speeds.

Straight Lines You Should Just Know

You ought to know these simple graphs straight off with no hesitation:

1) *Horizontal* and *Vertical* lines: "x = a" and "y = b"

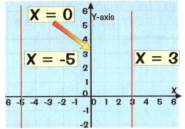

x=a is a vertical line through "a" on the x-axis

y=a is a horizontal line through "a" on the y-axis

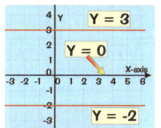

Don't forget: the y-axis is also the line x=0

Don't forget: the x-axis is also the line y=0

2) The *Main Diagonals*: "y = x" and "y = –x"

"Y = X" is the main diagonal that goes UPHILL from left to right.

"Y = -X" is the main diagonal that goes DOWNHILL from left to right.

3) Other *Sloping Lines* Through the origin: "y = ax" and "y = –ax"

y = ax and y = -ax are the equations for A SLOPING LINE THROUGH THE ORIGIN.

The value of "a" is the *GRADIENT* of the line, so the BIGGER the number, the STEEPER the slope — and a MINUS SIGN tells you it slopes DOWNHILL, as shown by the ones here:

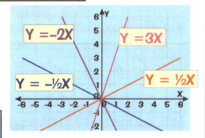

> The gradient of a horizontal line (eg y = 3) is 0.
> The gradient of a vertical line (eg x = 2) is ∞ (infinity — ooh).

All Other *Straight* Lines

Other straight-line equations are a little more complicated and the next two pages show three methods for drawing them. Mind you, the first step is identifying them in the first place. Remember:

All straight-line equations just contain *"something x, something y, and a number"*.

Straight lines:		NOT straight lines:	
x – y = 0	y = 2 + 3x	y = x³ + 3	2y – 1/x = 7
2y – 4x = 7	4x – 3 = 5y	1/y + 1/x = 2	x(3 – 2y) = 3
3y + 3x = 12	6y – x – 7 = 0	x² = 4 – y	xy + 3 = 0
5(x + 3y) = 5	12x – 7 = 3(x + 4y)	2x + 3y = xy	Y = ½SIN X

The Acid Test:

LEARN all the specific graphs on this page and also how to identify straight-line equations.

Now turn over the page and write down everything you've learned.

Plotting Straight-Line Graphs

Some people wouldn't know a straight-line equation if it ran up and bit them, but they're pretty easy to spot really — they just have two letters and a few numbers, but nothing fancy like squared or cubed, as shown on the bottom of the last page.

Anyway, in the Exam you'll be expected to be able to draw the graphs of straight-line equations. "$y = mx + c$" is the hard way of doing it (see P.31), but here's TWO NICE EASY WAYS of doing it:

1) The "Table of 3 values" method

You can EASILY draw the graph of ANY EQUATION using this EASY method:

> 1) Choose 3 VALUES OF X and draw up a wee table,
> 2) WORK OUT THE Y-VALUES,
> 3) PLOT THE COORDINATES, and DRAW THE LINE.

If it's a *straight-line equation*, the 3 points will be in a *dead straight line* with each other, which is the usual check you do when you've drawn it — if they aren't, then it could be a *curve* and you'll need to do *more values in your table* to find out what on earth's going on.

Example: *"Draw the graph of Y = 2X – 3"*

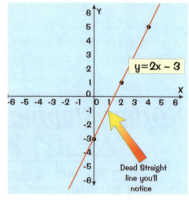

Dead Straight line you'll notice

1) DRAW UP A TABLE with some *suitable* values of X. Choosing X = 0, 2, 4 is usually cool enough.   i.e.

X	0	2	4
Y			

2) FIND THE Y-VALUES by putting each x-value into the equation:

X	0	2	4
Y	-3	1	5

   (e.g. When X = 4, $y = 2X - 3 = 2 \times 4 - 3 = 5$)

3) PLOT THE POINTS and DRAW THE LINE.

2) The "X = 0", "Y = 0" Method

> 1) Set x=0 in the equation and FIND Y — this is where it CROSSES THE Y-AXIS.
> 2) Set y=0 in the equation and FIND X — this is where it CROSSES THE X-AXIS.
> 3) Plot these two points and join them up with a straight line — and just hope it should be a straight line, since with only 2 points you can't really tell, can you!

Example: *"Draw the graph of 5x + 3y = 15"*

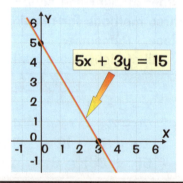

1) Putting x = 0 gives "3y = 15" $\Rightarrow$ y = 5
2) Putting y = 0 gives "5x = 15" $\Rightarrow$ x = 3
3) So plot y = 5 on the y-axis and x = 3 on the x-axis and join them up with a straight line:

Only doing 2 points is risky unless you're sure the equation is definitely a straight line — but then that's the big thrill of living life on the edge, isn't it.

The Acid Test: LEARN the details of these TWO EASY METHODS then turn over and write down all you know.

1) Draw these graphs using both methods   a) y = 4 + x   b) 4y + 3x = 12   c) y = 6 – 2x

Straight-Line Graphs: "Y = mx + c"

Using "y = mx + c" is perhaps the "proper" way of dealing with straight-line equations, and it's a nice trick if you can do it. The first thing you have to do though is <u>rearrange the equation</u> into the standard format "y = mx + c" like this:

<u>Straight line:</u>		<u>Rearranged into "y = mx +c"</u>	
y = 2 + 3x	→	y = 3x + 2	(m=3, c=2)
2y – 4x = 7	→	y =2x + 3½	(m=2, c=3½)
x – y = 0	→	y= x + 0	(m=1, c=0)
4x – 3 = 5y	→	y = 0.8x – 0.6	(m=0.8, c=-0.6)
3y + 3x = 12	→	y = -x + 4	(m=-1, c=4)

<u>REMEMBER</u>:   "<u>m</u>" equals the <u>GRADIENT</u> of the line.
"<u>c</u>" is the "<u>y-intercept</u>" (where the graph hits the y-axis).

<u>BUT WATCH OUT</u>: people mix up "m" and "c" when they get something like y = 5 + 2x.
REMEMBER, "m" is the number <u>IN FRONT OF THE "X"</u> and "c" is the number <u>ON ITS OWN</u>.

1) Sketching a *Straight Line* using y = mx + c

1) Get the equation into the form "<u>y = mx + c</u>".

2) *<u>Put a dot on the y-axis</u>* at the value of c.

3) Then go <u>ALONG ONE UNIT</u> and *up or down by the value of m* and make another dot.

4) *<u>Repeat</u>* the same "step" in *<u>both directions</u>*.

5) Finally check that the gradient <u>LOOKS RIGHT</u>.

The graph shows the process for the equation "y = 2x + 1":
1) "c" = 1, so put a first dot at y = 1 on the y-axis.
2) Go along 1 unit → and then up by 2 because "m" = +2.
3) Repeat the same step: 1→ 2↑ (or 1← 2↓).
4) CHECK: <u>a gradient of +2</u> should be <u>quite steep and uphill left to right</u> which it is, so it looks OK.

2) Finding the Equation of a Straight-Line Graph

This is the reverse process and is <u>EASIER</u>

1) From the axes, *<u>identify the two variables</u>* (e.g. "x and y" or "h and t").

2) *<u>Find the values</u>* of "<u>m</u>" (gradient) and "<u>c</u>" (y-intercept) from the graph.

3) Using these values from the graph, *<u>write down the equation</u>* with the standard format "y = mx + c".

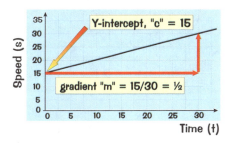

For the example above: "<u>S = ½t + 15</u>"

The Acid Test:
<u>LEARN</u> what straight-line equations look like and the <u>8</u> <u>RULES</u> for <u>drawing the lines</u> and <u>finding the equations</u>.

1) Sketch these graphs: a) y = 2 + x   b) y = x + 6   c) 4x – 2y = 0   d) y = 1 – ½x
e) x = 2y + 4   f) 2x – 6y – 8 = 0   g) 0.4x – 0.2y = 0.5   h) y = 3 – x + 2

Also in stage 2:

Quadratics

Quadratic functions are of the form <u>Y = anything with X^2 but not higher powers of X</u>.
Notice that all these X^2 graphs have the same <u>SYMMETRICAL bucket shape</u>.

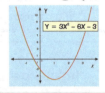

So when you plot a quadratic, remember that you're aiming for a symmetrical bucket shape — anything else is a sure sign that you've gone wrong.

Here's <u>how to tackle</u> questions on quadratics.

<u>Filling in</u> The Table of Values

<u>A typical question</u> would say *"Complete the table of values for the equation*
$y = x^2 - 4x + 3$ *"*

x	-2	-1	0	1	2	3	4	5	6
y			0			3			15

The rest of the question hinges on this table of values and one silly mistake here could cost you lots of marks — <u>YOU NEED TO MAKE SURE YOU GET THE NUMBERS RIGHT</u>:

1) First, <u>MAKE SURE YOU CAN REPRODUCE ANY VALUES THAT ARE ALREADY DONE</u>.

2) Once you've checked out your method, work out the other values <u>AT LEAST TWICE</u>.

3) Try to spot any <u>SYMMETRY or PATTERN</u> in the values, and check any that seem out of place.

You should be able to work out each value in one go on the calculator, but if things aren't working out you'll have to do a <u>SAFER METHOD</u>. For each value in the table you might be wise to write this out:

$$\underline{x=4} \qquad y = x^2 - 4x + 3$$
$$= 4^2 - 4\times4 + 3$$
$$= 16 - 16 + 3 = 3$$

<u>It's worth it, if it means you get it RIGHT rather than WRONG</u>!

<u>Plotting</u> the Points and <u>Drawing</u> the Curve

Here again there are <u>easy marks to be won and lost</u>. All these points matter:

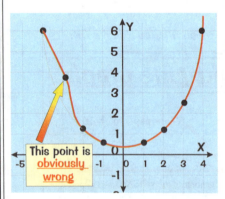

This point is <u>obviously wrong</u>

1) <u>Get the axes the right way round</u>: The values from the <u>FIRST row or column</u> are ALWAYS plotted <u>on the X-axis</u>.

2) Plot the points CAREFULLY, and don't muddle up the x and y values.

3) The points will ALWAYS form a <u>COMPLETELY SMOOTH CURVE</u>. <u>NEVER EVER let one point drag your line off</u> in some ridiculous direction. If one point seems out of place, <u>check the value in the table</u> and then the position where you've plotted it. When a graph is generated from an equation, <u>you never get spikes or lumps</u> — only MISTAKES.

4) A graph from an <u>ALGEBRA EQUATION</u> must always be a <u>SMOOTH CURVE</u> (or a dead straight line). You only use short straight-line sections to join points in "<u>Data Handling</u>".

The Acid Test:

LEARN the <u>3 Rules for tables of values</u> and the <u>4 points for drawing graphs</u>, then turn over and <u>write them down</u>.

1) <u>Complete the table of values</u> at the top of the page (applying the three rules of course).
2) Then <u>draw the graph</u>, taking note of the four points.
3) Using your graph, <u>find the value of y when x is 4.2</u>, and <u>the values of x when y=12</u>.

Pythagoras' Theorem and Bearings

Pythagoras' Theorem — $a^2 + b^2 = h^2$

1) <u>PYTHAGORAS' THEOREM</u> always goes hand in hand with *SIN*, *COS* and *TAN* because they're all involved with <u>RIGHT-ANGLED TRIANGLES</u>.

2) The big difference is that <u>PYTHAGORAS DOES NOT INVOLVE ANY ANGLES</u> — it just uses <u>two sides</u> to find the <u>third side</u>. (*SIN, COS* and *TAN* always involve <u>ANGLES</u>)

3) <u>THE BASIC FORMULA</u> for Pythagoras is $\boxed{a^2 + b^2 = h^2}$

4) <u>PLUG THE NUMBERS IN</u> and work it out.

5) <u>BUT GET THE NUMBERS IN THE RIGHT PLACE</u>. The 2 shorter sides squared add to equal the longest side squared.

6) <u>ALWAYS CHECK THAT YOUR ANSWER IS SENSIBLE</u>.

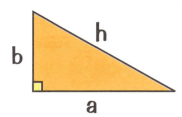

Example

"Find the missing side in the triangle shown."

<u>ANSWER</u>:

$$a^2 + b^2 = h^2$$
$$\therefore 3^2 + x^2 = 5^2$$
$$\therefore 9 + x^2 = 25$$

$$\therefore x^2 = 25 - 9 = 16$$
$$\therefore x = \sqrt{16} = \underline{4m}$$

(Is it <u>sensible</u>? — Yes, it's shorter than 5m, but not too much shorter)

5m — 3m

Bearings

To find or plot a bearing you must remember <u>the three key words</u>:

1) "FROM"

<u>Find the word "FROM" in the question</u>, and put your pencil on the diagram at the point you are going "<u>from</u>".

2) NORTH LINE

At the point you are going <u>FROM</u>, <u>draw in a NORTH LINE</u>.

3) CLOCKWISE

Now draw in the angle *CLOCKWISE* <u>from the north line to the line joining the two points</u>. This angle is the required bearing.

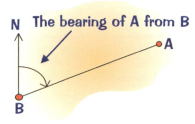
The bearing of A from B

Example

"Find the bearing of Q <u>from P</u>":

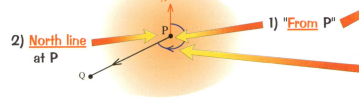

2) <u>North line</u> at P

1) "<u>From</u> P"

3) <u>Clockwise</u>, from the N-line. This angle is the <u>bearing of Q from P</u> and is <u>245⁰</u>.

N.B. <u>All bearings should be given as 3 figures</u>, e.g. 176^0, 034^0 (not 34^0), 005^0 (not 5^0), 018^0 etc.

The Acid Test:

LEARN the <u>6 facts about Pythagoras</u> and the <u>3 key words for bearings</u>. Then <u>turn over and write them down</u>.

1) Find the length of BC.
2) Find the bearing of T from H, by measuring from the diagram with a protractor.
3) CALCULATE the bearing of H from T.

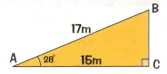
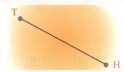

Pythagoras, Lines and Line Segments

Use Pythagoras to find the Distance Between Points

Now you've got the hang of Pythagoras' Theorem, you need to know when to apply it. In the Exam you'll have to spot when to use it for yourself.

Example: *"Point P has coordinates (8, 3) and point Q has coordinates (-4, 8). Find the length of the line PQ."*

If you get a question like this, follow these rules and it'll all become breathtakingly simple:

> 1) Draw a *sketch* to find the *right-angled triangle*.
>
> 2) Find the *lengths of the sides* of the triangle.
>
> 3) *Use Pythagoras* to find the *length of the diagonal*. (That's your answer.)

Solution:

①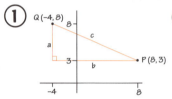

② Length of *side a* = 8 – 3 = **5**
Length of *side b* = 8 – -4 = **12**

③ *Use Pythagoras* to find *side c*:
$c^2 = a^2 + b^2 = 5^2 + 12^2 = 25 + 144 = 169$
So: $c = \sqrt{169} = 13$

Lines and Line Segments...

1) The example above asked you to find the length of the line PQ. To be really precise, the line PQ isn't actually a line — it's a **LINE SEGMENT**. Confused, read on...

2) A line is straight and continues to infinity (it goes on forever) in both directions. A line segment is just part of a line — it has 2 end points.

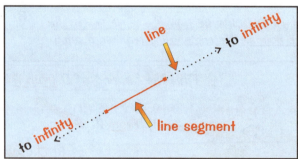

3) So the length PQ is just a chunk of the line running through P and Q. Don't worry too much about lines and line segments. The syllabus says you need to know the difference — and now you do. Just be aware that things which are actually line segments will often be referred to as lines.

The Acid Test:

LEARN the details on this page, then turn over and write them down.

1) Point A has coordinates (10, 15) and point B has coordinates (6, 12). Find the length of the line AB.

2) What is the difference between a line and a line segment?

Trigonometry — SIN, COS, TAN

There are several methods for doing Trig and they're all pretty much the same. However, *the method shown below has a number of advantages*, mainly because the *formula triangles* mean the same method is used every time (no matter which side or angle is being asked for). *This makes the whole topic a lot simpler*, and you'll find that once you've learned this method, the answers automatically come out right every time. It's just a joy.

Method

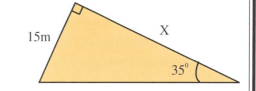

15m   X   35°

1) **Label the three sides O, A and H**
   (Opposite, Adjacent and Hypotenuse).

2) **Write down FROM MEMORY "SOH CAH TOA"**
   (Sounds like a Chinese word, "Sockatoa!")

3) **Decide WHICH TWO SIDES are INVOLVED O,H   A,H or O,A**
   and select SOH, CAH or TOA accordingly

4) **Turn the one you choose into a FORMULA TRIANGLE:**

S O H   **C A H**   **T O A**

$$\frac{O}{S^\theta \times H} \qquad \frac{A}{C^\theta \times H} \qquad \frac{O}{T^\theta \times A}$$

5) **Cover up the thing you want to find** (with your finger),
   and write down whatever is left showing.

6) **Translate into numbers and work it out.**

7) **Finally, check that your answer is SENSIBLE.**

Some *Nitty Gritty* Details

1) The <u>Hypotenuse</u> is the <u>LONGEST SIDE</u>. The <u>Opposite</u> is the side <u>OPPOSITE</u> the angle <u>being used</u> (θ), and the <u>Adjacent</u> is the side <u>NEXT TO</u> the angle <u>being used</u>.

2) In the formula triangles, S^θ represents SIN θ, C^θ is COS θ, and T^θ is TAN θ.

3) Remember, <u>TO FIND THE ANGLE — USE INVERSE</u>, i.e. press INV or SHIFT or 2nd, followed by SIN, COS or TAN (and make sure your calculator is in DEG mode).

4) You can only use SIN, COS and TAN on <u>RIGHT-ANGLED TRIANGLES</u> — you may have to add lines to the diagram to create one, especially with *isosceles triangles*.

The Acid Test:
LEARN the <u>7 Steps of the Method</u> and the Four Nitty Gritty Details. Then turn over and write them down.

Practising past paper questions is very important, but the whole point of doing so is to check and consolidate the methods <u>you have already learnt</u>. Don't make the mistake of thinking it's pointless learning these 7 steps. <u>If you don't know them all thoroughly, you'll just keep on getting questions wrong</u>.

Trigonometry — SIN, COS, TAN

Example 1) "Find x in the triangle shown."

1) Label O,A,H
2) Write down "SOH CAH TOA"
3) Two sides *involved*: O,H

4) So use

5) We want to find H so cover it up to leave: $H = \dfrac{O}{S^\theta}$

6) Translate :

$x = \dfrac{15}{SIN\ 35}$

Press `15` `÷` `SIN` `35` `=`   `26.151702`   So ans = **26.2m**

7) Check it's sensible: yes — it's about twice as big as 15, as the diagram suggests.

(N.B. on some calculators you press `35` `SIN` rather than `SIN` `35` — Know yours!)

Hyp
15m   x
Opp
35°
Adj

Example 2) "Find the angle θ in this triangle."

1) Label O, A, H
2) Write down "SOH CAH TOA"
3) Two sides *involved*: A,H

4) So use

5) We want to find θ so cover up C^θ to leave: $C^\theta = \dfrac{A}{H}$

6) Translate: $COS\ \theta = \dfrac{15}{25} = 0.6$

NOW USE INVERSE : $\theta = COS^{-1}(0.6)$

Press `INV` `COS` `0.6` `=`   `53.130102`   So ans. = **53.1°**

7) Finally, is it sensible? — Yes, the angle looks like about 50°.

Note the usual way of dealing with an *ISOSCELES TRIANGLE*: split it *down the middle* to get a *RIGHT ANGLE*:

25m   25m
θ
30m

Hyp
25m   Opp
θ   Adj
15m

The inverse cos function may appear as **COS⁻¹** *on your calculator.*

Angles of *Elevation* and *Depression*

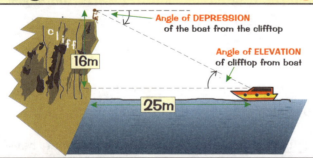

Angle of DEPRESSION
of the boat from the clifftop

Angle of ELEVATION
of clifftop from boat

cliff 16m   25m

1) The *Angle of Depression* is the angle *downwards* from the horizontal.

2) The *Angle of Elevation* is the angle *upwards* from the horizontal.

3) The Angles of Elevation and Depression are *EQUAL*.

The Acid Test:

Practise these two questions until you can apply the method *fluently* and without having to refer to it *at all*.

1) Find X   15m   28°   x

2) Find θ   15m   6m   θ

3) Calculate the angles of elevation and depression in the boat drawing above.

Circle Geometry

Now it's time for some lovely Geometry. Learn this page about Circles.

1) Don't muddle up these Two Circle Formulas

AREA of CIRCLE = π × (radius)²

$$A = \pi \times r^2$$

CIRCUMFERENCE = π × diameter

$$C = \pi \times D$$

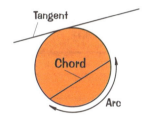

π = 3.141592....
= 3.14 (approx)

e.g. if the radius is 4cm, then
A = 3.14×(4×4)
= 50.24cm²

Circumference = distance round the outside of the circle

2) Arc, Chord and Tangent

A TANGENT is a straight line that just touches the outside of the circle.

A CHORD is a line drawn across the inside of a circle.

AN ARC is just part of the circumference of the circle.

3) Sectors and Segments are both Areas

SECTOR OF CIRCLE

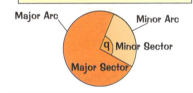

Major Arc   Minor Arc
q Minor Sector
Major Sector

SEGMENT OF CIRCLE

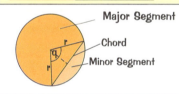

Major Segment
Chord
Minor Segment

4) Tangent and Radius Meet at 90⁰

A TANGENT is a line that just touches the edge of a circle (or other curve). If a tangent and radius meet at the same point, then the angle they make is EXACTLY 90⁰.

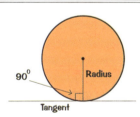

90⁰   Radius
Tangent

5) Equality of Tangents from a Point

The two tangents drawn from an outside point are always equal in length, so creating an "isosceles" situation, with two congruent right-angled triangles.

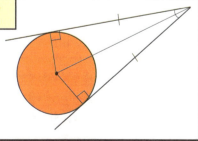

The Acid Test:

There are 5 SECTIONS on this page. They're all mighty important — LEARN THEM.

Now cover the page and write down everything you've learnt. Frightening isn't it.
1) A plate has a diameter of 14cm. Find the area and the circumference of the plate. Remember to show your working out.
2) A flower bed has a radius of 6m. Find the area and circumference of it.

Similarity and Enlargements

Enlarging a shape results in a similar shape — it has the same shape as the original, but is a different size. LEARN the 4 key features below.

1) If the Scale Factor is bigger than 1 the shape gets bigger.

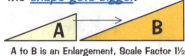

A to B is an Enlargement, Scale Factor 1½

2) If the Scale Factor is smaller than 1 (i.e. a fraction like ½) then the shape gets smaller. (Really this is a reduction, but you still call it an Enlargement, Scale Factor ½)

A to B is an Enlargement of Scale Factor ½

3) If the Scale Factor is NEGATIVE then the shape pops out the other side of the enlargement centre. If the scale factor is -1, it's exactly the same as a rotation of 180°.

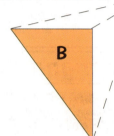

A to B is an enlargement of scale factor -2. B to A is an enlargement of scale factor -½.

4) The Scale Factor also tells you the relative distance of old points and new points from the Centre of Enlargement — this is very useful for drawing an enlargement, because you can use it to trace out the positions of the new points:

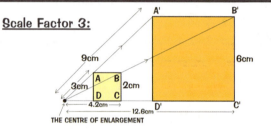

Scale Factor 3:

9cm, 6cm, 3cm, 2cm, 4.2cm, 12.6cm

THE CENTRE OF ENLARGEMENT

Areas and Volumes of Enlargements

Ho ho! This little joker catches everybody out. The increase in area and volume is **BIGGER** than the scale factor.

For example, if the Scale Factor is 2, the lengths are twice as big, each area is 4 times as big, and the volume is 8 times as big. Look at the rule below.

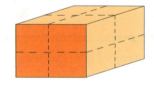

For a Scale Factor n:

The **SIDES** are n times bigger

The **AREAS** are n^2 times bigger

The **VOLUMES** are n^3 times bigger

Simple... but **VERY FORGETTABLE**

These ratios can also be expressed in this form:

Lengths	$n : m$	e.g. $3 : 4$
Areas	$n^2 : m^2$	e.g. $9 : 16$
Volumes	$n^3 : m^3$	e.g. $27 : 64$

A PARTICULAR EXAMPLE: 2 spheres have surface areas of $16m^2$ and $25m^2$. Find the ratio of their volumes.

<u>ANS</u>: $16 : 25$ is the areas ratio which must be $n^2 : m^2$, i.e. $n^2 : m^2 = 16 : 25$ and so $n : m = 4 : 5$ and so $n^3 : m^3 = \underline{64 : 125}$ The volumes ratio.

The Acid Test:

LEARN the 4 Key Features for Enlargements, plus the 3 Rules for Area and Volume Ratios. Then turn over and write them all down.

1) Draw the triangle A(2,1) B(5,2) C(4,4) and enlarge it by a scale factor of -1½, centred on the origin. Label the new triangle A' B' C' and give the coordinates of its corners.

2) Two similar cones have volumes of $27m^3$ and $64m^3$. If the surface area of the smaller one is $36m^2$, find the surface area of the other one.

Also in stage 3:

The Four Transformations

Transformations are about the most fun you can have without laughing.

T	ranslation	— ONE Detail
E	nlargement	— TWO Details
R	otation	— THREE Details
R	eflection	— ONE Detail
Y		

1) Use the word **TERRY** to remember the 4 types.

2) You must always remember to specify *all the details* for each type.

1) TRANSLATION

You must specify this ONE detail:

1) the **VECTOR OF TRANSLATION**
(See P.72 on vector notation)

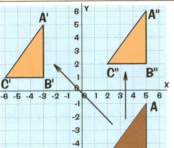

ABC to A'B'C' is a *translation of* $\begin{pmatrix} -8 \\ 6 \end{pmatrix}$

ABC to A"B"C" is a *translation of* $\begin{pmatrix} 0 \\ 7 \end{pmatrix}$

2) ENLARGEMENT

You must specify these 2 details:

1) The **SCALE FACTOR**
2) The **CENTRE** of Enlargement

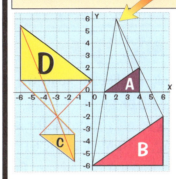

A to B is an enlargement of scale factor 2, and centre (2,6)

B to A is an enlargement of scale factor 1/2 and centre (2,6)

C to D is an enlargement of scale factor -2 and centre (-3,-2)

3) ROTATION

You must specify these 3 details:

1) **ANGLE** turned
2) **DIRECTION** (Clockwise or..)
3) **CENTRE** of Rotation

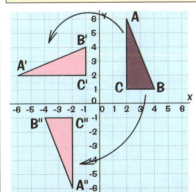

ABC to A'B'C' is a Rotation of 90°, anticlockwise, ABOUT the origin.

ABC to A"B"C" is a Rotation of half a turn (180°), clockwise, ABOUT the origin.

4) REFLECTION

You must specify this ONE detail:

1) The **MIRROR LINE**

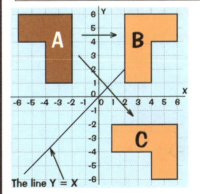

The line Y = X

A to B is a reflection IN the Y-axis.

A to C is a reflection IN the line Y=X

The Acid Test:

LEARN the names of the Four Transformations and the details that go with each. When you think you know it, *turn over and write it all down*.

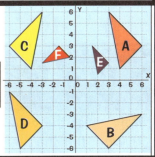

1) Describe *fully* these transformations: A→B, E→A, F→B, B→C, C→A, A→D, A→E, B→F.

Also in stage 2:

Areas, Solids and Nets

LEARN THESE FORMULAS for calculating the areas of rectangles and triangles.

1) Rectangle

Area of rectangle = length × width

Width

Length

$$A = l \times w$$

2) Triangle

Area of triangle = ½ × base × vertical height

$$A = \tfrac{1}{2} \times b \times h_v$$

Note that the height must always be the vertical height, not the sloping height.

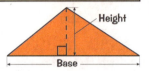

Height

Base

The alternative formula is this:
Area of triangle = ½ abSINC

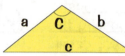

a   C   b

c

Surface Area and Nets

1) SURFACE AREA only applies to solid 3D objects, and it's simply the total area of all the outer surfaces added together.

2) There isn't usually a simple formula for surface area — you have to work out each side in turn and then ADD THEM ALL TOGETHER.

3) A NET is just a solid shape folded out flat.

4) So obviously: SURFACE AREA OF SOLID = AREA OF NET.

You need to know these 4 nets for the Exam. The area of each one can be found simply by using the formulas for rectangles and triangles above, and adding the sides.

1) Triangular Prism

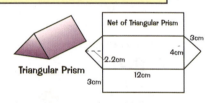

Net of Triangular Prism

3cm

4cm

2.2cm

12cm

3cm

Triangular Prism

2) Cube

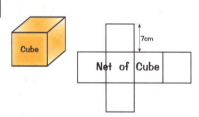

Cube

7cm

Net of Cube

3) Cuboid

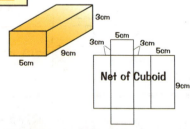

3cm

5cm   3cm   5cm

3cm

9cm   5cm

5cm

Net of Cuboid

9cm

4) Pyramid

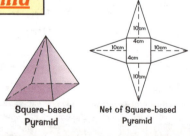

10cm

10cm   4cm   10cm

4cm

10cm

Square-based Pyramid

Net of Square-based Pyramid

The Acid Test:

LEARN the formulas for Areas of Rectangles and Triangles, the 4 details on Surface Area and Nets, and the FOUR NETS on this page.

Now cover the page and write down everything you've learnt.

1) Work out the area of all four nets shown above.

Volume or Capacity

VOLUMES — YOU MUST LEARN THESE TOO!

1) CUBOID (RECTANGULAR BLOCK)

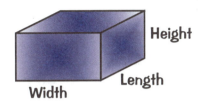

(This is also known as a '_rectangular prism_' — see below to understand why)

Volume of Cuboid = length × width × height

$$V = l \times w \times h$$

(The other word for volume is _CAPACITY_)

2) PRISM

A PRISM is a solid (3-D) object which has a CONSTANT AREA OF CROSS-SECTION — i.e. it's the same shape all the way through.

Now, for some reason, not a lot of people know what a prism is, but they come up all the time in Exams, so make sure YOU know.

Hexagonal Prism
(a flat one, certainly, but still a prism)

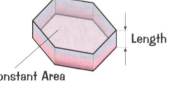

Constant Area of Cross-section

Length

Volume of prism = Cross-sectional Area × length

$$V = A \times l$$

Circular Prism
(or Cylinder)

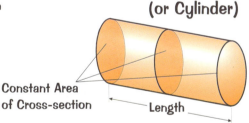

Constant Area of Cross-section

Length

Triangular Prism

Constant Area of Cross-section

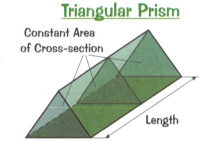

Length

As you can see, the formula for the volume of a prism is _very simple_. The _difficult_ part, usually, is _finding the area of the cross-section_.

The Acid Test:

LEARN this page. Then turn over and try to write it all down. Keep trying until you can do it.

Practise these two questions until you can do them both without any hesitation. Name the shapes and find their volumes:

a)

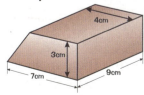

4cm

3cm

7cm   9cm

b)

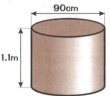

90cm

1.1m

Also in stage 2:

Mean, Median, Mode and Range

If you don't manage to *learn these 4 basic definitions* then you'll be passing up on some of the easiest marks in the whole Exam. It can't be *that* difficult can it?

1) *MODE*	=	*MOST* common
2) *MEDIAN*	=	*MIDDLE* value
3) *MEAN*	=	*TOTAL* of items ÷ *NUMBER* of items
4) *RANGE*	=	How far from the smallest to the biggest

THE GOLDEN RULE

Mean, median and mode should be *easy marks* but even people who've gone to the incredible extent of learning them still manage to lose marks in the Exam because they don't do *this one vital step*:

Always REARRANGE the data in ASCENDING ORDER

(and check you have the same number of entries!)

Example   *"Find the mean, median, mode and range of these numbers:"*

2, 5, 3, 2, 6, -4, 0, 9, -3, 1, 6, 3, -2, 3   (14)

1) FIRST... rearrange them: -4, -3, -2, 0, 1, 2, 2, 3, 3, 3, 5, 6, 6, 9   (14) ✓

2) MEAN = $\frac{\text{total}}{\text{number}}$ = $\dfrac{-4-3-2+0+1+2+2+3+3+3+5+6+6+9}{14}$

$$= 31 \div 14 = \underline{2.21}$$

3) MEDIAN = *the middle value* (only when they are *arranged in order of size*, that is!).

When there are two middle numbers as in this case, then the median is HALFWAY BETWEEN THE TWO MIDDLE NUMBERS.

> -4, -3, -2, 0, 1, 2, 2, 3, 3, 3, 5, 6, 6, 9
> ← seven numbers this side   ↑   seven numbers this side →
> Median = $\underline{2.5}$

4) MODE = *most* common value, which is simply $\underline{3}$. *(Or you can say "The modal value is 3".)*

5) RANGE = distance from lowest to highest value, i.e. from -4 up to 9, = $\underline{13}$.

REMEMBER: Mode = most (emphasise the 'o' in each when you say them).
Median = mid (emphasise the m*d in each when you say them).
Mean is just the average, but it's mean 'cos you have to work it out.

The Acid Test: LEARN The Four Definitions and THE GOLDEN RULE...

...then turn this page over and *write them down from memory*. Then apply all that you have *learnt* to this set of data: 1, 3, 14, -5, 6, -12, 18, 7, 23, 10, -5, -14, 0, 25, 8.

Frequency Tables

Frequency Tables can either be done in _rows_ or in _columns_ of numbers and they can be quite confusing, <u>but not if you learn these Eight key points</u>:

Eight Key Points

1) <u>ALL FREQUENCY TABLES ARE THE SAME</u>.

2) The word <u>FREQUENCY</u> just means <u>HOW MANY</u>, so a frequency table is nothing more than a <u>"How many in each group" table</u>.

3) The <u>FIRST ROW</u> (or column) just gives the <u>GROUP LABELS</u>.

4) The <u>SECOND ROW</u> (or column) gives the <u>ACTUAL DATA</u>.

Wait for it — we'll get to this on P.44.

5) You have to <u>WORK OUT A THIRD ROW</u> (or column) <u>yourself</u>.

6) The <u>MEAN</u> is always found using: | 3rd Row total ÷ 2nd Row Total |

7) The <u>MEDIAN</u> is found from the <u>MIDDLE VALUE in the 2nd row</u>.

8) The <u>RANGE</u> is found from <u>the extremes of the first row</u>.

Example

Here is a typical frequency table shown in both <u>ROW FORM</u> and <u>COLUMN FORM</u>:

No. of Sisters	Frequency
0	7
1	15
2	12
3	8
4	3
5	1
6	0

No. of Sisters	0	1	2	3	4	5	6
Frequency	7	15	12	8	3	1	0

 Column Form

 Row form

There's no real difference between these two forms and you could get either one in your Exam. Whichever you get, make sure you remember these <u>THREE IMPORTANT FACTS</u>:

1) <u>THE 1ST ROW</u> (or column) gives us the <u>GROUP LABELS</u> for <u>the different categories</u>: i.e. "no sisters", "one sister", "two sisters", etc.

2) <u>THE 2ND ROW</u> (or column) <u>is the ACTUAL DATA</u> and tells us <u>HOW MANY (people) THERE ARE</u> in each category i.e. 7 people had "<u>no sisters</u>", 15 people had "<u>one sister</u>", etc.

3) <u>BUT YOU SHOULD SEE THE TABLE AS _UNFINISHED_</u>, because it still needs <u>A THIRD ROW</u> (or column) and <u>TWO TOTALS</u> for the <u>2nd and 3rd rows</u>, as shown on the next page:

Frequency Tables

This is what the two types of table look like when they're completed:

No. of sisters	0	1	2	3	4	5	6	totals	
Frequency	7	15	12	8	3	1	0	46	(People asked)
No. x Frequency	0	15	24	24	12	5	0	80	(Sisters)

No. of Sisters	Frequency	No. x Frequency
0	7	0
1	15	15
2	12	24
3	8	24
4	3	12
5	1	5
6	0	0
TOTALS	46	80

(People asked)   (Sisters)

"Where does the third row come from?" ....I hear you cry!

THE THIRD ROW (or column) is ALWAYS obtained by MULTIPLYING the numbers FROM THE FIRST 2 ROWS (or columns).

THIRD ROW = 1ST ROW × 2ND ROW

Once the table is complete, you can easily find the MEAN, MEDIAN, MODE AND RANGE (see P.42) which is what they usually demand in the Exam: (see P.42)

Mean, Median, Mode and Range:

This is easy enough *if you learn it*. If you don't, you'll drown in a sea of numbers.

1) MEAN = $\dfrac{\text{3rd Row Total}}{\text{2nd Row Total}}$ = $\dfrac{80}{46}$ = 1.74 (Sisters per person)

2) MEDIAN: — imagine the original data *SET OUT IN ASCENDING ORDER*:

0000000 111111111111111 222222222222 33333333 444 5

↑

and the median is just the middle, which is here between the 23rd and 24th digits.
So for this data THE MEDIAN IS 2.

(Of course, when you get slick at this you can easily find the position of the middle value straight from the table.)

3) The MODE is *very easy* – it's just THE GROUP WITH THE MOST ENTRIES: i.e 1

4) The RANGE is 5 – 0 = 5   The first row tells us there are people with anything from "no sisters" right up to "five sisters" (but not 6 sisters). (Always give it as a single number.)

The Acid Test:

LEARN the 8 RULES for Frequency Tables, then turn over and WRITE THEM DOWN to see what you know.

Using the methods you have just learned and this frequency table, find the MEAN, MEDIAN, MODE and RANGE of the no. of phones that people have.

No. of Phones	0	1	2	3	4	5	6
Frequency	1	25	53	34	22	5	1

Grouped Frequency Tables

These are a bit trickier than simple frequency tables, but they can still look deceptively simple, like this one which shows the distribution of weights of a bunch of 60 school kids.

Weight (kg)	31 — 40	41 — 50	51 — 60	61 — 70	71 — 80
Frequency	8	16	18	12	6

Class Boundaries and Mid-Interval Values

These are the two little jokers that make Grouped Frequency tables so tricky.

1) THE CLASS BOUNDARIES are the precise values where you'd pass from one group into the next. For the above table the class boundaries would be at 40.5, 50.5, 60.5, etc. It's not difficult to work out what the class boundaries will be, just so long as you're clued up about it — they're nearly always "something.5" anyway, for obvious reasons.

2) THE MID-INTERVAL VALUES are pretty self-explanatory really and usually end up being "something.5" as well. Mind you a bit of care is needed to make sure you get the exact middle!

"Estimating" the Mean using Mid-Interval Values

Just like with ordinary frequency tables you have to *add extra rows and find totals* to be able to work anything out. Also notice *you can only "estimate" the mean from grouped data tables* — you can't find it exactly unless you know all the original values.

> 1) Add a 3rd row and enter MID-INTERVAL VALUES for each group.
> 2) Add a 4th row and multiply FREQUENCY × MID-INTERVAL VALUE for each group.

Weight (kg)	31 — 40	41 — 50	51 — 60	61 — 70	71 — 80	TOTALS
Frequency	8	16	18	12	6	60
Mid-Interval Value	35.5	45.5	55.5	65.5	75.5	—
Frequency × Mid-Interval Value	284	728	999	786	453	3250

1) ESTIMATING THE MEAN is then the usual thing of DIVIDING THE TOTALS:

$$\text{Mean} = \frac{\text{Overall Total (Final Row)}}{\text{Frequency Total (2nd Row)}} = \frac{3250}{60} = \underline{54.2}$$

2) THE MODE is still nice 'n' easy: the modal group is 51 — 60kg

3) THE MEDIAN can't be found exactly but you can at least say which group it's in. If all the data were put in order, the 30th/31st entries would be in the 51 — 60kg group.

The Acid Test:

LEARN all the details on this page, then turn over and write down everything you've learned. Good clean fun.

1) Estimate the mean for this table:
2) Also state the modal group and the approximate value of the median.

Length(cm)	15.5 —	16.5 —	17.5 —	18.5 — 19.5
Frequency	12	18	23	8

Cumulative Frequency

FOUR KEY POINTS

1) CUMULATIVE FREQUENCY just means ADDING IT UP AS YOU GO ALONG.
2) You have to ADD A THIRD ROW to the table — the RUNNING TOTAL of the 2nd row.
3) When plotting the graph, always plot points using the HIGHEST VALUE in each group (of row 1) with the value from row 3, i.e. plot 13 at 160.5, etc. (see below).
4) CUMULATIVE FREQUENCY is always plotted up the side of a graph, not across.

Example

Height (cm)	141 – 150	151 – 160	161 – 170	171 – 180	181 – 190	191 – 200	201 – 210
Frequency	4	9	20	33	36	15	3
Cumulative Frequency	4 (AT 150.5)	13 (AT 160.5)	33 (AT 170.5)	66 (AT 180.5)	102 (AT 190.5)	117 (AT 200.5)	120 (AT 210.5)

The graph is plotted from these pairs: (150.5,4) (160.5,13) (170.5,33) (180.5,66) etc.

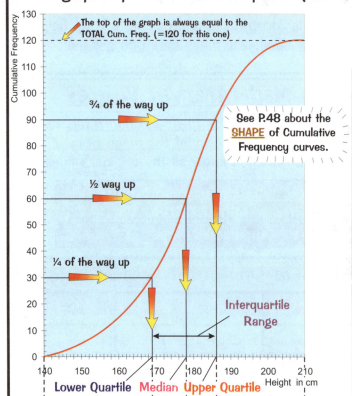

The top of the graph is always equal to the TOTAL Cum. Freq. (=120 for this one)

¾ of the way up

½ way up

¼ of the way up

See P.48 about the SHAPE of Cumulative Frequency curves.

Interquartile Range

Lower Quartile   Median   Upper Quartile

Height in cm

For a cumulative frequency curve there are THREE VITAL STATISTICS which you need to know how to find:

1) **MEDIAN**
   Exactly halfway UP, then across, then down and *read off the bottom scale*.

2) **LOWER AND UPPER QUARTILES**
   Exactly ¼ and ¾ UP the side, then across, then down and *read off the bottom scale*.

3) **THE INTERQUARTILE RANGE**
   The distance *on the bottom scale* between the lower and upper quartiles.

So from the cumulative frequency curve for this data, we get these results:
MEDIAN = 178 cm
LOWER QUARTILE = 169 cm
UPPER QUARTILE = 186 cm
INTERQUARTILE RANGE = 17 cm (186 – 169)

A Box Plot shows the Interquartile Range as a Box

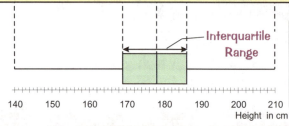

Interquartile Range

Height in cm

TO CREATE YOUR VERY OWN BOX PLOT:
1) *Draw the scale* along the bottom.
2) *Draw a box* the length of the *interquartile range*.
3) *Draw a line* down the box to show the *median*.
4) *Draw "whiskers"* up to the *maximum and minimum*.

(They're sometimes called "Box and Whisker diagrams".)

The Acid Test:

LEARN THIS PAGE, then cover it up and do these:

1) *Complete* this cumulative frequency table:
2) *Draw the graph*. Find the *3 Vital Statistics*.
3) Draw the box plot under the graph.

Weight (kg)	41 – 45	46 – 50	51 – 55	56 – 60	61 – 65	66 – 70	71 – 75
Frequency	2	7	17	25	19	8	2

Histograms and Frequency Density

Histograms

A histogram is like a bar chart with different width bars — the **AREA** of each bar gives the **FREQUENCY**, **NOT** the **HEIGHT** of the bars.

This changes them from nice easy-to-understand diagrams into seemingly incomprehensible monsters, and yes, you've guessed it, that makes them a *firm favourite* with the Examiners.

In fact things aren't half as bad as that — but only if you **LEARN THE THREE RULES:**

> 1) It's <u>not</u> the height, but the <u>AREA of each bar that matters.</u>
> 2) <u>Use the snip of information they give you</u> to find
>   <u>HOW MUCH IS REPRESENTED BY EACH AREA BLOCK.</u>
> 3) <u>Divide all the bars into THE SAME SIZED AREA BLOCKS</u>
>   and so work out the number for each bar (using **AREAS**).

EXAMPLE:

The histogram below represents the age distribution of people arrested for slurping boiled sweets in public places in 1995. Given that there were 40 people in the 55 to 65 age range, find the number of people arrested in all the other age ranges.

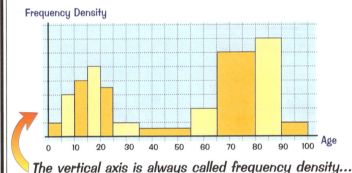

Frequency Density

The vertical axis is always called frequency density...

ANSWER:

The 55-65 bar represents *40 people* and contains *4 dotted squares*, so *each dotted square* must represent *10 people*.

The rest is easy. E.g. the 80-90 group has 14 dotted squares so that represents 14 × 10 = *140 people*.

> REMEMBER: <u>ALWAYS COUNT AREA BLOCKS</u> to find <u>THE NUMBER IN EACH BAR.</u>

Frequency Density is the Height of a Bar

You don't need to worry too much about this. It says in the syllabus that you need to understand frequency density, so here it is. Learn the formula and you'll be fine.

> **FREQUENCY DENSITY = FREQUENCY ÷ CLASS WIDTH**
>
> *Frequency density = the height of a bar.*
> *Frequency = the area of a bar.*
> *Class width = the width of the bar along the x-axis.*

EXAMPLE: For the 55-65 bar: Frequency = 40 people, class width = 10 years

Frequency density = frequency ÷ class width

So: Frequency density = 40 ÷ 10 = 4 — the *height of the bar.*

The Acid Test:
LEARN the <u>THREE RULES for Histograms</u> and the formula for <u>frequency density. Turn over and write it all down.</u>

1) Find the number of people arrested in each of the age ranges for the boiled sweet histogram above.
2) If the frequency is 25 and the class width is 5, what is the frequency density?

Also in stage 2:

Correlation, Dispersion and Spread

Shapes of Histograms and "Spread"

You can easily estimate the mean from the shape of a histogram — it's more or less **IN THE MIDDLE**.

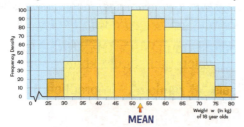
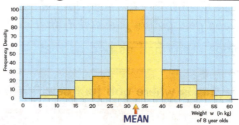

You must *LEARN the significance of the shapes* of these two histograms:

1) The first shows *high dispersion* (i.e. a *large spread* of results away from the mean).
   (i.e. the weights of a sample of 16 year olds will cover a very wide range)

2) The second shows a *"tighter"* distribution of results where most values are within a *narrow range* either side of the mean.
   (i.e the weights of a sample of 8 year olds will show very little variation)

Cumulative Freq. Curves and "Spread"

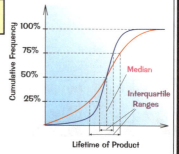

The shape of a **CUMULATIVE FREQUENCY CURVE** also tells us *how spread out* the data values are.

The *blue* line shows a *very tight distribution* around the **MEDIAN** and this also means the *interquartile range is small* as shown.

The *red* line shows a more *widely spread* set of data and therefore a *larger interquartile range*.

'Tight' distribution represents **CONSISTENT** results. E.g. the *lifetimes of light bulbs* would all be very close to the median, indicating a *good product*. The lifetimes of another product may show *wide variation*, which shows that the product is not as consistent. *They often ask about this "shape significance" in Exams.*

Scatter Graphs — Correlation and the Line of Best Fit

A scatter graph tells you how closely two things are related — the fancy word for this is *CORRELATION*. *Good correlation* means the two things are *closely related* to each other. *Poor correlation* means there is *very little relationship*. The *LINE OF BEST FIT* goes roughly *through the middle of the scatter of points*. (It doesn't have to go through any of the points exactly, but it may do.) If the line slopes *up* it's *positive correlation*, if it slopes *down* it's *negative correlation*. *Zero correlation* means there's no *linear relationship*.

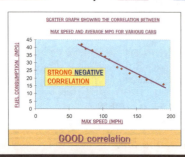

GOOD correlation

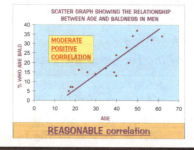

REASONABLE correlation

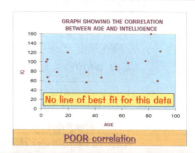

POOR correlation

The Acid Test:

LEARN THIS PAGE. Then *turn over* and *write down all the important details* from memory.

1) Draw two contrasting histograms showing speeds of cyclists and motorists.
2) Sketch two cumulative freq. curves for heights of 5 yr olds and 13 yr olds.

Sampling Methods

This is all about doing surveys of "populations" (not necessarily people) to find things out about them. Things start getting awkward when it's not possible to test the whole population, usually because there's just too many.

In that case you have to take a __SAMPLE__, which means you somehow have to select a limited number of individuals so that they properly represent the whole population.

There are __THREE DIFFERENT TYPES OF SAMPLING__ which you should know about:

__RANDOM__ — this is where you just select individuals "at random". In practice it can be surprisingly difficult to make the selection truly random.

__SYSTEMATIC__ — Select one at random, then select every, say, 10th or 100th one after that.

__STRATIFIED__ — this is used when a population is made up of groups (or categories).
A random sample is chosen in each group, proportional to the size of the group.

E.g. In a school there are 400 girls and 600 boys — 1000 students.
For a total sample of 50, you'd need to _randomly_ choose 20 girls and 30 boys.

Spotting Problems with Sampling Methods

In practice, the most important thing you should be able to do is to spot problems with sampling techniques, which means "look for ways that the sample might not be a true reflection of the population as a whole".

One mildly amusing way to practise is to think up examples of bad sampling techniques:

1) A survey of motorists carried out in London concluded that 85% of the British people drive black cabs.

2) Two surveys carried out on the same street corner asked, "Do you believe in God?" One found 90% of people didn't and the other found 90% of people did. The reason for the discrepancy? — one was carried out at 11 pm Saturday night and the other at 10.15 am Sunday morning.

3) A telephone survey carried out in the evening asked, "What do you usually do after work or school?" It found that 80% of the population usually stay in and watch TV. A street survey conducted at the same time found that only 30% usually stay in and watch TV. Astonishing.

Other cases are less obvious:
In a telephone poll, 100 people were asked if they use the train regularly and 20% said yes. Does this mean 20% of the population regularly use the train?

__ANSWER__: Probably not. There are several things wrong with this sampling technique:
  1) First and worst: the sample is far too small. At least 1000 would be more like it.
  2) What about people who don't have their own phone, e.g. students, tenants, etc.
  3) What time of day was it done? When might regular train users be in or out?
  4) Which part or parts of the region would you telephone?
  5) If the results were to represent, say, the whole country, then stratified sampling would be essential.

The Acid Test:
__LEARN__ the three sampling techniques, and make sure you understand the potential problems with sampling methods.

1) A survey was done to investigate the average age of cars on Britain's roads by standing on a motorway bridge and noting the registration of the first 200 cars. Give three reasons why this is a poor sampling technique and suggest a better approach.

Also in stage 3:

Time Series

Time Series — Measure the Same Thing over a Period of Time

A time series is what you get if you measure the same thing at a number of different times.

EXAMPLE: Measuring the temperature in your greenhouse at 12 o'clock each day gives you a time series — other examples might be profit figures, crime figures or rainfall.

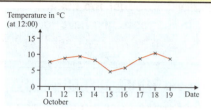

Temperature in °C (at 12:00)

___

THE RETAIL PRICE INDEX (RPI) IS A TIME SERIES: Every month, the prices of loads of items (same ones each month) — are combined to get an index number called the RPI, which is a kind of average. As goods get more expensive, this index number gets higher and higher. So when you see on TV that inflation this month is 2.5%, what it actually means is that the RPI is increasing at an annual rate of 2.5%.

Seasonality — The Same Basic Pattern

This is when there's a definite pattern that **REPEATS ITSELF** every so often. This is called **SEASONALITY** and the "so often" is called the **PERIOD**.

> To find the **PERIOD**, measure **PEAK TO PEAK** (or trough to trough).

This series has a *period of 12 months*. There are a few irregularities, so the pattern isn't exactly the same every 12 months, but it's about right.

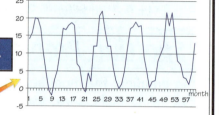

Trend — Ignoring the Wrinkles

This time series has lots of random fluctuations, but there's a definite upwards *trend*.

The pink line is the trend line. It's straight, so this is a linear *trend.*

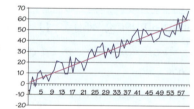

Moving Average — Smooths Out the Seasonality

It's easier to spot a trend if you can 'get rid of' the seasonality and some of the irregularities.

One way to smooth a series is to use a *moving average*.

This is a time series that definitely looks periodic — but it's difficult to tell if there's a trend.

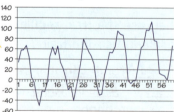

... but plot the moving average (at the mid-point of the period each time) (in pink — must be pink — that's dead important)...

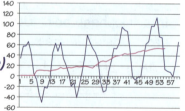

...and you can easily see the *upward trend*.

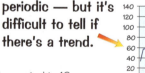

The period is 12, so you use 12 values for the moving average:

HOW TO FIND A MOVING AVERAGE:

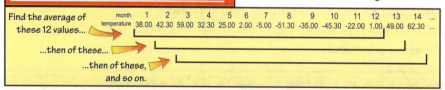

Find the average of these 12 values...

month	1	2	3	4	5	6	7	8	9	10	11	12	13	14	...
temperature	38.00	42.30	59.00	32.30	25.00	2.00	-5.00	-51.30	-35.00	-45.30	-22.00	1.00	49.00	62.30	...

...then of these...

...then of these, and so on.

The Acid Test:

LEARN the words TIME SERIES, SEASONALITY, PERIOD, TREND, MOVING AVERAGE. Cover the page and write a description of each.

1) My town's rainfall is measured every month for 20 yrs and graphed. There's a rough pattern, which repeats itself every 4 months. a) What is the period of this time series? b) Describe how to calculate a moving average.

Revision Summary for Stage One

These questions might seem a bit tricky, _but they're the very best revision you can do._ They follow the sequence of pages in Stage One, so you can easily look up anything you don't know. Keep going until you've got them sorted.

1) What are square, cube and prime numbers? Write down the first 10 of each.
2) What are a) multiples b) factors c) prime factors?
3) What are the LCM and HCF?
4) What is the method for rounding a number to three significant figures?
5) What is the possible error when rounding to a specified unit of accuracy?
6) How do you estimate a square root?
7) Describe the methods for multiplying, dividing, cancelling down and adding fractions.
8) Demonstrate the two methods for turning recurring decimals into fractions.
9) Explain what BODMAS is. Does your calculator know about it?
10) How do you enter a time in hours, minutes and seconds on your calculator?
11) What are the three steps for using conversion factors? Give three examples.
12) Give 8 metric, 5 imperial and 8 metric-to-imperial conversions.
13) How do you simplify awkward ratios, e.g. 3.25 : 4.5?
14) How do you split a total amount in a certain ratio?
15) Make up and complete your own example for each of the three types of percentage question.
16) What is the formula for compound growth and decay? Give 3 examples of its use.
17) What is the format of any number expressed in standard form?
18) Which is the standard form button? What would you press to enter 6×10^8?
19) Write down nine rules for powers and roots.
20) What is the method for multiplying pairs of brackets?
21) What are the six steps for solving equations?
22) Write down the 4 steps of the trial and improvement method.
23) What are the two formulas for finding the nth term of a sequence?
24) Give 5 important details relating to velocity-time graphs.
25) What is the "x = 0, y = 0" method of plotting straight-line graphs?
26) What do "m" and "c" represent in y = mx + c?
27) What's the formula for Pythagoras' theorem? Where can you use Pythagoras?
28) What are the three key words for bearings? How must bearings be written?
29) How do you decide whether to use SIN, COS or TAN in trig questions?
30) Draw a circle and show what an arc, a chord, a sector, a segment and a tangent are.
31) What three types of scale factor are there and what is the result of each?
32) How many details must be specified for each type of transformation?
33) Sketch the nets of a triangular prism, a cube, a cuboid and a pyramid.
34) Write down the formula for the volume of a prism.
35) Write down the definitions of mean, median, mode and range.
36) Write down eight important details about frequency tables.
37) How do you _estimate_ the mean from a grouped frequency table?
38) Draw a typical cumulative frequency curve, and indicate on it exactly where the median etc. are to be found.
39) Draw a box plot underneath your cumulative frequency curve from question 38.
40) What is the main difference between a histogram and a regular bar chart?
41) What does the shape of a histogram show about the dispersion of a set of data?
42) What does a scatter graph illustrate? What is the fancy word for this?
43) Name the four main sampling methods and give a brief description of each.
44) Which one of these is NOT a time series?
      a) measuring the temperature in 20 different countries at 12:00 today, GMT
      b) measuring the temperature in Britain at 12:00 every day for 100 days
45) How can you find out if a seasonal time series has an overall trend?

Reciprocals and Proportion

Reciprocals — Learn these 4 Facts

1) The reciprocal of a number is "one over" the number.

> The reciprocal of $5 = \frac{1}{5}$.

2) You can find the reciprocal of a fraction by turning it upside down.

> The reciprocal of $\frac{3}{8} = \frac{8}{3}$.

3) A number multiplied by its reciprocal gives 1.

> $\frac{6}{7} \times \frac{7}{6} = 1$

4) 0 has no reciprocal because you can't divide anything by 0.

The $\frac{1}{x}$ (or x^{-1}) Button Makes Reciprocals much Easier

This has two very useful functions:

1) Making divisions a bit slicker E.g. if you already have 2.3456326 in the display and you want to do 12 ÷ 2.3456326, then you can just press ÷ 12 = $\frac{1}{x}$ =, which does the division the wrong way up and then flips it the right way up.

2) Analysing decimals to see if they might be rational (i.e. something simple, see p.53), e.g. if the display is 0.1428571 and you press $\frac{1}{x}$ = you'll get 7, meaning it was 1/7 before.

Proportion — Two Amounts that are Linked Together

The two amounts in proportion questions will be either directly or inversely proportional. LEARN these definitions.

> DIRECTLY PROPORTIONAL — if one amount increases, the other increases too.

> INVERSELY PROPORTIONAL — if one amount increases, the other decreases.

So, if one amount changes, you can work out the new value for the other amount.
THE GOLDEN RULE is to work out one — if you know the amount of one thing, the rest is easy.

Example: A shop assistant earns £7 for 2 hours' work. How much would he earn if he worked for 5 hours?

Answer: First work out one — the amount he earns for ONE hour's work.
£7 ÷ 2 hours = £3.50 pounds for one hour.
So the pay for 5 hours is 5 × £3.50 = £17.50

The number of hours he works and the amount he earns are directly proportional.

Example: It takes 6 people 5 hours to dig a hole. How long would it take 10 people working at the same rate?

Answer: First work out one — how long it would take for ONE person to dig a hole.
6 people × 5 hours = 30 hours' work for one person.
So 10 people would take 30 ÷ 10 = 3 hours.

The number of people digging a hole and the time it takes are inversely proportional.

The Acid Test:
Make sure you know the difference between direct and inverse proportion.

1) What do you need to multiply $\frac{2}{9}$ by to get 1?

2) Which calculator button would you use to check if a decimal was a rational number?

3) 3.5 kg of bananas cost £2.80. How much would 5.5 kg of bananas cost?

Manipulating Surds and Use of π

RATIONAL NUMBERS The vast majority of numbers are rational. They are always either:

> 1) A whole number (either positive (+ve), or negative (−ve)), e.g. 4, -5, -12
> 2) A fraction p/q, where p and q are whole numbers (+ve or −ve), e.g. ¼, -½, ¾
> 3) A terminating or recurring decimal, e.g. 0.125   0.3333333333...   0.143143143143..

IRRATIONAL NUMBERS are messy!

> 1) They are always <u>NEVER-ENDING NON-REPEATING DECIMALS</u>. π is irrational.
> 2) A *good source* of <u>IRRATIONAL NUMBERS</u> is <u>SQUARE ROOTS AND CUBE ROOTS</u>.

Manipulating Surds

It sounds like something to do with controlling difficult children, but it isn't. Surds are expressions with irrational square roots in them. You <u>MUST USE THEM</u> if they ask you for an <u>EXACT</u> answer. There are a few simple rules to learn:

1) $\sqrt{a} \times \sqrt{b} = \sqrt{ab}$ e.g. $\sqrt{2} \times \sqrt{3} = \sqrt{2 \times 3} = \sqrt{6}$ — also $(\sqrt{b})^2 = b$, fairly obviously

2) $\frac{\sqrt{a}}{\sqrt{b}} = \sqrt{\frac{a}{b}}$ e.g. $\frac{\sqrt{8}}{\sqrt{2}} = \sqrt{\frac{8}{2}} = \sqrt{4} = 2$

3) $\sqrt{a} + \sqrt{b}$ — <u>NOTHING DOING</u>...   (in other words it is definitely NOT $\sqrt{a+b}$)

4) $(a + \sqrt{b})^2 = (a + \sqrt{b})(a + \sqrt{b}) = a^2 + 2a\sqrt{b} + b$ (NOT just $a^2 + (\sqrt{b})^2$)

5) $(a + \sqrt{b})(a - \sqrt{b}) = a^2 + a\sqrt{b} - a\sqrt{b} - (\sqrt{b})^2 = a^2 - b$

6) Express $\frac{3}{\sqrt{5}}$ in the form $\frac{a\sqrt{5}}{b}$ where a and b are whole numbers.
   To do this you must *"RATIONALISE the denominator"*, which just means multiplying top and bottom by $\sqrt{5}$: $\frac{3\sqrt{5}}{\sqrt{5}\sqrt{5}} = \frac{3\sqrt{5}}{5}$ so a = 3 and b = 5

7) If you want an *exact* answer, <u>LEAVE THE SURDS IN</u>. As soon as you go using that calculator, you'll get a *big fat rounding error* — and you'll get the answer <u>WRONG</u>. Don't say I didn't warn you...

> **Example:** A square has an area of 15 cm². Find the length of one of its sides.
> **Answer:** The length of a side is $\sqrt{15}$ cm.
>
> If you <u>have a calculator</u>, then you can work out $\sqrt{15} = 3.8729833...$cm.
> If you're working <u>without a calculator</u>, or are asked to give an <u>EXACT</u> answer,
> then just write: $\sqrt{15}$ cm. That's all you have to do.

Exact *calculations using* π — *Leave* π *in the answer*

π is another <u>irrational</u> number that often comes up in calculations, e.g. in finding the area of a circle. Most of the time you can use the nifty little π button on your calculator. But if you're asked to give an <u>exact</u> answer or, worse still, do the calculation <u>without a calculator</u>, just <u>leave</u> the π symbol in the calculation.

> **Example:** Find the area of a circle with radius 4 cm, without using a calculator.
> **Answer:** The area = $\pi r^2 = \pi \times 4^2 = 16\pi$ cm².

The Acid Test:
**LEARN the 7 rules for <u>manipulating surds</u>,
then <u>turn over and write it all down</u>.**

Simplify a) $(1 + \sqrt{2})^2 - (1 - \sqrt{2})^2$ b) $(1 + \sqrt{2})^2 - (2\sqrt{2} - \sqrt{2})^2$

Rounded Off Values

You should be confident about rounding numbers off to a certain number of decimal places or significant figures. *It gets tricky when they start asking about the maximum and minimum values possible* for a given level of accuracy in the rounding.

1) Finding the Upper and Lower bounds of a Single Measurement

The simple rule is this:

> The real value can be as much as HALF THE ROUNDED UNIT above and below the rounded-off value

E.g. If a length is given as 2.4 m to the nearest 0.1 m, the rounded unit is 0.1 m so the real value could be anything up to 2.4m ± 0.05m. This gives answers of 2.45m and 2.35m for the upper and lower bounds.

2) The Maximum and Minimum Possible Values of a Calculation

When a calculation is done using rounded-off values there will be a DISCREPANCY between the CALCULATED VALUE and the ACTUAL VALUE:

EXAMPLE: A floor is measured as being 5.3 m × 4.2 m to the nearest 10 cm. This gives an area of 22.26 m², but this is not the actual floor area because

the real values could be anything from 5.25 m to 5.35 m and 4.15 m to 4.25 m,

∴ Maximum possible floor area = $5.35 \times 4.25 = 22.7375$ m²,

∴ Minimum possible floor area = $5.25 \times 4.15 = 21.7875$ m².

3) Maximum Percentage Error

Having found the two possible extreme values, the one which is FARTHEST from the rounded value will give the maximum percentage error using this familiar formula:

$$\text{Percentage Error} = \frac{\text{Maximum Error}}{\text{Original}} \times 100$$

But watch out — the "original" is the EXTREME value, not the *rounded* one.

E.g. for the above rectangle the max error is 22.7375 – 22.26 = 0.4775 so the max percentage error is

$$\frac{0.4775}{22.7375} \times 100 = 2.1\%$$

4) Alas it is not always so simple...

In many formulas (especially in Exam Questions) it ISN'T the biggest input values that give the maximum result. Consider $z = x + \frac{1}{y}$. The maximum value for z will result from the *maximum* value for x coupled with the *minimum* value for y.

So when the question looks more complicated, the *safest method* is to work out the answer *using all four combinations* and see which combinations give the maximum and minimum results.

The Acid Test:

LEARN the FOUR POINTS on this page, then <u>turn over and write down</u> the important details for each of them.

1) x and y are measured as 2.32m and 0.45m to the nearest 0.01m. T is given by $T = (x - y)/y$. Find the maximum possible percentage error in T if the rounded values of x and y are used to calculate it.

Algebraic Fractions and The Difference of Two Squares

Algebra can look pretty tricky with all those letters standing in place of numbers. But if you take your time and look at the question properly, you'll often find you can either simplify questions by cancelling terms or pick out familiar expressions that you know how to tackle.

D.O.T.S. — The Difference Of Two Squares:

$$a^2 - b^2 = (a + b)(a - b)$$

 This is an IDENTITY — it works for all values of a and b.

The "difference of two squares" (D.O.T.S. for short) is where you have "one thing squared" take away "another thing squared" and in the Exam you'll more than likely be asked to factorise a D.O.T.S. expression (i.e. put it into two brackets as above). Too many people have more trouble than they should with this, probably because they don't make enough effort to learn it as a separate item in its own right. So learn it now and it'll be familiar come exam time and you'll know exactly what to do. Make sure you LEARN THESE important examples:

1) Factorise $9P^2 - 16Q^2$. Answer: $9P^2 - 16Q^2 = (3P + 4Q)(3P - 4Q)$
2) Factorise $1 - T^4$. Answer: $1 - T^4 = (1 + T^2)(1 - T^2)$
3) Factorise $3K^2 - 75H^2$. Answer: $3K^2 - 75H^2 = 3(K^2 - 25H^2) = 3(K + 5H)(K - 5H)$

Algebraic Fractions

The basic rules are exactly the same as for ordinary fractions (see P.8), and you should definitely be aware of the close similarity.

1) Multiplying (easy)

Multiply top and bottom separately and cancel if possible:

e.g. $\dfrac{st}{10w^3} \times \dfrac{35s^2tw}{6} = \dfrac{35s^3t^2w}{60w^3} = \dfrac{7s^3t^2}{12w^2}$

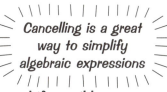 Cancelling is a great way to simplify algebraic expressions

2) Dividing (easy)

Turn the second one upside down, then multiply and cancel if possible:

e.g. $\dfrac{12}{p+4} \div \dfrac{4(p-3)}{3(p+4)} = \dfrac{\cancel{12}^{3}}{\cancel{p+4}} \times \dfrac{3\cancel{(p+4)}}{\cancel{4}(p-3)} = \dfrac{9}{p-3}$

3) Adding/subtracting (not so easy)

Always get a common denominator i.e. same bottom line (by cross-multiplying) and then ADD TOP LINES ONLY:

$\dfrac{t-2p}{3t-p} - \dfrac{1}{3} = \dfrac{3(t-2p)}{3(3t-p)} - \dfrac{1(3t-p)}{3(3t-p)} = \dfrac{3t-6p-3t+p}{3(3t-p)} = \dfrac{-5p}{3(3t-p)}$

The Acid Test:

LEARN THE DETAILS of both sections on this page. Then turn over and write down what you've learned.

1) Factorise: a) $X^2 - 16Y^2$ b) $49 - 81P^2Q^2$ c) $12Y^2X^6 - 48K^4M^8$

2) Simplify $\dfrac{5abc^3}{18de} \div \dfrac{15abd^2}{9ce}$ 3) Simplify $\dfrac{3}{5} + \dfrac{5g}{3g-4}$

Rearranging Formulas

Rearranging Formulas means making one letter the subject, e.g. getting "y= " from something like $2x + z = 3(y + 2p)$.

Generally speaking "solving equations" is easier, but don't forget:

> 1) EXACTLY THE SAME METHOD APPLIES TO BOTH FORMULAS AND EQUATIONS.
> 2) THE SAME SEQUENCE OF STEPS APPLIES EVERY TIME.

We'll illustrate this by making "y" the subject of this formula: $M = \sqrt{2K - \dfrac{K^2}{2y+1}}$

The Six Steps Applied to Formulas

1) Get rid of any square root signs by squaring both sides: $M^2 = 2K - \dfrac{K^2}{2y+1}$

2) Get everything off the bottom by cross-multiplying up to EVERY OTHER TERM:

$$M^2 = 2K - \frac{K^2}{2y+1} \quad \Rightarrow \quad M^2(2y+1) = 2K(2y+1) - K^2$$

3) Multiply out any brackets: $2yM^2 + M^2 = 4Ky + 2K - K^2$

4) Collect all subject terms on one side of the "=" and all non-subject terms on the other. Remember to reverse the +/− sign of any term that crosses the "="

+4Ky moves across the "=" and becomes −4Ky
+M² moves across the "=" and becomes −M²

$$2yM^2 - 4Ky = -M^2 + 2K - K^2$$

5) Combine together like terms on each side of the equation, and reduce it to the form "Ax = B", where A and B are just bunches of letters which DON'T include the subject (y). Note that the LHS has to be FACTORISED:

$$(2M^2 - 4K)y = 2K - K^2 - M^2$$

("Ax = B"   i.e. $A = (2M^2 - 4K)$, $B = 2K - K^2 - M^2$,   y is the subject)

6) Finally slide the A underneath the B to give "$X = \dfrac{B}{A}$", (cancel if possible) and that's your answer.   So $y = \dfrac{2K - K^2 - M^2}{(2M^2 - 4K)}$

The Seventh Step (if You Need It)

$M = \sqrt{2K - \dfrac{K^2}{2y^2+1}}$

If the term you're trying to make the subject of the equation is squared, this is what you do:

Follow steps 1) to 6), $y^2 = \dfrac{2K - K^2 - M^2}{(2M^2 - 4K)}$ and then...

(I've skipped steps 1) - 6) because they're exactly the same as the first example — but with y² instead of y.)

7) Take the square root of both sides and stick a ± sign in front of the expression on the right: $y = \pm\sqrt{\dfrac{2K - K^2 - M^2}{(2M^2 - 4K)}}$

Remember — square roots can be +ve or −ve. See P.1.

The Acid Test:

LEARN the 7 STEPS for rearranging formulas.
Turn over and write them down.

1) Rearrange " $F = \tfrac{9}{5}C + 32$ " from "F= ", to "C= " and then back the other way.

2) Make p the subject of these: a) $\dfrac{p}{p+y} = 4$ b) $\dfrac{1}{p} = \dfrac{1}{q} + \dfrac{1}{r}$ c) $\dfrac{1}{p^2} = \dfrac{1}{q} + \dfrac{1}{r}$

Simultaneous Equations

These are OK as long as you learn these **SIX STEPS** in every meticulous detail.

There are *Six Steps* here too:

We'll use these two equations for this example: $2x = 6 - 4y$ and $-3 - 3y = 4x$

1) REARRANGE BOTH EQUATIONS INTO THE FORM: $ax + by = c$
where a,b,c are numbers (which can be negative).
Also **LABEL THE TWO EQUATIONS** —① and —②

$$2x + 4y = 6 \qquad —①$$
$$-4x - 3y = 3 \qquad —②$$

2) You need to **MATCH UP THE NUMBERS IN FRONT** (the "coefficients")
of either the x's or y's in **BOTH EQUATIONS**.
To do this you may need to **MULTIPLY** one or both equations by a
suitable number. You should then **RELABEL** them: —③ and —④

$①×2:$ $4x + 8y = 12$ —③   (This gives us +4x in equation —③ to match
$-4x - 3y = 3$ —④   the –4x in equation —②, now called —④)

3) ADD OR SUBTRACT THE TWO EQUATIONS ...
...to eliminate the terms with the same coefficient.
If the <u>coefficients are the</u> **SAME** (both +ve or both –ve) then **SUBTRACT**.
If the <u>coefficients are</u> **OPPOSITE** (one +ve and one –ve) then **ADD**.

$③+④$ $0x + 5y = 15$ (In this case we have +4x and –4x so we **ADD**)

4) SOLVE THE RESULTING EQUATION to find whichever letter is left in it.

$$5y = 15 \Rightarrow \underline{y = 3}$$

5) SUB THIS BACK into equation ① and solve it to find the other quantity.

Sub in ①: $2x + 4×3 = 6 \Rightarrow 2x + 12 = 6 \Rightarrow 2x = -6 \Rightarrow \underline{x = -3}$

6) Then **SUBSTITUTE BOTH THESE VALUES INTO EQUATION** ② to make
sure it works out properly. If it doesn't then you've done
something wrong and you'll have to do it all again!

Sub x and y in ②: $-4×-3 - 3×3 = 12 - 9 = \underline{3}$
which is right, so it's worked.

So the solutions are: $\underline{x = -3}$, $\underline{y = 3}$

The Acid Test: LEARN the *6 Steps* for solving *Simultaneous Equations*.

Remember, you only know them when you can write them all out from memory, so
turn over the page and try it. Then apply the 6 steps to find F and G given that
$$2F - 10 = 4G \quad \text{and} \quad 3G = 4F - 15$$

Simultaneous Equations and Graphs

When you have _two graphs_ which represent _two separate equations_, there are two ways the question can present it: _TWO SIMULTANEOUS EQUATIONS_ or a _single MERGED EQUATION_. In either case _THE SOLUTIONS_ will simply be _WHERE THE TWO GRAPHS CROSS_ (fairly obviously!)

1) Two Graphs and Two Separate Equations

Example "Draw the graphs for "$Y = 2X + 3$" and "$Y = 6 - 4X$" and then use your graphs to solve them."

1) <u>TABLE OF 3 VALUES</u> (see P.30)
    for both equations:

X	0	2	-2
Y	3	7	-1

X	0	2	3
Y	6	-2	-6

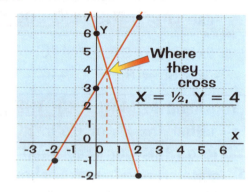

Where they cross
$X = ½, Y = 4$

2) <u>DRAW THE GRAPHS</u>:

3) <u>WHERE THEY CROSS</u>: $x = ½, y = 4$.
    And that's the answer!

$$x = ½ \text{ and } y = 4$$

2) Two Graphs but Just ONE Equation, or so it seems...

Also in stage 3:

Example "Using the graphs shown for $Y = 4 + ½X$ and $Y = 6 - X^2/3$, _solve the equation_: $X^2/3 + ½X - 2 = 0$."

<u>ANSWER</u>: _Learn_ these important steps:

1) _Equating the equations_ of the two graphs gives this:
    $6 - X^2/3 = 4 + ½X$ (a sort of _"merged" equation_)

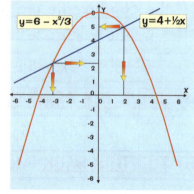

2) Now bring it all onto _one side_ and you end up with:
    $X^2/3 + ½X - 2 = 0$ (the equation in the question!)

3) Hence the _solutions_ to that equation are where the two initial equations ($Y = 4 + ½X$ and $Y = 6 - X^2/3$) are _equal_ — i.e. where their _graphs cross_, which as the graph shows is at: $x = 1.8$ or $x = -3.3$.

4) The _same_ question _could_ have been asked differently: "Using the graphs shown, _solve_ the two _simultaneous equations_: $Y = 4 + ½X$ and $Y = 6 - X^2/3$"
    <u>ANSWER</u>: From where the graphs cross: $X=1.8, Y=4.9$,   or $X=-3.3, Y=2.3$.

Even if you're not sure, you should _GUESS_ the answers to be the _points of intersection_ and just write them down.   Also note that for _simultaneous equations_ you give _BOTH_ the _X-values AND Y-values_ whilst for the _"merged equation"_ you _just give the X-values_. That's because the merged equation doesn't have any _Y_ in it to start with (even though the two equations it's derived from do) — tricky details, but you have to learn them.

The Acid Test:
<u>LEARN THE IMPORTANT DETAILS</u> on this page, then <u>turn over and write them all down</u>. Keep trying till you can.

1) Use graphs to find the solutions to these pairs of equations:
    a) $Y = 4x - 4$ and $Y = 6 - X$ b) $Y = 2x$ and $Y = 6 - 2x$
2) Draw the graphs of $y = 2x^2 - 4$ and $y = 2 - x$ and hence solve $2x^2 + x = 6$.

Inequalities

The thing to remember about inequalities is that they're not half as difficult as they look.

The 4 Inequality Symbols:

> means "Greater than"   ≥ means "Greater than or equal to"
< means "Less than"   ≤ means "Less than or equal to"

REMEMBER, the one at the BIG end is BIGGEST.

Algebra With Inequalities — this is generally a bit tricky

The thing to remember here is that inequalities are just like regular equations:
$$5X < X + 2$$
$$5X = X + 2$$

in the sense that all the normal rules of algebra apply...BUT WITH ONE BIG EXCEPTION:

Whenever you MULTIPLY OR DIVIDE BY A NEGATIVE NUMBER,
you must REVERSE THE INEQUALITY SIGN.

Example: "Solve 5X < 6X + 2"

ANS: Use normal algebraic rules to solve the equation for X:
$$5X < 6X + 2 \Rightarrow -X < 2$$

To get rid of the "−" in front of X you need to divide both sides by -1 — but remember
that means the "<" has to be reversed as well, which gives:

X > -2   i.e. "X is greater than -2" is the answer.

X > -2 is represented on this number line.

You have to reverse the inequality sign when you divide by a negative number

Graphing Inequalities — When You're Given More Than One

If you're given more than one inequality, you'll more than likely be asked to shade the region they define on a graph — the solution set. Learn this method.

Method: EXAMPLE: "Shade the region represented by: y ≤ x + 2, x + y ≤ 5 and y ≥ 0."

(Yuck, look at that horrible algebra)

STEP 1: CONVERT EACH INEQUALITY TO AN EQUATION:
$y \leq x + 2$ becomes $y = x + 2$,
$x + y \leq 5$ becomes $x + y = 5$,
$y \geq 0$ becomes $y = 0$

STEP 2: DO A TABLE OF 3 VALUES for
each equation, and draw the lines on a graph.
E.g. for $y = x + 2$:

x	0	2	4
y	2	4	6

STEP 3: SHADE THE DEFINED REGION,
and Bob's your Uncle, it's done.

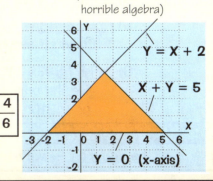

The Acid Test: LEARN: The 4 Inequality Signs and the Three Steps for graphing inequalities and shading the solution.

1) Find all the integer values of X which satisfy both $2X + 9 \geq 1$ and $4X < 6 + X$
2) Show on a graph the region defined by these conditions: $X + Y < 6$, $Y < 2X - 2$

Factorising Quadratics

There are several ways of solving a quadratic equation as detailed on the following pages. You need to know all the methods.

Factorising a Quadratic

"Factorising a quadratic" means "putting it into 2 brackets" — you'll need to remember that.

(There are several different methods for doing this, so stick with the one you're happiest with. If you have no preference then learn the one below.)

The standard format for quadratic equations is: $ax^2 + bx + c = 0$
Some exam questions have $a = 1$, making them much easier.
E.g. $x^2 + 3x + 2 = 0$ (See next page for when a is not 1)

Factorising Method When a = 1

1) ALWAYS rearrange into the STANDARD FORMAT: $ax^2 + bx + c = 0$.

2) Write down the TWO BRACKETS with the x's in: $(x\quad)(x\quad)=0$.

3) Then find 2 numbers that MULTIPLY to give "c" (the end number) but also ADD/SUBTRACT to give "b" (the coefficient of x).

4) Put them in and check that the +/– signs work out properly.

An Example   "Solve $x^2 – x = 12$ by factorising."

ANSWER: 1) First rearrange it (into the standard format): $x^2 – x – 12 = 0$

2) a=1, so the initial brackets are: $(x\quad)(x\quad)=0$

3) We now want to look at all pairs of numbers that multiply to give "c" (=12), but which also add or subtract to give the value of b:
   1×12 Add/subtract to give: 13 or 11
   2×6 Add/subtract to give: 8 or 4
   3×4 Add/subtract to give: 7 or ①   ⟶ This is what we're after (=±b)

4) So 3 and 4 will give b = ±1, so put them in: $(x\quad3)(x\quad4)=0$

5) Now fill in the +/– signs so that the 3 and 4 add/subtract to give -1 (=b),
   Clearly it must be +3 and –4 so we'll have: $(x + 3)(x – 4)=0$

6) As an ESSENTIAL check, EXPAND the brackets again to make sure they give the original equation:
   $(x + 3)(x – 4)=$ $x^2 + 3x – 4x – 12=$ $x^2 – x – 12$

We're not finished yet mind, because $(x + 3)(x – 4)=0$ is only the factorised form of the equation — we have yet to give the actual SOLUTIONS. This is very easy:

7) THE SOLUTIONS are simply the two numbers in the brackets, but with OPPOSITE +/– SIGNS: i.e. $x = -3$ or $+4$

Make sure you remember that last step. It's the difference between SOLVING THE EQUATION and merely factorising it.

Factorising Quadratics

When "a" is not 1

E.g. $3x^2 + 5x + 2 = 0$

The basic method is still the same but it's a lot messier. Chances are, the Exam question will be with a=1, so make sure you can do that type easily. Only then should you try to get to grips with these harder ones.

An Example

"Solve $3x^2 + 7x = 6$ by factorising."

1) First rearrange it (into the standard format): $3x^2 + 7x - 6 = 0$

2) Now because a = 3, the two x-terms in the brackets will have to multiply to give $3x^2$ so the initial brackets will have to be: $(3x\quad)(x\quad)=0$

(i.e. you put in the x-terms first, with coefficients that will multiply to give "a")

3) We now want to look at all pairs of numbers that multiply together to give "c" (=6, ignoring the minus sign for now):   i.e. 1×6 and 2×3

4) *Now the difficult bit*: to find the combination which does this:

> multiply with the 3x and x terms in the brackets and then add or subtract to give the value of b (=7):

The best way to do this is by trying out all the possibilities in the brackets until you find the combination that works. Don't forget that EACH PAIR of numbers can be tried in TWO different positions:

(3x 1)(x 6)	multiplies to give 18x and 1x which add/subtract to give	19x or 17x
(3x 6)(x 1)	multiplies to give 3x and 6x which add/subtract to give	9x or 3x
(3x 3)(x 2)	multiplies to give 6x and 3x which add/subtract to give	9x or 3x
(3x 2)(x 3)	multiplies to give 9x and 2x which add/subtract to give	11x or ⑦x

So (3x   2)(x   3) is the combination that gives b = 7, (give or take a +/−)

5) Now fill in the +/− signs so that the combination will add/subtract to give +7 (=b). Clearly it must be +3 and −2 which gives rise to +9x and -2x So the final brackets are: $(3x - 2)(x + 3)$

6) As an ESSENTIAL check, EXPAND the brackets out again to make sure they give the original equation:
$(3x - 2)(x + 3) = 3x^2 + 9x - 2x - 6 = 3x^2 + 7x - 6$

7) The last step is to get THE SOLUTIONS TO THE EQUATION: $(3x - 2)(x + 3)=0$

which you do by separately putting each bracket = 0 :

i.e. $(3x - 2)=0 \Rightarrow x = 2/3$ $(x + 3)=0 \Rightarrow x = -3$

Don't forget that last step. Again, it's the difference between SOLVING THE EQUATION and merely factorising it.

The Acid Test:

LEARN the 7 steps for solving quadratics by factorising, both for "a = 1" and "a ≠ 1".

1) Solve these by the factor method: a) $x^2 + 5x - 24 = 0$ b) $x^2 - 6x + 9 = 16$
c) $(x + 3)^2 - 3 = 13$ d) $5x^2 - 17x - 12 = 0$

The Quadratic Formula

The solutions to any quadratic equation $\underline{ax^2 + bx + c = 0}$ are given by this formula:

$$x = \frac{-b \pm \sqrt{b^2 - 4ac}}{2a}$$

LEARN THIS FORMULA — If you can't learn it, there's no way you'll be able to use it in the Exam, even if they give it to you. Using it should, in principle, be quite straightforward. As it turns out though there are quite a few pitfalls, so **TAKE HEED of these crucial details**:

Using The Quadratic Formula

1) Always write it down in stages as you go. Take it nice and slowly — any fool can rush it and get it wrong, but there's no marks for being a clot.

2) **MINUS SIGNS.** Throughout the whole of algebra, minus signs cause untold misery <u>because people keep forgetting them</u>. In this formula, there are two minus signs that people keep forgetting <u>the -b and the -4ac</u>.

The -4ac causes particular problems <u>when either "a" or "c" is negative</u>, because it makes the -4ac effectively +4ac — <u>so learn to spot it as a HAZARD before it happens</u>.

WHENEVER YOU GET A MINUS SIGN, <u>THE ALARM BELLS SHOULD ALWAYS RING</u>!

3) Remember you <u>divide ALL of the top line by 2a</u>, not just half of it.

4) Don't forget it's <u>2a</u> on the bottom line, not just a. This is another common mistake.

EXAMPLE:

"Find the solutions of $3x^2 + 7x = 1$ to 2 decimal places."
(The mention of decimal places in exam questions is a VERY BIG CLUE to use the formula rather than trying to factorise it!)

Method

1) First get it into the form $\underline{ax^2 + bx + c = 0}$: $3x^2 + 7x - 1 = 0$
2) Then carefully identify a, b and c: $\underline{a = 3,\ b = 7,\ c = -1}$
3) Put these values into the quadratic formula and <u>write down each stage</u>:

$$x = \frac{-b \pm \sqrt{b^2 - 4ac}}{2a} = \frac{-7 \pm \sqrt{7^2 - 4 \times 3 \times -1}}{2 \times 3} = \frac{-7 \pm \sqrt{49 + 12}}{6}$$

$$= \frac{-7 \pm \sqrt{61}}{6} = 0.1350 \text{ or } -2.468$$

So to 2 d.p., the solutions are: $\underline{x = 0.14 \text{ or } -2.47}$

4) Finally **AS A CHECK** put these values back into the <u>original equation</u>:
E.g. for x = 0.1350: $3 \times 0.135^2 + 7 \times 0.135 = 0.999675$,   which is 1, as near as ...

The Acid Test: LEARN the <u>4 CRUCIAL DETAILS</u> and the <u>4 STEPS OF THE METHOD</u> for using the Quadratic Formula, then <u>TURN OVER AND WRITE THEM ALL DOWN</u>.

1) Find the solutions of these equations (to 2 d.p.) using the quadratic formula:
   a) $x^2 + 10x - 4 = 0$ b) $3x^2 - 3x = 2$ c) $(2x + 3)^2 = 15$

Completing The Square

$$x^2 + 12x - 5 = (x + 6)^2 - 41$$

The SQUARE...   ...COMPLETED

Solving Quadratics by "Completing The Square"

This is quite a clever way of solving quadratics, but is perhaps a bit confusing at first. The name "Completing the Square" doesn't help — it's called that because of the method where you basically
1) write down a SQUARED bracket, and then
2) stick a number on the end to "COMPLETE" it.
It's quite easy really, so long as you make an effort to learn all the steps — some of them aren't all that obvious.

Method

1) As always, <u>REARRANGE THE QUADRATIC INTO THE STANDARD FORMAT</u>:
$$ax^2 + bx + c = 0$$

2) <u>If "a" is not 1 then divide the whole equation by "a" to make sure it is!</u>

3) Now <u>WRITE OUT THE INITIAL BRACKET</u>: $(x + b/2)^2$

   <u>NB:</u> <u>THE NUMBER IN THE BRACKET</u> is always <u>HALF THE (NEW) VALUE OF "b"</u>

4) <u>MULTIPLY OUT THE BRACKETS</u> and <u>COMPARE TO THE ORIGINAL</u>
   to find what extra is needed, and add or subtract the adjusting amount.

Example: "Express $x^2 - 6x - 7 = 0$ as a completed square, and hence solve it."

The equation is already in the standard form and "a" = 1, so:

1) The coefficient of x is -6, so the squared brackets must be: $(x - 3)^2$

2) <u>Square out the brackets</u>: $x^2 - 6x + 9$, <u>and compare</u> to the original: $x^2 - 6x - 7$.
   To make it like the original equation it needs -16 on the end, hence we get:

   <u>$(x - 3)^2 - 16 = 0$</u>   as the alternative version of $x^2 - 6x - 7 = 0$

Don't forget though, we wish to <u>SOLVE</u> this equation, which entails these 3 special steps:

1) <u>Take the 16 over</u> to get: $(x - 3)^2 = 16$.

2) Then <u>SQUARE ROOT BOTH SIDES</u>: $(x - 3) = \pm 4$ <u>AND DON'T FORGET THE $\pm$</u>

3) <u>Take the 3 over</u> to get: $x = \pm 4 + 3$ <u>so x = 7 or -1</u>

The Acid Test:
LEARN the <u>4 STEPS OF THE METHOD</u> for completing the square and the <u>3 SPECIAL STEPS</u> for <u>SOLVING THE EQUATION</u> you get from it.

1) <u>Now turn over and write it all down</u> to see what you've <u>learned</u>.   (Frightening, isn't it?)

2) Find the solutions of these equations (to 2 DP) by completing the square:
   a) $x^2 + 10x - 4 = 0$ b) $3x^2 - 3x = 2$ c) $(2x + 3)^2 = 15$

Four Graphs You Should Recognise

There are four graphs that you should know the basic shape of just from looking at their equations — it really isn't as difficult as it sounds.

1) X² BUCKET SHAPES: Y = ax² + bx + c   (where b and/or c can be zero)

Notice that all these graphs have the <u>same **SYMMETRICAL** bucket shape</u> and that if the x² bit has a "–" in front of it then the bucket is <u>*upside down*</u>.

Y = X²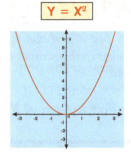

Y = 3X² – 6X – 3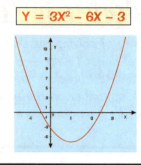

Y = –2X² – 4X + 3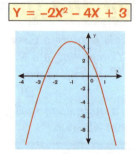

2) X³ GRAPHS: Y = ax³ + bx² + cx + d   (Note that b, c and/or d can be zero)

(Note that x³ must be the highest power and there must be no other bits like ¹/x etc.)

All X³ graphs have the <u>*same basic wiggle*</u> in the middle, but it can be a flat wiggle or a more pronounced wiggle. Notice that "<u>–X³ graphs</u>" always come <u>*down from top left*</u> whereas the <u>+X³</u> ones go <u>*up from bottom left*</u>.

Y = X³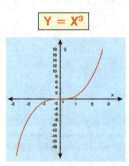

Y = X³ + 3X² – 4X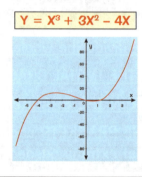

Y = –7X³ – 7X² + 42X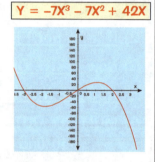

3) 1/X GRAPHS: Y = ᴬ/x, or XY = A,   where A is some number (+ or –)

Y = 4/X or XY = 4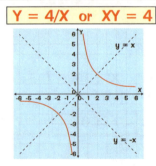

These graphs are <u>*all the same basic shape*</u>, except that the negative ones are in the opposite quadrants to the positive ones (as shown). The two halves of the graph don't touch. They're all <u>*symmetrical about the lines y=x and y=-x*</u>. This is also the type of graph you get with <u>*inverse proportion*</u>.   (See P.80)

Y = -4/X or XY = -4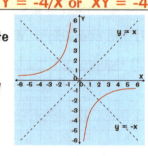

4) Kˣ GRAPHS: Y = Kˣ, where K is some positive number

Y = Kˣ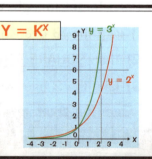

1) These graphs <u>*curve upwards*</u> when K > 1.
2) They're always <u>*above the x-axis*</u>.
3) They all <u>*go through the point (0, 1)*</u>.
4) For <u>*bigger values of K*</u>, the graph <u>*tails off towards zero more quickly*</u> on the left and <u>*climbs more steeply*</u> on the right.

The Acid Test:
LEARN the <u>4 Types of Graph</u>, both their equations and their shapes, then turn over and <u>sketch three examples</u> of each.

1) Describe the following graphs <u>*in words*</u>: a) y = 3x² + 2   b) y = 4 – x³   c) yx = 2
d) 2y = 1ˣ   e) x = -7/y   f) 3x² = y – 4x³ + 2   g) y = x – x²   h) y = 5ˣ

Solving Equations Using Graphs

This is an easy type of graph question — you just *draw a graph of the equation* and then *draw lines from one axis or the other to meet it*. Really you should be half EXPECTING that to happen, because that's *the most simple and obvious thing to do* with any graph.

The Answers are where The X- or Y-value Hits the Graph

The typical question will have a *nasty-looking equation* a bit like this: $y = 2x^2 - 3$ and a *graph* already drawn for you.

Then they'll ask you something like this:
"From the graph, find the values of x which make y = 4."

This is how you do it:

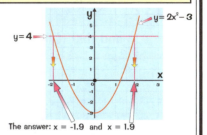

The answer: x = -1.9 and x = 1.9

The Easy Peasy Four-Step Method

1) Draw (or finish off) the *GRAPH* from a *TABLE OF VALUES*.   (See P.32)

2) Draw a line *ACROSS* (or *UP*) from the *Y-AXIS* (or *X-AXIS*) at the value *GIVEN*.

3) Where it *crosses the graph*, draw a line (or lines) *DOWN* (or *ACROSS*) to the *X-AXIS* (or *Y-AXIS*).

4) *READ OFF* the *VALUES* from the *X-AXIS* (or *Y-AXIS*) — and they're the *ANSWERS*.

Example: *A small piece of mouldy cheese is fired from a catapult. The height of the cheese, h, measured in metres, depends on the time in seconds, t, after being fired. h and t are linked by the following equation: $h = 25t - 5t^2$. Using a graphical method find a) the times at which the mouldy cheese is at a height of 25m and   b) its height after 2½ secs.*

ANSWER:

1) First *draw the graph from the equation*, doing your own *table of values* if necessary.

time	0	1	2	3	4	5
height	0	20	30	30	20	0

2) Draw the graph. Note the CURVED PEAK. DON'T EVER join the two points near the peak with a *ridiculous straight line*.

Eeek!

3) *Draw a line UP or ACROSS* from the axis (using the given value), *hit the curve* and *go ACROSS or DOWN* to the other axis and *read off the value*. Easy as that.

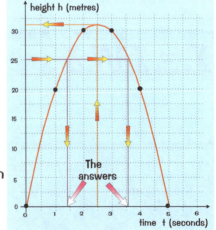

From the graph we can see the answers to this question are   a) 1.4s and 3.6s   b) 31m

The Acid Test: LEARN THE IMPORTANT DETAILS on this page, then turn over and write them all down. Keep trying till you can.

1) Using the above graph for $h = 25t - 5t^2$, find the values of t which give h = 15m.
2) Do a table of values and a graph for $y = x^2 + 2x - 3$.
  a) Find the values of x when y = −2.   b) Find the values of x which give y=0.

The Graphs of SIN, COS and TAN

You are expected to know these graphs and be able to **SKETCH** them *from memory*. It really isn't that difficult — the secret is to *notice their* **SIMILARITIES and DIFFERENCES**:

Y = SIN X

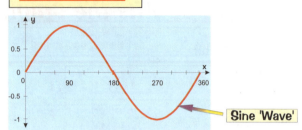

Sine 'Wave'

Y = COS X

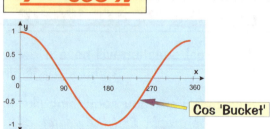

Cos 'Bucket'

1) *For 0° – 360°*, the shapes you get are a **SINE "WAVE"** (one peak, one trough) and a **COS "BUCKET"** (*Starts at the top*, dips, and *finishes at the top*).

2) The *underlying shape* of both the **SIN** and **COS** graphs are *identical* (as shown below) when you extend them (indefinitely) in both directions.

Y = SIN X

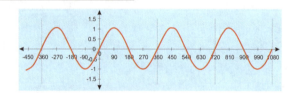

Y = COS X

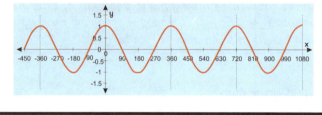

3) The only difference is that the SIN graph is shifted by 90° → compared to the COS graph.

4) Note that **BOTH GRAPHS** wiggle between *y-limits of exactly +1 and -1*.

5) *The key to drawing the extended graphs* is to first draw the 0 – 360° cycle of either the **SIN "WAVE"** or the **COS "BUCKET"** and then *repeat it in both directions as shown*.

Y = TAN X

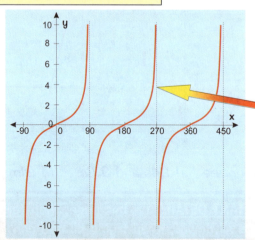

1) **The TAN graph BEARS NO RESEMBLANCE to the other two.**

2) *It behaves in a fairly bizarre way at 90°, 270° etc.* ....by disappearing up to *+ infinity* and then reappearing from *– infinity* on the other side of the *asymptote* (— a dotted line that the graph never quite touches).

3) *So, unlike the SIN and COS graphs*, Y = TAN X is **NOT LIMITED** *to values between +1 and -1*.

4) You'll also notice that whilst SIN and COS repeat *every 360°*, the TAN graph *repeats every 180°*.

The Acid Test:

LEARN The **FIVE** graphs above. **Then turn over and draw all five again in full detail.**

Congruence and Similarity

Congruence is another ridiculous maths word which sounds really complicated when it's not:
If two shapes are <u>CONGRUENT</u>, they are simply <u>the same</u> — <u>the same size and the same shape</u>.
That's all it is.   They can however be <u>MIRROR IMAGES</u>.

CONGRUENT
— same size,
same shape

SIMILAR
— same shape,
<u>different size</u>

Note that the angles
are always unchanged

Congruent Triangles — are they or aren't they?

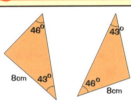

Probably the <u>trickiest area</u> of congruence is deciding whether <u>two triangles</u>, like the ones shown here, are CONGRUENT.

In other words, from the skimpy information given, are the two going to be the same or different. There are <u>THREE IMPORTANT STEPS</u>:

1) <u>The Golden Rule is definitely to DRAW THEM BOTH IN THE SAME ORIENTATION</u>
— only then can you compare them properly:

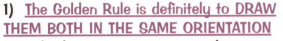

2) <u>Don't jump to hasty conclusions</u> — although the 8cm sides are clearly in different positions, it's always possible that <u>both top sides are 8cm</u>.
 In this case we can work out that they're <u>not</u> because the angles are different (so they can't be isosceles).

3) <u>Now see if any of these conditions are true</u>. If <u>ONE</u> of the conditions holds, the triangles are <u>congruent</u>.

1) SSS	three sides are the same	
2) AAS	two angles and a side match up	
3) SAS	two sides and the angle between them match up	
4) RHS	a right angle, the hypotenuse (longest side) and one other side all match up	

For <u>two triangles to be congruent</u>, <u>ONE OR MORE</u> of these four conditions must hold.

(<u>If none are true</u>, then you have proof that the triangles <u>aren't congruent</u>).

Congruence and Transformations

Remember <u>transformations</u>? (See page 39 if you don't), well...

WHEN A SHAPE IS <u>TRANSLATED</u>, <u>ROTATED</u> OR <u>REFLECTED</u>, THE IMAGE IS CONGRUENT TO THE ORIGINAL SHAPE. <u>ENLARGEMENTS</u> DON'T FOLLOW THIS RULE.

e.g.

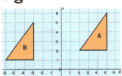

A to B is a <u>translation</u> of $\begin{pmatrix} -8 \\ -1 \end{pmatrix}$.

The lengths and angles are unchanged, so <u>A is congruent to B</u>.

e.g.

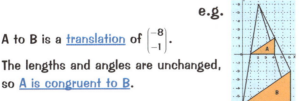

A to B is an <u>enlargement</u> of scale factor 2, and centre (2, 6).

The angles are unchanged but not the lengths, so <u>A is not congruent to B</u>.

The Acid Test:

LEARN the definitions of <u>similarity and congruence</u>, the <u>3 steps</u> for checking for <u>congruent triangles</u>, and the <u>rule about transformations</u>.

Then, *when you think you know it*, turn the page over and *write it all down again*, from *memory*, including the sketches and examples.

Lengths, Areas and Volumes

Now you might be thinking that this page is packed full of stuff that wouldn't fit anywhere else — and you'd be right. But learn it all anyway, ahh go on...

Also in stage 3:

Identifying Formulas Just by Looking at Them

This is pretty easy since we're only talking about the formulas for 3 things: **LENGTH**, **AREA** and **VOLUME**, and the rules are as simple as this:

> AREA FORMULAS always have lengths MULTIPLIED IN PAIRS
>
> VOLUME FORMULAS always have lengths MULTIPLIED IN GROUPS OF THREE
>
> LENGTH FORMULAS (such as perimeter) always have LENGTHS OCCURRING SINGLY

In formulas of course, *lengths are represented by letters*, so when you look at a formula you're *looking for groups of letters MULTIPLIED together* in ones, twos or threes. *BUT REMEMBER, π is NOT a length* so don't count it as one of your letters.

EXAMPLES:

πd (length)	$2l + 2w$ (length)	$4\pi(a + b)^2$ (area)
πr^2 (area)	$(4/3)\pi r^3$ (volume)	$3b(d + l)^2$ (volume)	$4\pi r^2 + 6d^2$ (area)
$4\pi r + 15L$ (length)	$Lwh + 6r^2L$ (volume)	$\dfrac{5ph^2 + d^3}{4\pi r}$ (area)	$5p^2L - 4k^3/7$ (volume)
$2\pi d - 14r/3$ (length)	$6hp + \pi r^2 + 7h^2$ (area)		

A CHORD BISECTOR IS A DIAMETER

A **CHORD** is any line <u>drawn across a circle</u>. And no matter where you draw a chord, the perpendicular line (at 90°) that <u>cuts it exactly in half</u>, will <u>go through the centre of the circle</u> and so will be a <u>DIAMETER</u>.

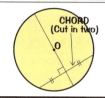

CHORD
(Cut in two)

SECTORS AND ARCS

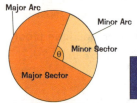

Major Arc
Minor Arc
Minor Sector
Major Sector
θ

> Area of Sector = $\dfrac{\theta}{360}$ × Area of full Circle

(Pretty obvious really isn't it?)

> Length of Arc = $\dfrac{\theta}{360}$ × Circumference of full Circle

(Obvious again, no?)

SURFACE AREA AND NETS

1) Remember, the <u>SURFACE AREA</u> of a 3D object is just the <u>total area of all the outer surfaces added together</u>.
2) <u>SURFACE AREA OF SOLID = AREA OF NET</u>.
3) <u>Nets</u> for <u>prisms, cubes, cuboids and pyramids</u> are covered on p.40.
4) You need to learn how to calculate the surface area of <u>spheres, cones and cylinders</u> too.
5) The <u>nets</u> for these are <u>difficult to draw</u>, so <u>MAKE SURE YOU LEARN THE FORMULAS</u>.

SPHERES:
Surface area = $4\pi r^2$

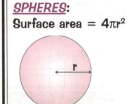

CONES:
Surface area = $\pi r l + \pi r^2$

curved area of cone   area of circular base

CYLINDERS:
Surface area = $2\pi rh + 2\pi r^2$

Especially note that the <u>length of the rectangle</u> is equal to the <u>circumference</u> of the circular ends.

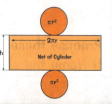

Cylinder
Net of Cylinder
πr^2
$2\pi r$
πr^2

The Acid Test:

LEARN this page. Then turn over and try to write it all down.

1) Draw the net of a cone.
2) Work out the surface area of a cylindrical drink can of height 12.5cm and diameter 7.2cm.

Volumes

If you don't want to learn any more formulas — look away now...

1) Sphere

$$\text{Volume of sphere} = \frac{4}{3}\pi r^3$$

EXAMPLE: The moon has a radius of 1700km, find its volume.

<u>Ans</u>: $V = \frac{4}{3}\pi r^3 = (4/3) \times 3.14 \times 1700^3 = \underline{2.1 \times 10^{10}}$ <u>km³</u>   *(A lot of cheese)*

2) Prisms

Finding the <u>volumes of prisms</u> was covered back in Stage 1 (page 41).
Just to remind you:

$$\underline{\text{Volume of prism}} = \frac{\text{Cross-sectional Area}}{} \times \text{length}$$

$$\mathbf{V = A \times l}$$

3) Pyramids and Cones

<u>*A pyramid is any shape that goes up to a point at the top*</u>. Its base can be any shape at all. If the base is a circle then it's called a <u>cone</u> (rather than a circular pyramid).

Cone

Square-based Pyramid

Tetrahedron

<u>Volume of Pyramid</u> = ⅓ x Base Area x Height

<u>Volume of Cone</u> = ⅓ x πr^2 x Height

This surprisingly simple formula is true for any pyramid or cone, whether it goes up "vertically" (like the three shown here) or off to one side (like the one below).

The Acid Test:

<u>LEARN this page</u>. Then turn over and try to write it all down. <u>Keep trying until you can do it</u>.

Practise these questions until you can do them all the way through without any hesitation.

1) Name the shape below and find its volume:

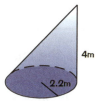

4m

2.2m

2)   A ping pong ball has a diameter of 4cm. A tennis ball has a diameter of 7cm. Find the volume of both balls. Are the relative volumes about what you would expect? (See P.38)

Loci and Constructions

A LOCUS (another ridiculous maths word) is simply:

A LINE that shows all the points which fit in with a given rule

Make sure you learn how to do these PROPERLY using a RULER AND COMPASSES as shown on these two pages.

1) The locus of points which are "A FIXED DISTANCE from a given POINT"

This locus is simply a CIRCLE.

Pair of Compasses

A given point

The LOCUS of points equidistant from it

2) The locus of points which are "A FIXED DISTANCE from a given LINE"

This locus is a sort of OVAL SHAPE.

It has straight sides (drawn with a ruler) and ends which are perfect semicircles (drawn with compasses).

Semicircle ends drawn with compasses

A given line

The LOCUS of points equidistant from it

3) The locus of points which are "EQUIDISTANT from TWO GIVEN LINES"

1) Keep the compass setting THE SAME while you make all four marks.

2) Make sure you leave your compass marks showing.

3) You get two equal angles — i.e. this LOCUS is actually an ANGLE BISECTOR.

Step 1

Step 2

A given line

The LOCUS

Second Compass marks

First Compass marks

The other given line

4) The locus of points which are "EQUIDISTANT from TWO GIVEN POINTS"

(In the diagram below, A and B are the two given points)

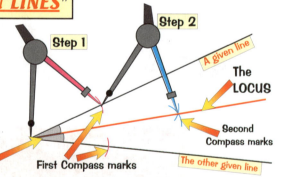

Step 1

Step 1

Step 3

The LOCUS

A

Step 2

B

Step 2

This LOCUS is all points which are the same distance from A as they are from B.

This time the locus is actually the PERPENDICULAR BISECTOR of the line joining the two points.

Loci and Constructions

Constructing accurate 60° angles

1) They may well ask you to draw an _accurate 60° angle_.

2) One place they're needed is for drawing an _equilateral triangle_.

3) Make sure you _follow the method_ shown in this diagram, and that you can do it _entirely from memory_.

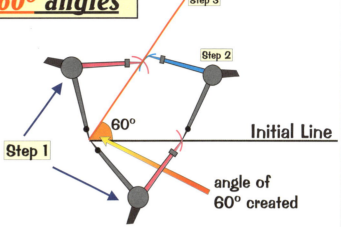

Step 3

Step 2

Step 1

60°

Initial Line

angle of 60° created

Constructing accurate 90° angles

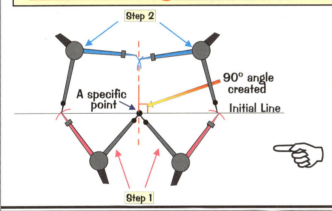

Step 2

A specific point

90° angle created

Initial Line

Step 1

1) They might want you to draw an _accurate 90° angle_.
2) They won't accept it just done "_by eye_" or with a ruler — if you want the marks you've got to do it _the proper way_ with _compasses_ like I've shown you here.
3) Make sure you can _follow the method_ shown in this diagram.

Drawing the Perpendicular from a Point to a Line

1) This is similar to the one above but _not quite the same_ — make sure you can do _both_.

2) Again, they won't accept it just done "_by eye_" or with a ruler — you've got to do it _the proper way_ with _compasses_.

3) _Learn_ the diagram.

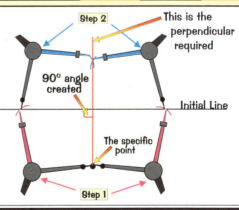

Step 2

This is the perpendicular required

90° angle created

Initial Line

The specific point

Step 1

The Acid Test: LEARN EVERYTHING ON THESE TWO PAGES

Now cover up these two pages and draw an example of each of the four loci.
Also draw an equilateral triangle and a square, both with fabulously accurate 60° and 90° angles.
Also, draw a line and a point and construct the perpendicular from the point to the line.

Vectors

5 MONSTROUSLY IMPORTANT THINGS you need to know about _Vectors_:

1) _The Four Notations_

The vector shown here can be referred to as:

$$\binom{7}{4} \text{ or } \underline{a} \text{ or } \mathbf{a} \text{ (in bold type) or } \overrightarrow{AB}$$

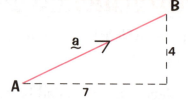

It's pretty obvious what these mean. Just make sure you know which is which in the column vector ($x\rightarrow$ and $y\uparrow$) and what a negative value means in a column vector.

2) _Scalar Multiple of a Vector_

A scalar, unlike a vector, doesn't have a direction — it's just a number like 2, 5, 27 etc. Multiplying a vector by a scalar is done in the obvious way.

EXAMPLE: ANSWER:

Given that vector **a** $= \binom{2}{4}$ and vector **b** = 2**a**, find **b**. $\mathbf{b} = 2\binom{2}{4} = \binom{2\times 2}{2\times 4} = \binom{4}{8}$

3) _Adding And Subtracting Vectors_

Vectors must always be added END TO END, so that the _arrows all point WITH each other_, not AGAINST each other.

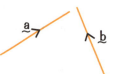
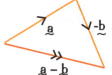

Adding and subtracting
COLUMN VECTORS is really easy: E.g. if **a** $= \binom{5}{3}$ and **b** $= \binom{-2}{4}$, then $2\mathbf{a} - \mathbf{b} = 2\binom{5}{3} - \binom{-2}{4} = \binom{12}{2}$.

4) _Splitting Into Components_

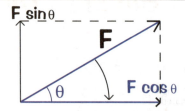

Any vector can be split into two components that are at 90° to each other. These two components will always be _Fcos θ and Fsin θ_. The main difficulty is knowing which one is which. Learn this:

When you turn F through angle θ as shown, you get FCOSθ (So the _other one_ must be Fsinθ)

5) _A Typical Exam Question_

This is a common type of question and it illustrates a very important vector technique:

To obtain the _unknown vector_ just '_get there_' by any route _made up of known vectors_.

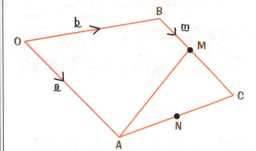

Applying this rule we can easily obtain the following vectors in term of **a**, **b** and **m**, (given that M and N are mid points):

1) $\overrightarrow{AM} = -\underline{a} + \underline{b} + \underline{m}$ (i.e. get there via O and B)

2) $\overrightarrow{OC} = \underline{b} + 2\underline{m}$ (i.e. get there via B and M)

3) $\overrightarrow{AC} = -\underline{a} + \underline{b} + 2\underline{m}$ (A to C via O, B and M)

"Real-Life" Vector Questions

These are the type of vector question you're most likely to get in the Exam, so make sure you learn all the little tricks on this page.

1) The Old "Swimming Across the River" Question

This is a really easy question: You just <u>ADD the two velocity vectors END TO END</u> and draw the <u>RESULTANT vector</u> which shows both the <u>speed and direction of the final course</u>. Simple huh?

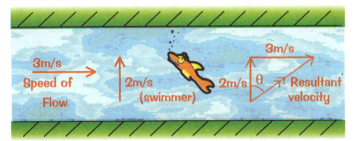

Overall Speed =
$$\sqrt{3^2 + 2^2} = \sqrt{13} = 3.6 m/s$$

Direction: $TAN\ \theta = 3 \div 2$
$$\theta = TAN^{-1}\ (1.5) = 56.3^0$$

<u>As usual with vectors</u>, you'll need to use <u>Pythagoras and Trig</u> to find the length and angle but that's no big deal is it? Just make sure you **LEARN** the two methods in this question.

The example shown above is absolutely dog-standard stuff and you should definitely see it that way, rather than as one random question of which there may be hundreds — there aren't!

2) The Old "Swimming Slightly Upstream" Question

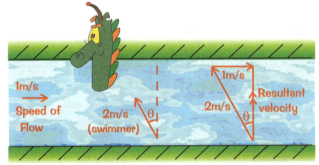

1) $SIN\ \theta = OPP/HYP$
$$= 1/2$$
so $\theta = SIN^{-1}\ (0.5) = 30^0$

2) <u>Speed</u> $= \sqrt{2^2 - 1^2} = \sqrt{3} =$
$$1.73\ m/s$$

The general idea here is to <u>end up going directly across the river</u>, and <u>ONCE AGAIN the old faithful method</u> of <u>DRAWING A VECTOR TRIANGLE</u> makes light work of the whole thing — 2 vectors joined <u>END TO END</u> to give the resultant velocity. However, in this case the resultant is drawn in **FIRST** (straight across), so that <u>the angle θ has to be worked out to fit</u> as shown above.

3) The Old "Queen Mary's Tugboats" Question

The problem here is to find the overall force from the two tugs.

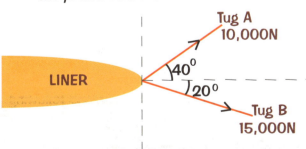

This can be tackled in two ways:
1) By working out the <u>COMPONENTS of the two force vectors</u> along both dotted lines (**F COS** θ and **F SIN** θ etc.)
<u>OR:</u>
2) By <u>adding the vectors END TO END</u> to make a vector triangle and using the <u>SINE & COSINE RULES</u> (See P.86).

The Acid Test:

LEARN the 3 EXAMPLES on this page, then <u>turn over and write them out</u>, but with <u>different numbers</u>.

1) Work out the overall force on the Queen Mary in example 3, using **BOTH** methods.

Speed and Density Formulas

Formula triangles are <u>EXTREMELY POTENT TOOLS</u> for dealing with common formulas. They're <u>VERY EASY</u>, so make sure you know how to use them.

Speed = Distance ÷ Time

Questions on <u>speed</u> are always coming up in exams, and they never give you the formula. Either you learn it beforehand or you wave goodbye to <u>several easy marks</u>.

It makes life easier if you learn the speed formula as this **FORMULA TRIANGLE**.

D
S × T

How Do You Use Formula Triangles?

1) <u>COVER UP the thing you want to find</u> and just <u>WRITE DOWN what is left showing</u>.

2) Now <u>PUT IN THE VALUES</u> for the other two things and <u>WORK IT OUT</u>.

EXAMPLE: "A car travels 90 miles at 36 miles per hour. How long does it take?"
ANSWER: We want to find the time, so cover up T in the triangle which leaves D/S, so T = D/S = Distance ÷ speed = 90 ÷ 36 = 2.5 hours

Of course you have to *remember the order of the letters* in the triangle (SDT), and we have the word *SoDiT* to help you.

So if it's a question on speed, distance and time just say: **SOD IT**.

Density *is Another Important* Example:

The standard formula for density is:

DENSITY = MASS ÷ VOLUME

But <u>the best method</u> of learning it by far is to <u>remember</u> this **FORMULA TRIANGLE**.

If you remember it as $D^M V$ or <u>DiMoV</u> (the Russian Agent) you won't go far wrong.

EXAMPLE: "Find the volume of an object with a mass of 40 g and a density of 6.4 g/cm³."
ANSWER:
To find the volume, <u>cover up V</u>. This leaves M/D, <u>so V = M ÷ D</u> = 40 ÷ 6.4 = 6.25 cm³.

IF YOU <u>LEARN THE FORMULA TRIANGLES</u>, YOU WILL FIND QUESTIONS ON SPEED AND DENSITY <u>VERY EASY</u>.

The Acid Test:

LEARN the <u>Formula Triangles</u>, for <u>density</u> and <u>speed</u>. Then turn over and <u>write them from memory</u>.

1) First see page 11 to remind yourself and then find the time taken, in hours, mins and secs, for a purple-nosed buffalo walking at 3.2 km/h to cover 5.2 km.
2) A metal object has a volume of 45 cm³ and a mass of 743 g. What is its density?
3) Another piece of the same metal has a volume of 36.5 cm³. What is its mass?

Probability

This is where most people start getting into trouble, and d'you know why?
I'll tell you — it's because they don't know the three simple steps and the two rules to apply:

The Steps

1) <u>Always break down</u> a complicated-looking probability question into <u>A SEQUENCE</u> of <u>SEPARATE SINGLE EVENTS</u>.

2) <u>Find the probability of EACH</u> of these <u>SEPARATE SINGLE EVENTS</u>.

3) <u>Apply the AND/OR rule</u>:

The Rules:

1) The AND Rule:

Which means:

$$P(A \text{ and } B) = P(A) \times P(B)$$

The probability of <u>Event A</u> **AND** <u>Event B</u> **BOTH** happening is equal to the two separate probabilities <u>MULTIPLIED together</u>.

(strictly speaking, the two events have to be <u>INDEPENDENT</u>. All that means is that one event happening does not in any way stop the other one from happening. Contrast this with *mutually exclusive* below.)

2) The OR Rule:

Which means:

$$P(A \text{ or } B) = P(A) + P(B)$$

The probability of <u>Either Event A OR Event B happening</u> is equal to the two separate proabilities <u>ADDED together</u>.

(Strictly speaking, the two events have to be <u>MUTUALLY EXCLUSIVE</u> which means that if one event happens, the other one *can't* happen. Pretty much the opposite of *independent* events (see above).)

The way to remember this is that it's the wrong way round — i.e. you'd want the AND to go with the + but it doesn't: It's "<u>AND with ×</u>" and "<u>OR with +</u>".

Example

"Find the probability of picking two kings from a pack of cards (assuming you don't replace the first card picked)."

<u>ANSWER</u>:

1) <u>SPLIT</u> this into TWO SEPARATE EVENTS
— i.e. picking the <u>first king</u> *and* *then* <u>picking the second king</u>.

2) *Find the SEPARATE probabilities* of these two *separate events*:

P(1st king) = $\frac{4}{52}$ P(2nd king) = $\frac{3}{51}$ (— note the change from 52 to 51)

3) *Apply the AND/OR Rule*:   BOTH events must happen, so it's the AND Rule:

so <u>multiply</u> the two separate proabilities: $\frac{4}{52} \times \frac{3}{51} = \frac{1}{221}$

The Acid Test:

LEARN the <u>Three Simple Steps</u> for <u>multiple events</u>, and <u>the AND/OR Rule</u>.

1) Now turn over and write these rules down <u>from memory</u>. Then apply them to this:
2) Find the probability of picking 2 queens plus the ace of spades from a pack of cards.

Relative Frequency

This isn't the number of times your granny comes to visit.
It's a way of working out probabilities.

Fair or Biased?

The probability of rolling a three on a dice is $\frac{1}{6}$ — you know that each
of the 6 numbers on a dice is equally likely to be rolled, and there's only 1 three.

BUT this only works if it's a fair dice. If the dice is a bit wonky (the technical term is "biased")
then each number won't have an equal chance of being rolled. That's where Relative
Frequency comes in — you can use it to work out probabilities when things might be wonky.

Do the Experiment Again and Again and Again and Again

You need to do an experiment over and over again and then do a quick calculation.
(Remember, an experiment could just mean rolling a dice.)
Usually the results of these experiments will be written in a table.

The Formula for Relative Frequency

$$\text{Probability of something happening} = \frac{\text{Number of times it has happened}}{\text{Number of times you tried}}$$

You can work out the relative frequency as a fraction but usually
decimals are best for comparing relative frequencies.

The important thing to remember is:

> The more times you do the experiment,
> the more accurate the probability will be.

Example:

So, back to the wonky dice. What is the probability of rolling a three?

Number of Times the dice was rolled	10	20	50	100
Number of threes rolled	2	5	11	23
Relative frequency	$\frac{2}{10}=0.2$	$\frac{5}{20}=0.25$	$\frac{11}{50}=0.22$	$\frac{23}{100}=0.23$

So, what's the probability? We've got 4 possible answers, but the best is the one
worked out using the highest number of dice rolls.
This makes the probability of rolling a three on this dice 0.23.
And since for a fair, unbiased dice, the probability of rolling a three is $\frac{1}{6}$ (about 0.17), then
our dice is biased.

The Acid Test:

LEARN the formula for
calculating **RELATIVE FREQUENCY**

1) Bill picks a card at random out of a pack and then replaces the card. He does this 100 times,
and picks a total of 13 aces. Do you think the pack is biased? Why?

Probability — Tree Diagrams

General Tree Diagram

Tree Diagrams are all pretty much the same, so it's a pretty darned good idea to learn these basic details (which apply to <u>ALL</u> tree diagrams) — ready for the one in the Exam.

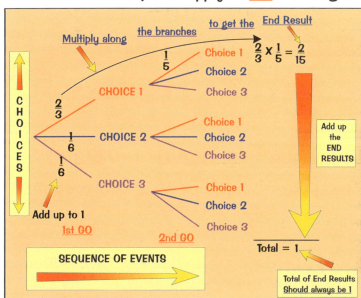

1) Always <u>**MULTIPLY ALONG THE BRANCHES**</u> (as shown) to get the END RESULTS.

2) <u>*On any set of branches which all meet at a point*</u>, the numbers must always <u>ADD UP TO 1</u>.

3) *Check that your diagram is correct* by <u>making sure the End Results ADD UP TO ONE</u>.

4) *To answer any question*, simply <u>ADD UP THE RELEVANT END RESULTS</u> (see below).

A likely Tree Diagram Question

<u>EXAMPLE</u>: "A box contains 5 red disks and 3 green disks. Two disks are taken <u>without replacement</u>. Draw a tree diagram and hence find the probability that both disks are the same colour."

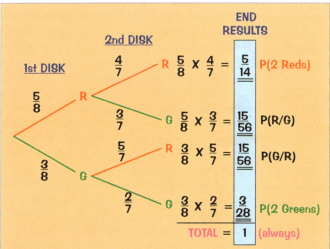

<u>*Once the tree diagram is drawn*</u> all you then need to do to answer the question is simply <u>select the RELEVANT END RESULTS</u> and then <u>ADD THEM TOGETHER</u>:

| 2 REDS | (5/14) |
| 2 GREENS | (3/28) |

$$\frac{5}{14} + \frac{3}{28} = \frac{13}{28}$$

If you can, use a calculator for this. Otherwise, use the fraction rules on P.8.

The Acid Test:

LEARN the <u>GENERAL DIAGRAM</u> for Tree Diagrams and the <u>4 points</u> that go with them.

1) O.K. let's see what you've learnt shall we:
   TURN OVER AND WRITE DOWN EVERYTHING YOU KNOW ABOUT TREE DIAGRAMS.

2) A bag contains 6 red tarantulas and 4 black tarantulas. If two girls each pluck out a tarantula at random, draw a tree diagram to find the probability that they get different coloured ones.

Probability

Four Extra Details for the Tree Diagram method:

1) Always break up the question INTO A SEQUENCE OF SEPARATE EVENTS.

E.g. "3 coins are tossed together" – just split it into 3 separate events.
You need this sequence of events to be able to draw any sort of tree diagram.

2) DON'T FEEL you have to draw COMPLETE tree diagrams.

Learn to adapt them to what is required. E.g. "What is the chance of throwing a dice 3 times and getting 2 sixes followed by an even number?"

This diagram is all you need to get the answer: $\frac{1}{6} \times \frac{1}{6} \times \frac{1}{2} = \frac{1}{72}$

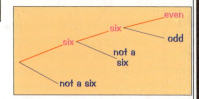

3) WATCH OUT for CONDITIONAL PROBABILITIES...

...where the fraction on each branch depends on what happened _on the previous branch_, e.g. bags of sweets, packs of cards etc, where the _bottom_ number of the fractions _also_ changes as items are removed. E.g. $\frac{11}{25}$ then $\frac{10}{24}$ etc.

4) With "AT LEAST" questions, it's always (1 – Prob of "the other outcome"):

For Example, _"Find the probability of having AT LEAST one girl in 4 children"_
There are in fact _15 different ways_ of having "AT LEAST one girl in 4 children" which would take a long time to work out, even with a tree diagram.
The clever trick you should know is this:
The prob of _"AT LEAST something or other"_ is just (1 – prob of "the other outcome") which in this case is (1 – prob of "all 4 boys") = (1 – 1/16) = _15/16_.

Example

"Herbert and his two chums, along with five of Herbert's doting aunties, have to squeeze onto the back seat of his father's Bentley, en route to Royal Ascot. Given that Herbert does not sit at either end, and that the seating order is otherwise random, find the probability of Herbert having his best chums either side of him."

The untrained probabilist wouldn't think of using a tree diagram here, but see how easy it is when you do. _This is the tree diagram you'd draw:_

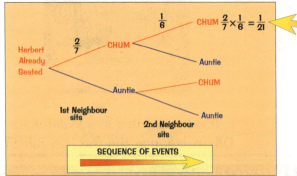

So the answer is 1/21.

Of course you'd have to do a bit of thinking to decide to place Herbert first and then have the two events as each of his "neighbours" are placed beside him, but that sort of trick is pretty standard really.

The Acid Test:

LEARN THE WHOLE OF THIS PAGE. Then _turn over and write down_ all the key points and the example too.

1) As it turned out the Bentley could only seat 6 people across so the last two in had to sit on other people's laps. Find the probability that Herbert had his best chums either side and no doting Auntie on his lap.

2) Find TEN probability questions, and practise tackling them with TREE DIAGRAMS.

Revision Summary for Stage Two

I know these questions seem difficult, _but they're the very best revision you can do_. The whole point of revision, remember, is <u>to find out what you _don't_ know</u> and then learn it <u>until you do</u>. These searching questions test how much you do know _better than anything else ever can_. Keep practising until you can glide through them smoothly.

1) How do you find the reciprocal of a fraction?
2) What is the reciprocal of zero?
3) Give an example of two amounts that are; a) directly proportional
$\qquad\qquad\qquad\qquad\qquad\qquad\qquad$ b) inversely proportional.
4) What is an irrational number? Give two examples.
5) What is a surd? Write down all you know about manipulating surds.
6) What should you do if you're asked to find the <u>exact</u> area of a circle?
7) How do you determine the upper and lower bounds of a rounded measurement?
8) What does D.O.T.S. stand for? Give two examples of it.
9) Give details of the three techniques for doing algebraic fractions, with examples.
10) What are the six steps for rearranging formulas? Why might you need a seventh step?
11) Write down the six steps for doing simultaneous equations.
12) What is the meaning of life? Why are we here?
$\qquad$ And why do we have to do so much algebra?
13) Explain briefly how simultaneous equations can be solved using two graphs?
14) What do the four inequality symbols mean?
15) What are the rules of algebra for inequalities? What's the big exception?
16) What are the three steps for doing graphical inequalities?
17) What does "factorising a quadratic" mean you have to do?
18) What check should you do to make sure you've done it right?
19) Write down the formula for solving quadratics.
20) What are the four main steps for turning a quadratic into a completed square?
21) Describe in words and with a sketch the different forms of these graphs:
$\qquad\qquad$ $y = ax^2 + bx + c$; $y = ax^3 + bx^2 + cx + d$; $xy = a$; $y = k^x$
22) What are the four steps for solving an equation using graphs?
23) Draw the graphs of SIN, COS and TAN, over 0°-360° and then -1080° to 1080°.
24) What do "congruent" and "similar" mean?
25) What do "SSS", "AAS", "SAS" and "RHS" mean?
26) How can you tell if a formula is a length, an area or a volume just by looking at it?
27) What's special about a chord bisector?
28) How do you work out the length of an arc?
29) Write down the surface area formulas for: a) a sphere   b) a cone   c) a cylinder.
30) Write down the volume formulas for: a) a sphere   b) a cone   c) a pyramid.
31) What is a locus? Describe with diagrams the four you should know.
32) Demonstrate how to draw accurate 60° and 90° angles.
33) Draw a diagram to show how you split a vector into its components.
34) In a typical exam question, what's the basic rule for finding an unknown vector?
35) Produce your own "swimming slightly upstream" question and work it out.
36) Write down formula triangles for speed and density.
37) What is the AND/OR rule for probability?
38) Draw a general tree diagram with all the features that tree diagrams have.
39) How do you work out the "at least" type of probability question?

Direct and Inverse Proportion

Direct Proportion: y = kx	Inverse Proportion: y = k/x
BOTH INCREASE TOGETHER	One INCREASES, one DECREASES

1) The graph of y against x is _a straight line through the origin: y = kx_

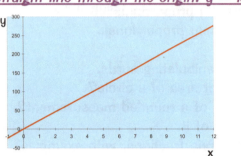

The graph of y against x is the well known $y = k/x$ graph:

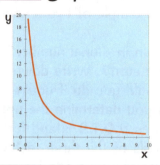

2) In a table of values the MULTIPLIER is the same for X and Y, i.e. if you double one of them, you double the other; if you times one of them by 3, you times the other by 3, etc.

$\times 3 \quad \times 2 \quad \times 4$

X	2	6	8	12	14	56
Y	3	9	12	18	21	84

$\times 3 \quad \times 2 \quad \times 4$

In a table of values the MULTIPLIER for one of them becomes a DIVIDER for the other, i.e. if you double one, you halve the other, if you treble one, you divide the other by three, etc.

$\times 3 \quad \times 2 \quad \div 4$

X	2	6	8	12	40	10
Y	30	10	7.5	5	1.5	6

$\div 3 \quad \div 2 \quad \times 4$

3) The RATIO x/y is the same for all pairs of values, i.e. from the table above:

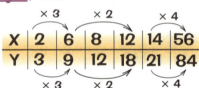

$$\frac{2}{3} = \frac{6}{9} = \frac{8}{12} = \frac{12}{18} = \frac{14}{21} = \frac{56}{84} = 0.6667$$

The PRODUCT XY (X times Y) is the same for all pairs of values, i.e. from the table above:

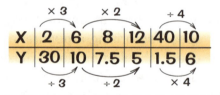

$2 \times 30 = 6 \times 10 = 8 \times 7.5 = 12 \times 5$
$= 40 \times 1.5 = 10 \times 6 = \underline{60}$

Inverse Square Variation

You can have all sorts of relationships between x and y, like $y = kx^2$ or $y = k/x^3$ etc. as detailed on P.81. The most important type is $y = k/x^2$ and is called "INVERSE SQUARE" variation. DON'T MIX UP THIS NAME with inverse proportion, which is just $y = k/x$.

The Acid Test:

LEARN the 3 KEY FEATURES for both Direct and Inverse proportion. Then turn over and write them all down.

1) Give examples of 2 real quantities that exhibit a) direct   and   b) inverse proportion.
2) Make up your own tables of values which show
    a) DIRECT PROPORTION   b) INVERSE PROPORTION

Variation

This concerns Exam questions which involve statements like these:

"y is proportional to the square of x" "t is proportional to the square root of h"
"D varies with the cube of t" "V is inversely proportional to r cubed"

To deal successfully with things like this <u>you must remember this method</u>:

Method

1) Convert the sentence into a proportionality using the symbol " $\propto$ " which means "<u>is proportional to</u>".

2) Replace " $\propto$ " with "=k" to make an EQUATION:

The above examples would become:	Proportionality	Equation
"y is proportional to the square of x"	$y \propto x^2$	$y = kx^2$
"t is proportional to the square root of h"	$t \propto \sqrt{h}$	$t = k\sqrt{h}$
"D varies with the cube of t"	$D \propto t^3$	$D = kt^3$
"V is inversely proportional to r cubed"	$V \propto 1/r^3$	$V = k/r^3$

(Once you've got it in the form of an equation with k, <u>the rest is easy</u>)

3) Find a PAIR OF VALUES of x and y somewhere in the question, and <u>SUBSTITUTE them into the equation</u> with the <u>sole purpose of finding k</u>.

4) Put the value of k back into the equation and it's now ready to use.   e.g. $y = 3x^2$

5) INEVITABLY, they'll ask you to find y, having given you a value for x (or vice versa).

Example:

The time taken for a duck to fall down a chimney (it happens!) is inversely proportional to the square of the diameter of the flue. If she took 25 seconds to descend a chimney of diameter 0.3m, how long would it take her to get down one of 0.2m diameter?

(Notice there's no mention of "writing an equation" or "finding k" — it's up to <u>YOU</u> to remember the method for yourself.)

<u>ANSWER</u>:
1) Write it as a <u>proportionality</u>, then an <u>equation</u>: $t \propto 1/d^2$ i.e. $t = k/d^2$
2) <u>Sub in the given values</u> for the two variables: $25 = k/0.3^2$
3) Rearrange the equation to <u>find k</u>: $k = 25 \times 0.3^2 = 2.25$
4) Put k <u>back in</u> the formula: $t = 2.25/d^2$
5) <u>Sub in new value</u> for d: $t = 2.25/0.2^2 = \underline{56.25 \text{secs}}$

The Acid Test:

LEARN the FIVE STEPS of the METHOD plus the <u>four</u> examples. Then <u>turn over and write them all down</u>.

1) The frequency of a pendulum is inversely proportional to the square root of its length. If the pendulum swings with a frequency of 0.5 Hz when the length is 80cm, what frequency will it have with a length of 50cm, and what length will give a frequency of 0.7 Hz?

Simultaneous Equations

You know the method for solving linear simultaneous equations. When one's quadratic, it's a bit trickier.

Six Steps For TRICKY Simultaneous Equations

Example: Solve these two equations simultaneously: $7x + y = 1$ and $2x^2 - y = 3$

1) Rearrange the quadratic equation so that you have **one term on its own**. And label the equations ① and ② .

$7x + y = 1$ — ①

$y = 2x^2 - 3$ — ②

2) Substitute the quadratic expression into the **other equation**. Label your new equation ③.

$7x + y = 1$ — ①

$y = \boxed{2x^2 - 3}$ — ②

$7x + (2x^2 - 3) = 1$ — ③

In this example you just shove the expression for y into equation ①, in place of y.

3) Rearrange to get a **quadratic equation**. And guess what... You've got to **solve it**.

$2x^2 + 7x - 4 = 0$

That factorises into:

$(2x - 1)(x + 4) = 0$

So, $2x - 1 = 0$ OR $x + 4 = 0$

In other words, *x = 0.5* OR *x = -4*

Check this step by multiplying out again:
$(2x - 1)(x + 4) = 2x^2 - x + 8x - 4 = 2x^2 + 7x - 4$ ☺

Remember — if it won't factorise, you can either use the formula or complete the square. Have a look at P.62-63 for more details.

4) Stick the values back in one of the **original equations** (pick the easy one).

① $7x + y = 1$ **Substitute in x = 0.5**: $3.5 + y = 1$, so *y = 1 - 3.5 = -2.5*

① $7x + y = 1$ **Substitute in x = -4**: $-28 + y = 1$, so *y = 1 + 28 = 29*

5) Substitute both pairs of answers back into the other **original equation** to **check** they work.

② $y = 2x^2 - 3$

Substitute in x = 0.5 and y = -2.5: $-2.5 = (2 \times 0.25) - 3 = -2.5$ — jolly good.

Substitute in x = -4 and y = 29: $29 = (2 \times 16) - 3 = 29$ — *smashing.*

6) Write the pairs of answers out again, *CLEARLY*, at the bottom of your working.

The two pairs of answers are: *x = 0.5 and y = -2.5* OR *x = -4 and y = 29*

The Solutions are the Points of Intersection on a Graph...

1) Solutions to simultaneous equations can be found easily using graphs.
2) You'll more than likely be given the graphs of two equations and asked to solve them.
3) Just remember this:

> THE POINTS WHERE THE GRAPHS INTERSECT ARE THE SOLUTIONS OF THE SIMULTANEOUS EQUATIONS.

See page 58 for an example.

The Acid Test:

LEARN the 6 Steps for solving TRICKY Simultaneous Equations.

1) Use the 6 steps to solve: a) $f = g^2 + 4$ and $f - 6g - 4 = 0$ b) $g = 4f^2 - 3$ and $g + 11f = 0$
2) By drawing a graph, solve the simultaneous equations $y = 2x^2 - 4$ and $y = 2 - x$.

Gradients and Graphs of Circles

Parallel Lines have the Same Gradients

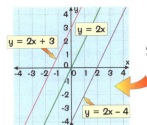

1) The equation of a straight line is $y = mx + c$, where m is the gradient and c is the y-intercept.

2) Parallel lines have the same value of m — i.e. the same gradient.

EXAMPLE: The lines $y = 2x + 3$,
$y = 2x$
and $y = 2x - 4$ are all parallel.

Perpendicular Gradients are Linked

The gradients of two perpendicular lines multiply to give –1.

> If the gradient of the first line is m, the gradient of the other line will be $\dfrac{-1}{m}$, because $m \times \dfrac{-1}{m} = -1$.

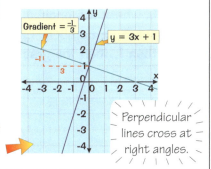

Perpendicular lines cross at right angles.

EXAMPLE: The line $y = 3x + 1$ has the gradient 3. A line which is perpendicular to this line will have the gradient $\dfrac{-1}{3}$.

Circles have Equations

The equation for a circle with centre (0, 0) and radius r is: $x^2 + y^2 = r^2$

E.g. $x^2 + y^2 = 4$ is a circle with centre (0, 0). $r^2 = 4$, so the radius, r, is 2.
$x^2 + y^2 = 100$ is a circle with centre (0, 0) too. $r^2 = 100$, so the radius, r, is 10.

You might be given two simultaneous equations to solve, where one is the equation of a circle. Eeek.

Example: *"By drawing graphs, solve the simultaneous equations $x^2 + y^2 = 16$ and $y = 2x + 1$."*

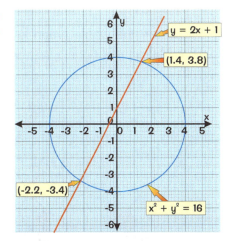

1) DRAW BOTH GRAPHS.
$x^2 + y^2 = 16$ is the equation of a circle, centre (0, 0) and radius $\sqrt{16} = 4$.
$y = 2x + 1$ is a straight line with gradient 2. It crosses the y-axis at 1.

2) LOOK FOR WHERE THE GRAPHS CROSS.
The straight line crosses the circle at two points. Reading the x and y values of these points gives the solutions x = 1.4, y = 3.8 and x = -2.2, y = -3.4 (to 1 decimal place).

The Acid Test:

1) What are the gradients of lines perpendicular to these lines?
   a) $y = 4x + 3$ b) $y = \frac{1}{2}x - 5$ c) $y = 5 - 2x$
2) What are the radii of the following circles?
   a) $x^2 + y^2 = 1$ b) $x^2 + y^2 = 49$ c) $x^2 + y^2 = 20$

Graphs: Shifts and Stretches

Don't be put off by function notation involving f(x). It doesn't mean anything complicated, it's just a fancy way of saying "An expression in x".

In other words "y = f(x)" just means "y = some totally mundane expression in x, which we won't tell you, we'll just call it f(x) instead to see how many of you get in a flap about it".

In a question on transforming graphs they will either use function notation or they'll use a known function instead. There are only four different types of graph transformations so just LEARN them and be done with it. Here they are in order of difficulty:

1) Y-Stretch: $y = k \times f(x)$

This is where the original graph is stretched along the y-axis by multiplying the whole function by a number, i.e. y = f(x) becomes y = kf(x) (where k = 2 or 5 etc.). If k is less than 1, then the graph is squashed down in the y-direction instead:

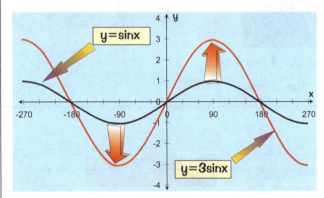

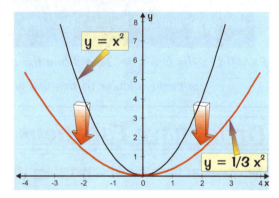

This graph shows $y = f(x)$ and $y = 3f(x)$
(y = SIN X and Y = 3 SIN X)

This graph shows $y = f(x)$ and $y = \frac{1}{3} f(x)$
(y=x² and y=1/3 x²)

2) Y-Shift: $y = f(x) + a$

This is where the whole graph is slid UP OR DOWN the y-axis with no distortion, and is achieved by simply adding a number onto the end of the equation: $y = f(x) + a$.

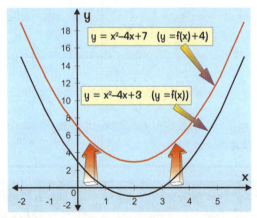

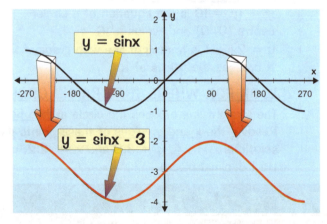

This shows $y = f(x)$ and $y = f(x) + 4$
i.e. y = x² – 4x + 3, and
$$y = (x^2 - 4x + 3) + 4$$
$$\text{or } y = x^2 - 4x + 7$$

This shows $y = f(x)$ and $y = f(x) - 3$
i.e. y = sin x and y = sinx – 3

Graphs: Shifts and Stretches

3) X-Shift: Y = f(x – a)

This is where <u>the whole graph slides to the left or right</u> and it only happens when you <u>replace "x"</u> everywhere in the equation <u>with "x – a"</u>. These are a bit tricky because they go "<u>the wrong way</u>". In other words if you want to go from <u>y = f(x) to y = f(x – a)</u> you must move the whole graph a distance "a" in the <u>POSITIVE</u> X-direction →   (and vice versa).

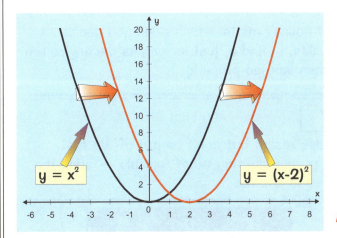

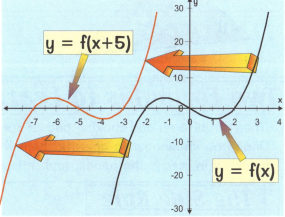

This graph shows <u>y=f(x)</u> and <u>y=f(x–2)</u>
(i.e. y =x² and y =(x–2)²)

This graph shows <u>y=f(x)</u> and <u>y=f(x+5)</u>
i.e. y=x³ – 4x, and y=(x+5)³ – 4(x+5)

4) X-Stretch: Y = f(kX)

These go "<u>the wrong way</u>" too — when k is a "<u>multiplier</u>" it *scrunches the graph up*, whereas when it's a "<u>divider</u>", it *stretches* the graph out (the opposite of the y-stretch).

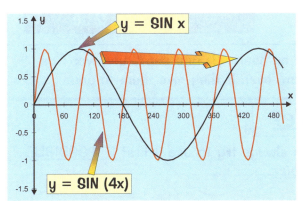

This graph shows
   <u>y = SIN X</u> and <u>y = SIN(4X)</u>.
The one that is all squashed up is y = SIN(4X).
   The way to sketch it is simply that with a multiplier of 4, it will be 4 times as squashed up.
(*Each full cycle of up-and-down takes ¼ the amount of x-axis as the original graph, so you fit 4 of them into 1 of the other graph.*)

Remember, if k is a <u>divider</u>, then the graph <u>spreads out</u>. So if the squashed up graph above was the original, <u>y = f(x)</u>, then the more spread out one would be <u>y = f(x/4)</u>.

The Acid Test:

LEARN the <u>Four types of Graph Transformations</u>, both the effect on the formula and the effect on the graph. <u>Then turn over</u> and <u>draw two examples of each type</u>.

1) Sketch these graphs: a) y = x²   b) y = x² – 4   c) y = 3x²   d) y = (x – 3)²
   e) y = cos x   f) y = cos (x + 30⁰)   g) y = cosx + 3   h) y = 2cosx – 4

The Sine and Cosine Rules

Normal trigonometry using SOH CAH TOA etc. can only be applied to right-angled triangles. The Sine and Cosine Rules on the other hand allow you to tackle any triangle at all with contemptuous ease.

Labelling The Triangle

This is very important. You must label the sides and angles properly so that the letters for the sides and angles correspond with each other:

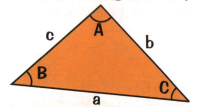

Remember, *side "a" is opposite angle A* etc.

It doesn't matter which sides you decide to call a, b, and c, just as long as the angles are then labelled properly.

Two Formulas to Learn:

They're quite an odd-looking pair of formulas really, but don't be put off by that. Once you know how to operate them they're just like any other formula — stick the numbers in, crank the handle and out pops the answer.

The Sine Rule

You don't use the whole thing with both "=" signs of course, so it's not half as bad as it looks — you just choose the two bits that you want:

$$\frac{a}{SIN\,A} = \frac{b}{SIN\,B} = \frac{c}{SIN\,C}$$

e.g. $\dfrac{b}{SIN\,B} = \dfrac{c}{SIN\,C}$ or $\dfrac{a}{SIN\,A} = \dfrac{b}{SIN\,B}$

The Cosine Rule

$$a^2 = b^2 + c^2 - 2bc\,COS\,A$$

or $$COS\,A = \frac{b^2 + c^2 - a^2}{2\,bc}$$

You should **LEARN** these three formulas off by heart. If you can't, you won't be able to use them successfully in the Exam, even if they give them to you.

When Do You Use Which Rule?

1) Basically, THE SINE RULE is *much simpler* so always try to use it first IF POSSIBLE.
2) However, *you don't usually have a lot of choice*.

The good news is that there are only FOUR basic questions, TWO which need the SINE RULE and TWO which need the COSINE RULE as detailed on the next page. However, once you know 4 BITS OF DATA (e.g. 2 sides and 2 angles, or 3 sides and 1 angle) then the rest is easily worked out (with the SINE RULE preferably).

The Acid Test:

LEARN the proper labelling, the Three Formulas, and how to decide which rule to use.

Now turn over and write down everything on this page.

The Sine and Cosine Rules

The Four *Examples*

Amazingly enough there are <u>BASICALLY ONLY FOUR</u> questions where the SINE and COSINE rules would be applied. *Learn the exact details of these four basic examples:*

1) TWO ANGLES given plus ANY SIDE:

— SINE RULE NEEDED

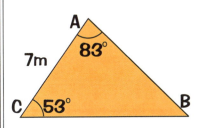

1) Don't forget the obvious: $B = 180 - 83 - 53 = \underline{44^0}$

2) Then use $\dfrac{b}{\text{SIN}\,B} = \dfrac{c}{\text{SIN}\,C}$ $\Rightarrow$ $\dfrac{7}{\text{SIN}\,44} = \dfrac{c}{\text{SIN}\,53}$ *(Remember — side c is opposite angle C.)*

3) Which gives $\Rightarrow c = \dfrac{7 \times \text{SIN}\,53}{\text{SIN}\,44} = \underline{8.05\text{m}}$

Finding BC is easy using the SINE RULE.

2) TWO SIDES given plus an ANGLE NOT ENCLOSED by them:

— SINE RULE NEEDED

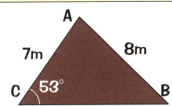

1) Use: $\dfrac{b}{\text{SIN}\,B} = \dfrac{c}{\text{SIN}\,C}$ $\Rightarrow$ $\dfrac{7}{\text{SIN}\,B} = \dfrac{8}{\text{SIN}\,53}$

2) $\Rightarrow$ $\text{SIN}\,B = \dfrac{7 \times \text{SIN}\,53}{8} = 0.6988$ $\Rightarrow B = \text{SIN}^{-1}(0.6988) = 44.3^0$

Finding angle A and the side BC is easy using the SINE RULE.

3) TWO SIDES given plus THE ANGLE ENCLOSED by them:

— COSINE RULE NEEDED

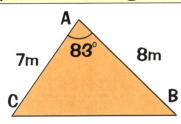

1) Use: $a^2 = b^2 + c^2 - 2bc\,\text{COS}\,A$

$= 7^2 + 8^2 - 2 \times 7 \times 8 \times \text{COS}\,83$

$= 99.3506$ $\Rightarrow$ $a = \sqrt{99.3506} = \underline{9.97\text{m}}$

Finding angles C and B is easy using the SINE RULE.

4) ALL THREE SIDES given but NO ANGLES:

— COSINE RULE NEEDED

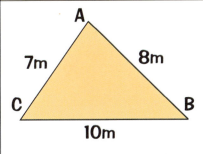

1) Use: $\text{COS}\,A = \dfrac{b^2 + c^2 - a^2}{2bc}$

$= \dfrac{49 + 64 - 100}{2 \times 7 \times 8} = \dfrac{13}{112} = 0.11607$

2) Hence $A = \text{COS}^{-1}(0.11607) = \underline{83.3^0}$

The rest is easy using the SINE RULE.

The Acid Test:

LEARN the FOUR BASIC TYPES as above.
Then cover the page and do these:

1) Write down *a new version* of each of the 4 examples above and then use the *SINE* and *COSINE RULES* to find *ALL of the sides and angles* for each one.

2) A triangle has two sides of 12m and 17m with an angle of 70^0 between them. Find all the other sides and angles in the triangle.   (A sketch is essential, of course).

3-D Pythagoras and Trigonometry

3D questions on Pythagoras and trig might seem a bit mind-boggling
at first — but you're really just using those same old rules.

Angle Between Line and Plane — Use a Diagram

Learn The 3-Step Method

1) Make a RIGHT-ANGLED triangle using the line, a line in
   the plane and a line between the two.

2) Draw this right-angled triangle again so that you can
   see it clearly. Label the sides. You might have to use
   Pythagoras to work out the length of one of the sides.

3) Use trigonometry to calculate the angle.

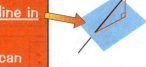

Example: *"ABCDE is a square-based pyramid. It is 12 cm high and the square base has sides of length 7 cm. Find the angle the edge AE makes with the base."*

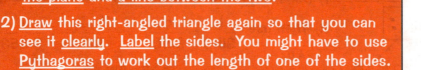

X is the centre
of the square
base.

1) First draw a right-angled triangle using the edge AE, the base and a line between
   the two (in this case the central height). Call the angle you're trying to find θ.

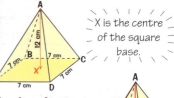

2) Now draw this triangle clearly and label it.

To find θ, you need to know the length of side EX.

So, using Pythagoras — $EX^2 = 3.5^2 + 3.5^2 = 24.5 \Rightarrow EX = \sqrt{24.5}$ cm

You know the lengths of the **opposite** *and* **adjacent** *sides, so use* **tan**.

3) Now use trigonometry to find the angle θ:

$$\tan\theta = \frac{12}{\sqrt{24.5}} = 2.4... \quad \theta = \underline{67.6°} \text{ (1 d.p.)}$$

Use Right-Angled Triangles To Find Lengths too

Example:

1) First use Pythagoras to find the length FH.

   $FH^2 = 3^2 + 3^2 = 18 \Rightarrow FH = \sqrt{18}$ cm

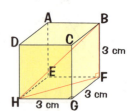

2) Now use Pythagoras again to find the length BH.

   $BH^2 = 3^2 + (\sqrt{18})^2 = 27 \Rightarrow BH = \sqrt{27}$ cm $= \underline{5.2 \text{ cm}}$ (1 decimal place)

The Acid Test:

LEARN THE 3-STEP METHOD —
then try the questions below.

1) Calculate the angle that the line AG makes with the base of this cuboid.
2) Calculate the length of AG.

Angles of Any Size

YOU CAN ONLY DO THIS IF YOU'VE LEARNT THE GRAPHS ON PAGE 66.

SIN, COS and TAN for Angles of Any Size

There is ONE BASIC IDEA involved here:

> If you draw a horizontal line at a given value for SIN X then it will pick out an infinite number of angles on the X-axis which all have the same value for SIN X.

Example 1: "Find 6 different angles X such that Sin X = 0.94."

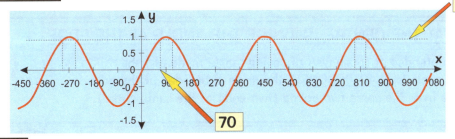

Method

1) SKETCH the extended SIN X graph.

2) Put a HORIZONTAL LINE across at 0.94.

3) DRAW LINES DOWN to the X-axis wherever the horizontal CROSSES THE CURVE.

4) Use your CALCULATOR to find INV SIN 0.94, to get the first angle (70° in this case).

5) The SYMMETRY is surely obvious. You can see that 70° is 20° away from the peak, so all the other angles are clearly 20° either side of the peaks at 90°, 450°, etc.

> Hence we can say that the SIN X = +0.94 for all the following angles:
> ..... -290°, -250°, 70°, 110°, 430°, 470°, 790°, 830°....

Example 2: "Find three other angles which have the same Cosine as 65°."

ANSWER: 1) Use the calculator to find COS 65° = +0.423.
2) Draw the extended COS curve and a horizontal line across at + 0.423.
3) Draw the vertical lines from the intersections and use symmetry.

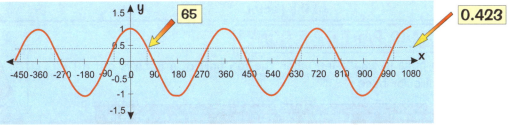

Since 65° is 25° below 90° the other angles shown must be: -425°, -295°, -65°, etc

The Acid Test:
LEARN the methods above.
Then turn over and write it all down.

1) Find the first 4 positive values and first two negative values for X such that
    a) SIN X = 0.5   b) COS X = -0.67   c) TAN X = 1

Circle Geometry

1) ANGLE IN A SEMICIRCLE = 90⁰

A triangle drawn from the <u>two ends of a diameter</u> will **ALWAYS** make an <u>angle of 90⁰ where it meets</u> the edge of the circle.

2) ANGLES IN THE SAME SEGMENT ARE EQUAL

All triangles drawn from a chord will have <u>the same angle where they touch the circle</u>. Also, the two angles on opposite sides of the chord <u>add up to 180⁰</u>.

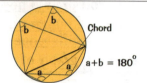

3) ANGLE AT THE CENTRE IS TWICE THE ANGLE AT THE EDGE

The angle subtended at (posh way of saying "angle made at") the centre of a circle is <u>EXACTLY DOUBLE</u> the angle subtended at the edge of the circle from the same two points (two ends of the same chord).

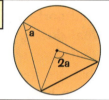

4) OPPOSITE ANGLES OF A CYCLIC QUADRILATERAL ADD UP TO 180⁰

A <u>*cyclic quadrilateral*</u> is a <u>4-sided shape with every corner touching the circle</u>. Both pairs of opposite angles add up to 180⁰.

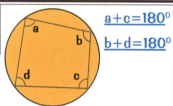

$a+c=180^0$
$b+d=180^0$

5) ANGLE IN OPPOSITE SEGMENT IS EQUAL

This is quite a tricky one to remember. If you draw a <u>tangent</u> and a <u>chord</u> that meet, then <u>the angle between them</u> is always <u>equal</u> to "<u>*the angle in the opposite segment*</u>" (i.e. the angle made at the edge of the circle by two lines drawn from the chord).

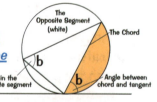

6) THE AREA OF A SEGMENT

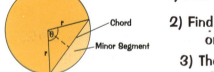

<u>FINDING THE AREA OF A SEGMENT</u> is a slightly involved business but worth learning:

1) Find the <u>area of the sector</u> using the formula on page 68.

2) Find the <u>area of the triangle</u>. You can use A = ½ ab sin C, or in this case, A = ½ r² sin θ.

3) Then just <u>subtract</u> the area of the triangle from the area of the sector.

7) A FRUSTUM IS PART OF A CONE

A <u>frustum of a cone</u> is what's left when the top part of a cone is cut off parallel to its circular base

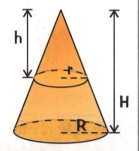

| VOLUME OF FRUSTUM | = | VOLUME OF THE ORIGINAL CONE | − | VOLUME OF THE REMOVED CONE |

$$= \tfrac{1}{3}\pi R^2 H - \tfrac{1}{3}\pi r^2 h$$

The Acid Test:

LEARN The <u>SEVEN RULES</u> above. Then turn over and write all seven out again in full detail.

Revision Summary for Stage Three

Here we are again — more lovely questions for you to test yourself with. Remember, you have to keep practising these questions *over and over again* until you can answer them all. Seriously you do. That's the best kind of revision there is. Enjoy.

Keep learning these basic facts until you know them.

1) Explain the difference between direct proportion and inverse proportion.
2) Sketch the graph of y against x when; a) x and y are directly proportional
                                          b) when x and y are inversely proportional
3) What's the difference between inverse proportion and inverse square proportion?
4) What sort of statements are involved in the subject of "variation"?
5) What does $y \propto x^2$ mean?
6) What does $y \propto 1/x^2$ mean?
7) What are the five essential steps involved in dealing with variation questions?
8) Explain how to solve simultaneous equations when one is quadratic.
9) What must you do to check your solution is correct?
10) Which value in the equation $y = mx + c$ is the same for all parallel lines?
11) How are the gradients of perpendicular lines linked?
12) What is the general formula for a circle with centre (0, 0)?
13) What is the radius of a circle with equation $x^2 + y^2 = 49$ and centre (0, 0)?
14) How can you use a graph to solve a pair of simultaneous equations
    where one is a circle?
15) What does the notation $y = f(x)$ mean? Is it really complicated?
16) How many types of shift and stretch are there for graphs?
17) Illustrate each of the different types.
18) Explain how the equation is modified for each of these.
19) Give an example of each type, both the modified equation and a sketch.
20) Write down the SINE and COSINE rules and draw a properly labelled triangle.
21) List the four different types of questions and which rule you need for each.
22) What are the three steps for finding the angle between a line and a plane in a 3D shape?
23) What is the method for dealing with SIN, COS and TAN for angles of any size.
24) Illustrate the method by finding 6 angles whose cosine is -0.5.
25) What are the three steps needed to find the area of a segment?
26) What do the opposite angles of a cyclic quadrilateral add up to?
27) Draw a diagram to illustrate the rule "Angles in the same segment are equal".
28) What can you say about the angles x and y below?

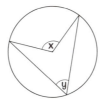

29) What is the formula for calculating the volume of a frustum of a cone?

Answers

STAGE ONE

P1 Squares, Cubes, Square Roots and Negative Numbers: **1) a)** 81, 25, 36, 1, 64, 225 **b)** 8, 27, 125, 1, 64, 1000 **2) a)** 14.142 **b)** 3 or –3 **c)** –3

P2 Prime Numbers: **1)** 2, 3, 5, 7, 11, 13, 17, 19, 23, 29, 31, 37, 41, 43, 47 **2) a)** 101, 103, 107, 109 **b)** none **c)** 503, 509

P3 Multiples, Factors and Prime Factors: **1)** 7, 14, 21, 28, 35, 42, 49, 56, 63, 70; 9, 18, 27, 36, 45, 54, 63, 72, 81, 90; **2)** 1, 2, 3, 4, 6, 9, 12, 18, 36; 1, 2, 3, 4, 6, 7, 12, 14, 21, 28, 42, 84; **3) a)** $990 = 2 \times 3 \times 3 \times 5 \times 11$ **b)** $160 = 2 \times 2 \times 2 \times 2 \times 2 \times 5$

P4 LCM and HCF: **1)** 8, 16, 24, 32, 40, 48, 56, 64, 72, 80 and 9, 18, 27, 36, 45, 54, 63, 72, 81, 90 LCM = 72 **2)** 1, 2, 4, 7, 8, 14, 28, 56 and 1, 2, 4, 8, 13, 26, 52, 104 HCF = 8 **3)** 63 **4)** 12 **P5 Rounding Off:** **1)** 3.57 **2)** 0.05 **3)** 12.910 **4)** 3546.1

P6 Rounding Off: **1) a)** 3.41 **b)** 1.05 **c)** 0.07 **d)** 3.60 **2 a)** 568 (Rule 3) **b)** 23400 (Rule 3) **c)** 0.0456 (Rules 1 and 3) **d)** 0.909 (Rules 1, 2 and 3) **3)** 16 feet 6 in. to 17 feet 6 in. **P7 Accuracy and Estimating:** **1) a)** 35g **b)** 134 mph **c)** 850g **2) a)** Approx 600 miles × 150 miles = 90,000 square miles **b)** Approx 7cm × 7cm × 12cm = 590cm³ **3) a)** 3.4 or 3.5 **b)** 10.1 or 10.2 **c)** 7.1, 7.2 or 7.3 **d)** 5.4 or 5.5

P8 Fractions: **1) a)** 3/8 **b)** $27/10 = 2^{7}/_{10}$ **c)** 11/15 **d)** x=13, **e)** y=1 **2) a)** 8/15 **b)** $8/3 = 2^{2}/_{3}$ **c)** 7/24 **d)** 3/7 **e)** 3/4 **f)** $112/15 = 7^{7}/_{15}$ **g)** $2^{4}/_{11}$

P9 Fractions and Decimals: **1)** 1/7 **2)** 7/200

P11 Calculator Buttons: **1)** See P.10 **2) a)** `6` `xʸ` `8` `=` **b)** `6` `EXP` `8` **c)** `50` `xʸ` `(` `(−)` `4` `aᵇ/c` `5` `)` `=` or `50` `xʸ` `(−)` `0.8` `=` **d)** `(` `4` `aᵇ/c` `3` `aᵇ/c` `5` `)` `x³` `(` `1` `aᵇ/c` `6` `)` `=` or `6` `ˣ√` `4.6` **3)** `(` `23.3` `+` `35.8` `)` `÷` `(` `36` `×` `26.5` `)` `=` **4) a)** 4hrs 34mins (12secs) **b)** 5.5397 hrs

P12 Conversion Factors: **1)** 2,300m **2)** £174 **3)** 3.2cm

P13 Metric and Imperial Units: **1)** 15.75 litres **2)** 200 or 220 yards **3)** 115 cm **4)** 62.9p per litre **5)** 104 km/h

P15 Ratios: **1) a)** 5:7 **b)** 2:3 **c)** 3:5 **2)** 17½ bowls of porridge **3)** £3500 : £2100 : £2800

P16 Percentages: **1)** 40% **2)** £20,500 **3)** 1.39% **P17 Compound Growth and Decay:** **1)** 48 stick insects **2)** 0.15m/s. Forever.

P19 Standard Index Form: **1)** 9.58×10^{5} **2)** 1.8×10^{-4} **3)** 4560 **4)** 2×10^{21}

P20 Powers: **1) a)** 3^{8} **b)** 4 **c)** 8^{12} **d)** 1 **e)** 7^{6} **2) a)** 1 **b)** 64 **c)** 0.0016 or 1/625 **d)** 1/5 **e)** 2 **3) a)** 1.53×10^{17} **b)** 15.9 **c)** 2.89

P22 Basic Algebra: **1) a)** 0 **b)** –6 **c)** X **2) a)** 18 **b)** –216 **c)** 2 **d)** –27 **e)** –336 **3)** 4x + y – 4 **4)** 6p²q – 8pq³ **5)** 8g² + 16g – 10 **6)** 7xy²(2xy + 3 – 5x²y²) **P23 Substitution:** **2)** 25

P24 Solving Equations: **1) a)** x = 2 **b)** x = -0.2 or -1/5 **c)** x = ±√6 **P25 Trial and Improvement:** **1)** X = 1.6

P26 Number Patterns: **a)** 162, 486 **b)** 18, 29 **c)** 23, 30 **d)** 16, 8 **P27 Finding the nth Term:** **1a)** 3n + 1 **b)** 5n – 2 **c)** ½n(n + 1) **d)** n² – 2n + 4

P28 D/T and V/T Graphs: **1)** 0.5km/h **2)** Accels. 6m/s² 2m/s² -8m/s² (deceleration), Speeds: 30m/s, 50m/s

P30 Plotting Straight-line Graphs: **P31 Straight-line Graphs:"y = mx + c"**

P32 Quadratics:

x	-2	-1	0	1	2	3	4	5	6
y	15	8	3	0	-1	0	3	8	15

3) y = 3.8, x = –1.6 or 5.6

P33 Pythagoras and Bearings: **1)** BC = 8m **2)** 298° **3)** 118°

P34 Pythagoras, Lines and Line Segments **1)** 5 units **2)** A line continues to infinity, whereas a segment is part of a line.

P36 Trigonometry: **1)** x = 26.5 m **2)** 23.6° **3)** 32.6° (both)

P37 Circle Geometry: **1)** Area = 154 cm² Circumference = 44.0 cm **2)** A = 113 m² C = 37.7 m

P38 Similarity and Enlargements: **1)** A'(-3, -1.5), B'(-7.5, -3), C'(-6, -6) **2)** 64 m²

P39 Transformations: A → B, Rotation of 90° clockwise about the origin. E → A, Enlargement, scale factor 2, centre (0,0) F → B, Enlargement, scale factor -2, centre (0,0) B → C, Reflection in the line Y = X. C → A, Reflection in the Y-axis. A → D, Translation of $\binom{-9}{-7}$, A → E, Enlargement, scale factor ½, centre (0,0) B → F, Enlargement, scale factor -½, centre (0,0)

P40 Areas, Solids and Nets: **1)** 128.8 cm² **2)** 294 cm² **3)** 174 cm² **4)** 96 cm²

P41 Volume or Capacity: **a)** Trapezoidal Prism, V = 148.5 cm³ **b)** Cylinder, V = 0.70 m³

P42 Mean, Median, Mode: First: -14, -12, -5, -5, 0, 1, 3, 6, 7, 8, 10, 14, 18, 23, 25 Mean = 5.27, Median = 6, Mode = -5, Range = 39

P44 Frequency Tables:

No. of Phones	0	1	2	3	4	5	6	TOTALS
Frequency	1	25	53	34	22	5	1	141
No. × Frequency	0	25	106	102	88	25	6	352

Mean = 2.5, Median = 2, Mode = 2, Range = 6

P45 Grouped Frequency Tables:

Length(cm)	15.5 —	16.5 —	17.5 —	18.5 — 19.5	TOTALS
Frequency	12	18	23	8	61
Mid-Interval Value	16	17	18	19	—
Freq × M I V	192	306	414	152	1064

Mean = 17.4, Modal Group = 17.5 — 18.5, Median ≈17.5

P46 Cumulative Frequency:

Weight (kg)	41 – 45	46 – 50	51 – 55	56 – 60	61 – 65	66 – 70	71 – 75
Frequency	2	7	17	25	19	8	2
Cum. Freq.	2	9	26	51	70	78	80

Median = 58 kg, Lower Quartile = 53 kg Upper Quartile = 62 kg Interquartile range = 9 kg

Answers

P47 Histograms and Frequency Density: **1)** 0–5: 10, 5–10: 30, 10–15: 40, 15–20: 50, 20–25: 35, 25–35: 20, 35–55: 20, 55–65: 40, 65–80: 180, 80–90: 140, 90–100: 20 **2)** 5

P48 Correlation, Dispersion and Spread: **1)**

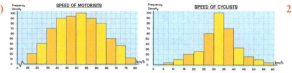

2)

P49 Sampling Methods:

1) Sample too small, motorways not representative of average motorist, only done at one time of day and in one place, not easy to get accurate age from registration letter. Better approach: A more detailed survey which deals with all the above problems — surveying people emerging from various Post Offices with new tax discs might be good. Stratified sampling would be essential in choosing the Post Offices.

P50 Time Series: 1) a) period = 4 months **b)** Find the average of the readings from months 1-4, then the average from months 2-5, then from months 3-6, etc. (& you could plot these on a graph to see the trend.)

STAGE TWO

P52 Reciprocals, Inverse Operations and Proportion: **1)** 9/2 **2)** or X^{-1} **3)** £4.40

P53 Manipulating Surds and Use of π: **1)** $4\sqrt{2}$ **2)** $1 + 2\sqrt{2}$

P54 Rounded Off Values: **1)** $(4.22472 - 4.1556) \div 4.22472 = 0.01637 = 1.64\%$

P55 Algebraic Fractions and D.O.T.S.: **1) a)** $(X + 4Y)(X - 4Y)$ **b)** $(7 + 9PQ)(7 - 9PQ)$ **c)** $12(YX^3 - 2K^2M^4)(YX^3 + 2K^2M^4)$ **2) a)** $(c^4/6d^3)$ **b)** $2(17g - 6)/5(3g - 4)$

P56 Rearranging Formulas: **1)** $C = 5(F-32)/9$ **2) a)** $p = -4y/3$ **b)** $p = rq/(r + q)$ **c)** $p = \pm\sqrt{\{rq/(r+q)\}}$

P57 Simultaneous Equations: F = 3 G = -1

P58 Simultaneous Equations and Graphs: **1) a)** x = 2, y = 4 **b)** x = 1.5, y = 3 **2)** x = 1.5 or -2

P59 Inequalities: **1) a)** -4, -3, -2 , -1, 0, 1 **2)**

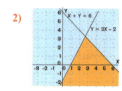

P61 Factorising Quadratics: **1) a)** x = 3 or -8 **b)** x = 7 or -1 **c)** x = 1 or -7 **d)** x = 4 or -3/5

P62 The Quadratic Formula: **1) a)** x = 0.39 or -10.39 **b)** x = 1.46 or -0.46 **c)** x = 0.44 or -3.44

P63 Completing the Square: **2) a)** x = 0.39 or -10.39 **b)** x = 1.46 or -0.46 **c)** x = 0.44 or -3.44

P64 Four Graphs You Should Recognise: **1) a)** x^2 bucket shape **b)** $-x^3$ wiggle (top left to bottom right) **c)** +ve inverse proportion graph **d)** Straight line parallel to x-axis **e)** –ve inverse proportion graph **f)** $+x^3$ wiggle (bottom left to top right) **g)** $-x^2$ upside down bucket shape **h)** K^X curve upwards through (0, 1)

P65 Solving Equations Using Graphs: **1)** t = 0.7 or 4.3 **2) a)** x = –2.4, 0.4 **b)** x = -3, 1

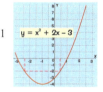

P68 Lengths, Areas and Volumes: **1)** 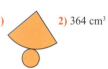 **2)** 364 cm³

P69 Volumes: **1)** Cone, 20.3 m³ **2)** 33.5 cm³, 179.6 cm³

P73 "Real-Life" Vectors:

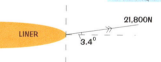

P74 Speed and Density Formulas: **1)** 1 hr 37 mins 30 secs **2)** 16.5 g/cm³ **3)** 602.7 g

P75 Probability: **2)** $(4/52) \times (3/51) \times (1/50) = (12/132600) = (1/11050)$

P76 Relative Frequency: **1)** Probability of Bill drawing an ace = (13/100) = 0.13 Expected probability of drawing an ace = (4/52) = 0.077. 0.13 is much greater than 0.077 so YES, the pack is biased.

P77 Probability — Tree Diagrams: **2)** 8/15 **P78 Probability:** **1)** $(2/7) \times (1/6) \times (5/6) \times (4/5) = (40/1260) = (2/63)$

STAGE THREE

P80 Direct and Inverse Proportion: 1) a) Total cost and No.of tins of Bone-tingling Fireball Soup **b)** No. of people working on a job and time taken to complete it. **P81 Variation:** **1) a)** 0.632 Hz **b)** 40.8 cm

P82 Simultaneous Equations: **1) a)** f = 4 & g = 0 OR f = 40 & g = 6 **b)** f = -3 & g = 33 OR f = 1/4 & g = -11/4

2) Solutions are: x = -2, y = 4 or x = 1.5, y = 0.5

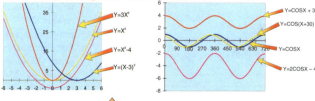

P85 Graphs: Shifts and Stretches:

P83 Gradients and Graphs of Circles: **1) a)** -1/4 **b)** -2 **c)** 1/2 **2) a)** 1 **b)** 7 **c)** $\sqrt{20} = 2\sqrt{5}$

P87 Sine and Cosine Rules: **2)** 17.13m, 68.8°, 41.2°

P88 3-D Pythagoras and Trigonometry: **1)** 25.1° **2)** 7.07 cm

P89 Angles of Any Size: 1) a) x = -330°, -210°, 30°, 150°, 390°, 510° **b)** x = -228°, -132°, 132°, 228°, 492°, 588° **c)** -315°, -135°, 45°, 225°, 405°, 585°

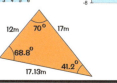

Index

Projects Inspired Myth, Magic and Fantasy

Julie Ashfield, Natalie Deane,
Flora Ellis, Jean Evans, Valerie Hughes,
Rebecca Mellor and Katharine Newall

Acknowledgements

Julie Ashfield (pp. 6–11, 20–21, 24–25, 36–37, 40–41, 44–45, 54–59, 68–69) would like to thank the staff and students at All Saints C.W Primary Cardiff, Bryn Hafod Primary Cardiff, Marlborough Primary Cardiff, Willowbrook Primary Cardiff for their wonderful work on the projects.

Natalie Deane (pp. 12–13, 16–19, 22–23, 34–35), Kirklees Advanced Skills Teacher for Primary Art, Craft & Design would like to thank her brilliant Co-designer / Display Technician, Jenny Hayer for all her work on these projects. Essential thanks also goes to the artist Mike Barrett <http://www.emelbi.com/> who led the after school club during which the pupil work was created for 'Super sidekicks', to the Illustrator Julia Ogden for the inspiration behind 'Illustrating characters' and to sculptor Samantha Bryan <http://brainsfairies.co.uk/> for the original 3D character crafting concepts. Thanks also to all the pupils at Battyeford CE Primary who created the fabulous artwork.

Flora Ellis (pp. 64–67) would like to thank the children of Class 2 at Sherborne C of E Primary, Mr Pudifoot and in particular, Moira Cooper for her help.

Jean Evans (pp. 26–33, 42–43) would like to thank staff working with Classes 4 and 6 at Dodmire School for their endless support and encouragement. The children were a joy – wonderfully creative and brimming with enthusiasm. Thanks also to Alison Whelan, Reception class teacher at Heighington CE Primary School, and to Hannah Morris, student teacher, for their creative input. Very special thanks go to her daughter, Charlotte Spiers, for listening, trying out ideas and believing that anything is possible.

Valerie Hughes (pp. 38–39, 70–72) would like to thank the staff and pupils at Longcot and Fernham CE Primary School for their hard work.

Rebecca Mellor (pp. 14–15, 60–63) would like to say a big thank you to the Reception class at Woodhouse Primary School.

Katharine Newall (pp. 46–53) would like to thank Miss Becki Holmes and her class at Marshlands Primary School, and Mrs Fiona Binsley and her class at Gilberdyke Primary School, for all of their help, enthusiasm and hard work producing the displays.

Published by Collins
An imprint of HarperCollins*Publishers*
77–85 Fulham Palace Road
Hammersmith
London
W6 8JB

© HarperCollins*Publishers* Limited 2013

10 9 8 7 6 5 4 3 2 1

ISBN-13 978 0 00 750121 2

Julie Ashfield, Natalie Deane, Flora Ellis, Jean Evans, Valerie Hughes, Rebecca Mellor and Katharine Newall assert their moral rights to be identified as the authors of this work.

British Library Cataloguing in Publication Data
A Catalogue record for this publication is available from the British Library

Cover design by Steve Evans Design and Illustration
Photography by Elmcroft Studios

Internal design by Linda Miles, Lodestone Publishing Limited
Edited by Alison Sage and Fiona Undrill
Proofread by Ros and Chris Davies

Printed and bound by Printing Express Limited, Hong Kong

Browse the complete Collins catalogue at
www.collinseducation.com

MIX
Paper from
responsible sources
FSC™ C007454

Contents

Introduction

Encouraging children to explore books and a love of reading is something that all teachers aim to promote but classrooms are busy places and it is sometimes difficult to dedicate time to this very valuable part of education and anchor it in a meaningful scheme of work. In this book, teachers from all over the country give their ideas about inspiring and practical hands-on projects that can be displayed to provide a creative record of the children's learning journey through each book or genre. The chapters are organised into themes that include projects that are suitable for either 4–7 year olds or 7–11 year olds and the age rage is indicated in the top left hand corner of each double-page spread. Chapters 3 and 7 are aimed specifically towards Key Stage 1 and all other chapters include a range of projects suitable for either Key Stage 1 or Key Stage 2 levels.

Chapter 1: Into the Woods
Some of the classic fairytales are based in woodlands and forests. Chapter 1 explores stories in nature, including a sustained piece of work on *Little Red Riding Hood* and a visit to the tropical rainforest. Into the Woods examines how to promote children's confidence in art and how to get them talking and thinking about their work so that curiosity about a new idea spills into all aspects of the school curriculum.

Chapter 2: Out of This World
Leaving the Earth, these projects explore space travel and aliens for the youngest children, and venture into other worlds for the older ones. The chapter features a trip through the wardrobe to Narnia and a chance to meet some of the stranger creatures in *Alice in Wonderland*.

Chapter 3: Can You Believe it?
Folk tales are the inspiration for this chapter, which is mainly aimed at younger children. Stories such as *The Enormous Turnip* and *Chicken Licken* offer humour through the ludicrous, while *The Bad-Tempered Ladybird*, *Tiddler* and *funnybones* allow learning opportunities by encouraging creative pupil response.

Chapter 4: Faraway Lands
These projects look at fantasy stories in other lands, from Africa to Australia, showing how different art can be in different cultures.

Chapter 5: Once Upon a Time …
Every generation reinvents the classic fairy stories. This chapter looks at *Cinderella* and *Jack and the Beanstalk* and shows how stories of giants and fairies, magic carpets and godmothers are still relevant today.

Chapter 6: Dragons and Other Beasts
Strange and wonderful creatures have lived in our imaginations for many thousands of years. These projects look at dragons and other mythical beings from *Beowulf* to the modern day.

Chapter 7: The Golden Age of Greece
These stories are part of the fabric of language from almost every country. Based at one point on a long-forgotten truth, they aim to warn or explain through their telling. There is the story of *Theseus and the Minotaur*, which remembers a time when the Cretan civilization was powerful as well as Icarus, who flew too close to the Sun.

Using display effectively

When making a display, it is important that children should be involved at every stage in the choices that are made, in order for them to get maximum enjoyment and learning advantage. Children will be very quick to notice if their displays look interesting, challenging and exciting. They will also remember what they have done and the confidence developed through successful projects will make them want to make discoveries in other fields. A display can be used and reused many times in different circumstances and for different subjects. It is a stepping stone towards further learning and a foundation for exploration.

Adapting projects for older and younger readers

The projects in this book have been designed with a particular age group in mind and as part of a longer, sustained piece of work. However, advice and instructions have been given on how to age them up or down, depending on the age and the ability of the children who are taking part.

Break-out boxes throughout the book assist teachers in getting the most out of each project. The further ideas boxes provide suggestions for how to adapt projects for older or younger children and offer advice on how to extend the activities. Cross-curricular link boxes suggest activities that tie the project into the curriculum so that each activity becomes the basis for a larger piece of work. Resources boxes contain a comprehensive list of materials required for each activity.

Safety precautions

All equipment should be carefully supervised and different ages will need different levels of help to make these projects work to their full advantage. Adults should naturally accompany children on any trips out of the school and it is common sense that the teacher should always use a glue gun, craft knife or guillotine. Safety glasses may also be required when working with wire and other materials to create 3D projects. Please check your school's own safety policy.

Skills and techniques

Throughout these projects children can employ and develop various creative skills including collage, painting, printing, fabric printing, drawing from life, 3D work, sculpture, clay, ink washing, model-making, papier mâché and making salt dough. In addition to artistic techniques, these projects also engage children with a wider variety of educational and fun activities including role-play, writing and games.

We hope you and your pupils enjoy the projects as much as we have.

Julie Ashfield, Natalie Deane, Flora Ellis, Jean Evans, Valerie Hughes, Rebecca Mellor and Katharine Newall

The Labours of Hercules

Into the Woods

Woodland wonders

Storybooks can be an exciting stimulus for artwork, particularly if children are involved in the learning objectives and understand that their investigations can be used to form part of a display. *Into the Forest* by Anthony Brown offers possibilities for a range of techniques but the focus of this project is exploring texture and working with textiles, including painting, printing onto fabric and using dye sticks.

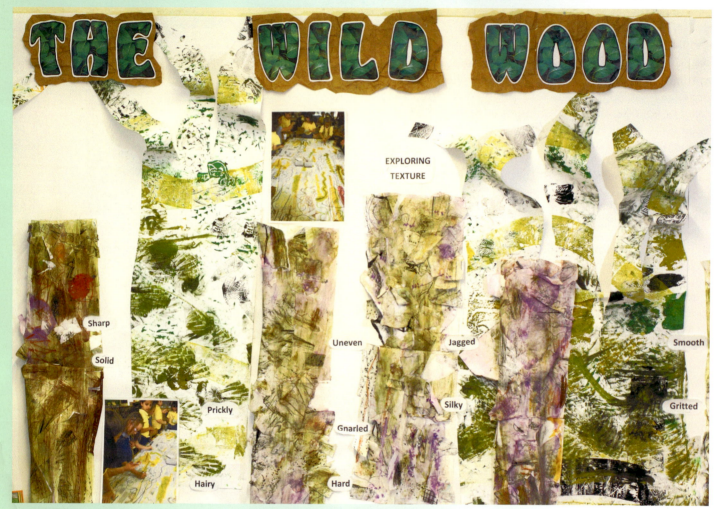

Painting and printing textures on fabric

Approach

1   In groups, visit a park, woodland, or a school ground where there are trees. Ask children to collect textures in their sketchbooks, encouraging them to touch and feel tree trunks and take photos. Collect twigs, leaves and ferns to take back to school.

2   Back in the classroom, share the children's sketchbook ideas and make a list of related vocabulary.

Resources

- *Into the Forest* by Anthony Brown
- Sketchbooks
- Graphic materials: marker pens, graphite sticks and wax crayons
- Cameras
- Collection bags
- Oil pastels, chalk pastels
- Paper

3   Fern and ivy leaves are ideal for discussing outline shape and making observational drawings. It is important to talk about the size of the drawings in relation to the size of the A4 paper, encouraging children to fill the space on the page.

4   Spread out the collected material onto covered tables and lay long lengths of paper over the top. Children should work collaboratively to make large-scale rubbings with oil pastels and chalk pastels. These will be used to create tree trunks for the wild wood display.

5   To complete the display, create a title, for example The Wild Wood using an online lettering resource.

6   Work collaboratively on a large scale using fabric paints, inks and dye sticks. Most fabric paints are concentrated and can be diluted with water to create paler shades or mixed to make new colours.

7   Demonstrate the technique by painting a patch of fabric with water, then adding the fabric paint. The paint 'bleeds' into the water and spreads out. Leave to dry before adding another layer of detail with dye sticks.

8   Sticky-back foam sheets are much easier to use as printing blocks, particularly for young children. Designs can be drawn directly onto the foam, then cut out and assembled instantly onto a card base.

9   Encourage children to create their own printing block based on their ivy or fern observational drawings. These blocks can be painted with fabric printing ink and printed repeatedly.

Further ideas

Extend the project by designing and creating costumes for fairytale forest characters. Children can colour and print recycled materials and design and create costumes for fairytale characters living in the forest, such as Jack from *Jack and the Beanstalk*, the giant, Rapunzel, and Little Red Riding Hood.

Resources

- Recycled materials
- Fabric paints, dye sticks, inks, water and paint brushes
- Sticky-back foam sheets
- Ballpoint pens
- Card
- Scissors

Cross-curricular links

Geography: research why trees and forests are so important to people all over the world.

Literacy: read *The Minpins* by Roald Dahl and write a fairy story about people and creatures living in a wood.

Science: Discuss how trees and plants grow. Explore seeds and fruits.

Fairytale settings

There are many fairy tales set in woodlands and forests. *Little Red Riding Hood* is a starting point for this project as the story offers rich opportunity for role play. Young children will enjoy the story and project, as they create their own imaginative class forest.

To extend this project to older children, look at the representation of wolves in writing such as 'Little Red Riding Hood and the Wolf' in Roald Dahl's *Revolting Rhymes*, Ann Jungman's *Sash and the Wolf Cub*, JRR Tolkien's *The Hobbit* and Laura Ingalls Wilder's *The Little House in the Big Woods*.

Resources

- A suitable version of *Little Red Riding Hood*
- Graphic materials
- Computer, printer
- Collection boards
- Wax crayons
- Images of wolves, plastic animal models
- Oil pastels
- A5, A4 and A3 paper
- Black crayons, black marker pens, graphite sticks

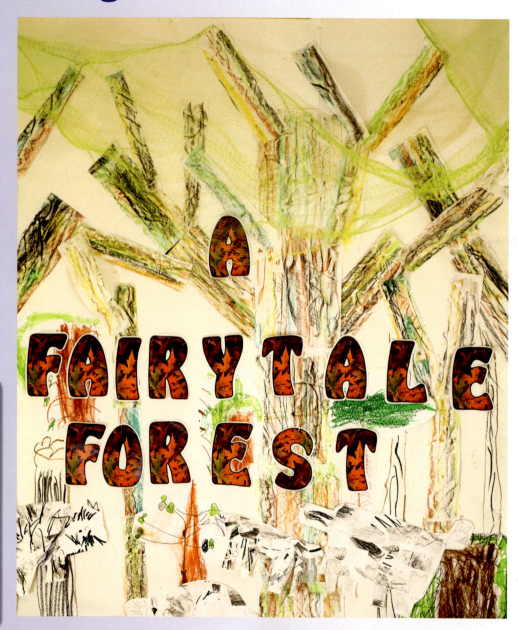

Mark-making and role-play

Approach

1 Before introducing the story, take children on a trip to a local forest to experience first-hand a similar setting to that of *Little Red Riding Hood*. Give each child a board to collect leaves and twigs on.

2 Back in the classroom, make rubbings of the leaves and twigs directly from the boards. To do this, cover the board with the leaves and twigs in A4 paper and rub wax crayons and oil pastels in a range of forest colours (greens, reds, yellows, browns and blacks) over the paper. Prepare a display board backed in white paper and arrange and stick the children's A4 rubbing sheets onto the display to form larger tree trunks. As the forest trees 'grow' taller, introduce narrower strips of rubbings to create branches for the tree.

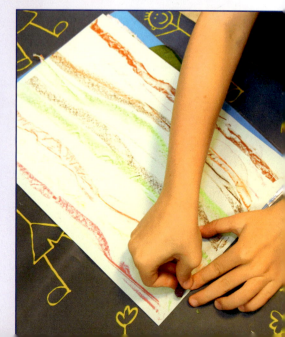

3   Encourage children to draw and colour their own imaginative tree drawings on A3 paper to add to the forest display. Some may want to draw a tree directly onto the white display paper background.

4   Read the story and capture the children's ideas in mind maps to display for each character.

5   Explain to children that they are now going to make wolves to add to the forest. First, they will need to create the impression of fur, using black crayons, graphite sticks and marker pens. Ask children to experiment making marks on A5 paper that resemble wolf fur.

6   Spend time looking at images of wolves and plastic animal models. Discuss the 2D and 3D shapes that the children are familiar with. Talk about the shape of a wolf's legs, body, head and tail. Children can now draw their own wolf on A3 paper, aiming to fill up the page. Add collage to the paper wolves using torn pieces from the mark-making sheets.

7   Cut out the wolves and add to the forest display.

8   To complete the display, create a title, for example, A Fairytale Forest using an online lettering resource.

9   Role-play in a real or a fairytale forest. You can use fabrics from the previous project for dressing up.

Cross-curricular links

Drama: write and act out a version of *Little Red Riding Hood*, including other fairytale characters.
Literacy: write a fantasy story about animals living in a forest.
Maths: use 3D shapes to make model animals.
Science: Research habitats and food chains involving wolves.

Tropical rainforests

Many children's stories explore conservation issues. Jean Craighead George's
One Day in the Tropical Rainforest also offers possibilities for investigating line, shape, and colour through observation and imaginative drawing. These elements are the focus for this display.

Imaginative drawings

Approach

1   Talk about the main characteristics of the rainforest in preparation for reading *One Day in the Tropical Rainforest* in class.

2   Explain that the project will create a 3D display illustrating the main features of a tropical rainforest. The children must decide what to include. Make a word picture (use an online 'word cloud' creator) using the vocabulary they found in their research.

Resources

- *One Day in the Tropical Rainforest* by Jean Craighead George
- Computer
- Sketchbooks
- Choice of graphic materials
- Oil pastels, chalk pastels
- Coloured drawing inks
- A4, A3 and A1 paper
- Glue sticks
- Thin card

3 Highlight which visual elements will be the focus of the artwork: line and mark for trees, shape and colour for plants and flowers. Allow the children time to experiment making lines and drawing shapes.

4 With the experience of their previous mark-making work, talk about the different types of lines children could use, encouraging them to create imaginative drawings of trees.

5 Divide children into groups and ask them collaboratively to scale their drawings up to A1 size or larger. Using oil pastels, children can colour these large-scale tree drawings and then cut them out. They will form the structure for the display and should be stuck to a display board covered in white backing paper.

6 In the next session, bring in plants and flowers or look at pictures of them in books or on the internet. Discuss different types of outline shapes of rainforest plants and flowers. On A3 paper or thin card, ask children to make observational drawings. Encourage them to colour their drawings using oil pastels or coloured inks.

7 Ask children to cut out their drawings and add to the display to create a 3D effect. Talk about how this could be done, putting larger plants and flowers in place before smaller ones.

8 Children now have all the skills to explore their own ideas for a group 3D layered display. Create outline shapes of birds and animals. The bird outlines can be coloured with oil pastels and collaged with scraps from magazines.

Cross-curricular links

Art: research artist Henri Rousseau.

Geography: Discuss what makes a rainforest. Why are they located where they are?

ICT: use a storyboard and the display to make a video of the rainforest.

Literacy: write a storyboard about life in a rainforest.

Music: add a soundtrack to the video. Children can compose their own music.

Science: research endangered species. What can be done to save them?

Out of This World

Space explorers

Q Pootle 5 by Nick Butterworth inspires children to think about the themes of friendship, trust and our environment. This text is useful for encouraging play and exploration with KS1 children using scrap. The approaches used here will suit any space-based project. The splash and drag background effects in ink also work well for landscapes or seascapes.

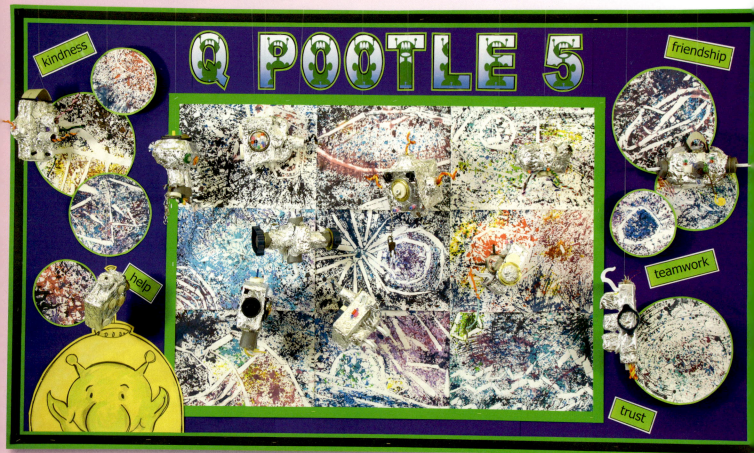

3D scrap spacecraft

Approach

1 Encourage children to use sketchbooks to plan their spacecraft. Get them to draw several different designs. Talk about the designs and how they might work.

2 Create a spacecraft 'body' by using a small cardboard box, some cardboard tubes and insulation foam (cut into a variety of lengths). Secure everything onto the box with masking tape.

3 Cover the body with scraps of tin foil coated with PVA glue, and leave to dry for 24 hours.

Resources
- *Q Pootle 5* by Nick Butterworth
- A4 or A3 white card, masking tape, sticky tape
- Mixed ink powder or drawing inks, small/medium brushes and palettes
- Small cardboard boxes, insulation foam and cardboard tubes
- Tin foil, PVA glue and hogs-hair brushes
- Selection of scrap materials: pipe cleaners, buttons, beads, nuts, washers, and so on.
- Video camera, editing software

Be careful with metal scraps and check for sharp edges before using.

4 Secure scrap items, pipe cleaners and wires onto the spacecraft body to create detail, using sellotape or PVA glue. The teacher may need to fix small heavy metal items with a glue gun.

5 On a white card background use masking tape torn into thin strips to create space-like patterns (look at secondary source space imagery with the children for inspiration). Provide palettes, ink powders or drawing inks (preferably with a limited range of colours) and brushes. Show the children how to grip the paintbrush and tap on the handle, controlling this movement to create a splash. Avoid shaking the brush up and down. Build up the ink splashes in layers, concentrating around the edges of the masking tape and ensuring coverage across the paper. Use the paintbrush end to create drags of ink lines, as well as using wet ink splashed onto the paper. Remove the masking tape to show the white lines beneath the ink. Attach the 'planetary' discs to the display.

6 To complete the display, create a title, for example, Q Pootle 5 using an online lettering resource.

Further ideas

To extend the space project to older children, add small models of people and film the spacecraft moving across a space-themed background. You could also make a time-lapse film using stop motion animation software.

This project can be carried out by younger children by developing a photocopy sheet depicting household objects. Encourage children to cut out the objects and use them to collage and make individual spacecraft.

Cross-curricular links

Design and Technology: design and make your own Moon party food.
Craft and create new uses for scrap items and see if you can sell your products in school!
Geography: how can we create a greener society?
History: ask the children to research how people recycled waste 100 years ago. How has our country's waste changed and what do we do with our waste today?
Science: find out what happens to a variety of scrap materials if left to 'decay' in a range of environments.

Catching stars

How to Catch a Star is an inspirational text for young children. In it, the little boy tries to catch a star for himself but there are many problems to solve along the way.

Wishes and stars

Approach

1   Discuss *How to Catch a Star* with the children with an emphasis on stars. Talk about wishing upon a star. Share music linked to this idea, for example "When You Wish Upon a Star" written by Harline and Washington.

2   Provide the children with star-shaped foil. Demonstrate how to emboss the foil using a variety of tools such as wooden and plastic sticks, pencils, pens or the tips and edges of shells.

3   Write wishes on stars and think of the best place to hang them. Suggest a 'wishing tree' in the garden.

4   Create some larger stars cut in half and introduce the concept of two halves equalling a whole. Ask the children to work in pairs to decorate their two halves.

5   On a large sheet of paper, sketch the main character from the story reaching for the star. Paint the sketch using watercolours and add it to the display.

6   Back the foil stars on shiny gold paper and the wish stars on blue and silver paper. Display on a blue background to create the impression of the night sky.

Resources
- *How to Catch a Star* by Oliver Jeffers
- Card stars
- Thick foil: copper, silver or gold
- Shiny gold, silver and blue paper
- Pencils
- Wooden sticks
- Plastic tools
- Paper
- Watercolour paints
- Cartridge paper
- Scissors
- PVA glue

Star catchers

Approach

1 Begin by asking the children: *how would you catch a star? What would you use?* Try to solve this problem as a group. Discuss dream catchers and how Native Americans created these as a way to protect their children. The belief is that the night air is filled with dreams; bad dreams get trapped in the web of the dream catcher whilst good dreams slide down the feathers to the sleeping child.

2 Before working with the children, an adult should make wire hoops by bending lengths of wire so that the ends touch. Use pliers and gloves to wrap around the wire ends. Use tape to fix them in place and make the sharp ends safe.

3 Provide the children with twine, embroidery, weaving threads and wool to wrap around the frame. Depending on the age or ability of the children, knot or tape these in place.

4 Attach foil or paper stars and beads to attract the light.

5 Add feathers and stars to the hanging ends.

6 Hang the star catcher in trees outdoors. Add shimmering stars for a dramatic display. Alternatively, display on a dark background to give a night sky effect.

Resources
- Pre-made wire or willow hoops
- Garden twine
- Sticky tape
- Embroidery wool/ thread
- Feathers
- Beads
- Foil stars / sequins

Shimmering stars

Approach

1 Tear up different yellow-coloured paper. Use transparent or fine paper such as tissue for a 'stained-glass' effect.

2 Using a plastic sheet as a canvas, spread a layer of glue and stick the paper down. Ensure that the base is entirely covered.

3 Add another layer of glue and then more paper. Continue this until you have at least four layers of paper. Ensure that all the edges are stuck down and apply a final layer of glue on top.

4 Sprinkle stars and glitter on top of the wet glue and allow to dry.

5 Cut out star shapes and display the stars.

Resources
- Plastic sheets
- Cellophane
- Tissue paper
- PVA glue
- Glitter
- Small gold stars

Cross-curricular links

Literacy: write a star poem focusing on how stars look.

Music: listen to a piece of music from "The Planets" by Holst. Use instruments and conductor cards (cards with symbols for how to play the instruments – quiet or loud, fast or slow, and so on) to create a 'Stars' composition.

Science: use models of the Earth and Sun to look into how the Earth rotates around the Sun and gives us the seasons.

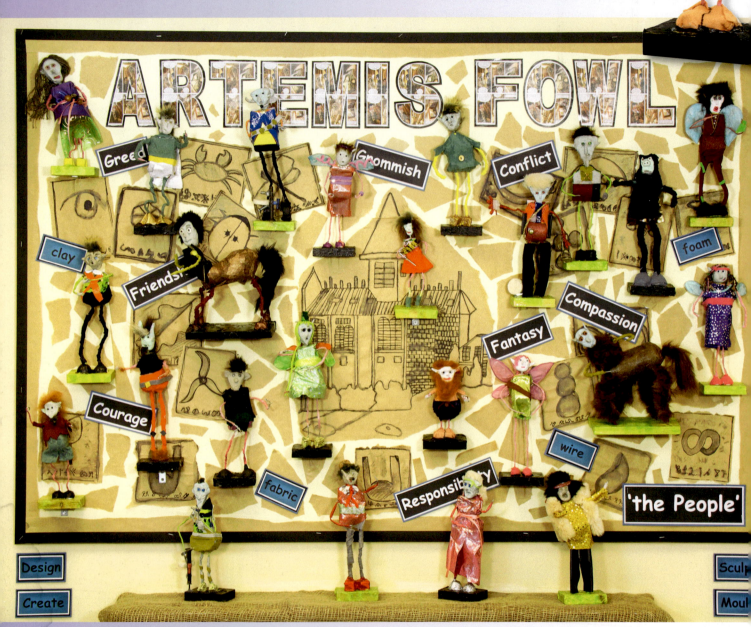

Capturing characters

For inspiration, take a look at *Artemis Fowl: The Graphic Novel* with upper KS2 pupils and encourage them to sculpt their own characters to enter the world of 'the People'. Create a fact file using the following headings: name; classification; known pseudonym; specialised skills; distinguishing features; weapon of choice. Pupils could talk about their ideas and materials with a partner to hone their communication skills prior to making their drawn and annotated design.

Resources

- *Artemis Fowl: The Graphic Novel* by Eoin Colfer
- Self-hardening clay
- 2 mm aluminium craft wire
- PVA glue, containers and small flat hogs-hair brushes
- Pencils, matchsticks, modelling tools, buttons and beads
- Scrap fabrics, felt, fake fur and wool
- Dense foam, cut into rectangles
- Wooden bases: 10 cm × 10 cm × 3 cm wooden pieces with two × 2 mm holes drilled in
- L-shaped corner braces for fixing bases into display

Pupils must be supervised when using wire. Safety glasses may also be required. The use of glue guns should always be supervised by an adult.

Miniature 3D characters

Approach

1. To form the character's head, use a small ball of self-hardening clay. Mould the ball and squeeze out the ears and nose from the clay shape. To create the eye sockets and mouth, use fine clay tools, matchsticks or a pencil. Push a piece of 2 mm aluminium wire into the clay head whilst damp to form a 'neck'. When hardened, create a wash of ink over the clay head for skin colour. Add details to the head using beads, fur, wool, and so on. Put aside.

2. To make the body use a small piece of cut foam. Push a piece of 2 mm wire through the top of the torso to create arms, and the bottom of the torso to make legs (make the legs quite long so you have enough wire to place the figure on a small wooden base for display). Add PVA glue where the arms and legs enter/exit the body and leave to dry.

3. Cover the body and limbs with strips of tissue paper to act as a skin (leave a gap of about 2 cm from the bottom of the legs). Use felt and other samples of material to craft and create clothing. Glue on small buckles, beads and smaller items to bring the character to life.

4. Stabilise the body by pushing the wire at the base of the legs into the wooden base. Glue gun around the wire.

5. Push a hole into the foam and push the wire from the head down into the body. Glue gun the head into position.

6. Create shoes, boots, hooves, and so on for the character out of pieces of foam. Cover in fur, felt or tissue paper.

7. Taking inspiration from the Gnommish alphabet in the *Artemis Fowl* books, create a new language for the fairies. Draw symbols onto brown paper backgrounds with a black marker pen and wash with a brush and water.

8. To complete the display, create a title, for example, Artemis Fowl using an online lettering resource.

Further ideas

Younger children can enjoy this activity by making a character torso. Create the head with a polystyrene ball instead of clay, add wire for features and a range of buttons/beads for the eyes, mouth, and so on.

Cross-curricular links

Design and Technology: design and create a human-free zone for your character.

Geography: using a globe, send a fairy on a mission. Use compass skills and research to plot a journey identifying countries and cities you cross from start to finish.

Literacy: The *Artemis Fowl* stories involve a 'Time Stop'. Tell a story about 24 hours which includes an 8-hour 'Time Stop'.

Science: create a fact file for the oak tree and the plant and animal life it supports.

In groups, survey a section of an oak tree and share the findings.

Super sidekicks

Inspired by Japanese Manga-style comics, these large-scale graphic characters and their sidekicks can be developed with KS2 children, using a limited range of acrylic paint colours and black and white acrylic-based pens. Loosely based on the *Artemis Fowl* 'fairy' this project uses continuous drawing to form character sketches. *Artemis Fowl* explores kinship and a sense of team friendship that is explored through the slogans accompanying each pupil's image.

Resources

- *Artemis Fowl: The Graphic Novel* by Eoin Colfer
- A4 card
- Pencils, graphitones and graphite sticks
- Fine and thick-line black marker pens (non-colourfast for water wash)
- A1 recycled board
- Black, white, red and blue acrylic paints
- Black and white acrylic-based pens (with a variety of tips)
- Variety of brushes
- Disposable palettes
- Water pots
- Foam insulation tubing and glue gun (for display only)
- Sponge roller
- Aprons

Manga-style characters

Approach

1. Encourage pupils to use a graphitone or black marker pen to create a continuous line sketch of a 'character' from their imagination. Once the outline is complete, add layers of tone/shadow and wash with water to develop the effect. Focus on the eyes as a central feature.

2. Develop a 'sidekick'. Look at children's cartoon characters such as Pokémon available on the internet. Talk about sidekicks and their purpose as a friend or conscience.

3 Prepare large boards or sheets of thick card (A2 or A1) with a wash of white acrylic paint. You can use a sponge roller to speed up the process. Pupils should look at their original character and sidekick sketches. Using a pencil, they need to scale up their sketches, transferring them onto the prepared board.

4 Use a limited colour palette of acrylic paints to block out sections of the portrait.

5 Refine and add detail and pattern onto the painted characters with the acrylic-based pens. Make sure the acrylic paint is fully dry before using the pens.

6 To display, cut out the characters and stick them onto a coloured background. Using a glue gun, stick pieces of foam insulation to the back of the cut-outs and attach them to the display for a 3D effect.

7 Talk with children about creating short statements linked to the theme of friendship. Develop statements that can be written in bubble-writing alongside their characters. Use acrylic-based pens to create this on top of the background colour.

Further ideas

To make this activity suitable for younger children, use superheroes such as Batman or Disney characters for inspiration. Provide head outlines for characters that children can trace onto heavy paper or card. Encourage children to draw on facial features. Paint the image in two colours and overlay with acrylic-based pens for extra interest.

⚠ Acrylic paint and acrylic-based pens can mark children's clothing so provide them with aprons. **Tip:** advise parents to wash acrylic-paint splashed clothing in cold water prior to an ordinary warm wash. The use of glue guns should always be supervised by an adult.

Cross-curricular links

History: the term 'cartoon' originates from the Middle Ages. Research and create a timeline of cartoonists and styles from the early 20th century to now.

PSHE: ask children to discuss what makes a good friend.

Different angles

Children are often fascinated by other worlds and the concept of space travel. *Thief* by Malorie Blackman can be used as a stimulus for a painting project which explores how a world might look from outer space.

Imaginative landscape paintings

Approach

1. Look carefully at aerial images of different types of landscapes. Talk about the images and what they could be showing. What happens to an object when you see it from above? What might we see from outer space?

2. Ask children to draw four rectangles in their sketchbooks. They should choose four small sections from the aerial photographs that they find interesting and reproduce them in the rectangles. These are small-scale investigations which will give children ideas for larger paintings.

3. Add colour to the small studies using a range of media.

4. Show children colourful circular paintings by Ingeborg Scott from the internet. Share the artist's own words with them: *My journey in painting has taken me from representational art, focussing on portrait and still life, to the more audacious expressions of my recent work. Even so, the subject matter of my art still retains its roots in naturalistic shape and design, part-inspired by my love of our planet.*

Resources

- *Thief* by Malorie Blackman
- Ingeborg Scott artwork images
- Sketchbooks
- Images of aerial views of landscapes
- Marker pens
- A3, A2, A1 paper
- Ready-mix paint in primary colours
- Paintbrushes
- Oil pastels
- Scissors
- PVA glue
- Split pins
- Rubber bands
- Yoghurt pots and other small scrap
- Modroc (Plaster of Paris bandages)

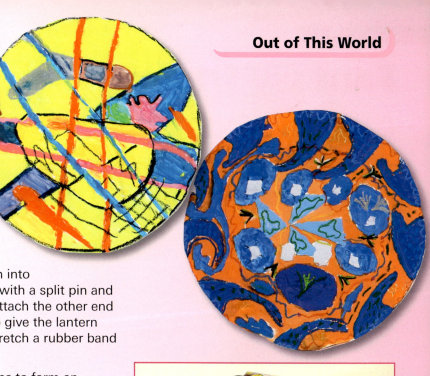

5 To make the outline for an imaginary landscape, use a classroom wastepaper bin and draw a circle on A3 cartridge paper. Begin painting by adding the palest colours first and paint in different parts to allow other parts to dry. The paintings can be done over several sessions and outlined in oil pastel when finished.

6 In groups, on sheets of A1 paper, encourage children to paint a larger landscape.

7 Take the most vibrant paintings and slice them into strips 4–5 cm wide. Join the strips at one end with a split pin and fan out into a circle. With a second split pin, attach the other end of the strips to make a loose lantern-shape. To give the lantern tension and make a 'ball' shape, attach and stretch a rubber band from one split pin to the other.

8 Cut the remaining pictures into small rectangles to form an interesting mosaic border for the display.

9 Divide children into groups and on sheets of A2 paper, build 3D alien landscapes from glued-down yoghurt pots and other small pieces of scrap. Cover with Modroc and allow to dry. Paint with acrylic paints and 'varnish' with a mixture of PVA glue and water.

10 Create a title using an online display source. Arrange the rectangular imaginative models and the circular world on the display board so that they look like planets from outer space. Hang the 3D planets next to the display.

Cross-curricular links

Geography: research iconic world landmarks viewed from space.

History: research the first moon landing.

Literacy: write an imaginative account of landing on another planet.

Science: Research spacecraft and the equipment astronauts use in space.

Fantasy friends

The fantasy world of Narnia and its characters can appeal to both boys and girls. Read *The Lion, the Witch and the Wardrobe* with children as a stimulus for their imagination and to provide ideas for making sculptures.

Giant sculptures

Approach

1   Talk about the characters of Narnia and show as much reference material as possible, for example online clips from the film. Ask children to make sketches of their chosen characters. Show them the materials they will be using to make their sculptures. Tell them to include in the sketches details about how they will use the material in their sculptures.

2   To make the sculpture begin with individual parts. Build the torso and limbs separately before joining them together as one. Build the head separately and decorate.

3   To make the head, push and glue a long piece of 3 mm modelling wire into a polystyrene ball. Stand it in a piece of foam or wood to make it easier to work on. The wire will form the 'neck'.

4   Use thin wire to form the nose, horns or eyebrows (depending on the character) and glue the wire where it enters the polystyrene.

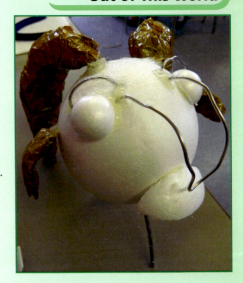

5 Add small pieces of polystyrene balls to make the eyes, lips and ears, and glue these into place. Use PVA-coated tissue paper to create a layer of 'skin' to cover the head and disguise the wire and polystyrene.

6 Add fur, buttons, beads, wool, and so on to create features for the character.

7 To make the body, cut foam insulation pieces to suit the character's torso and limbs. Push 3 mm wire through the limbs so that they can be bent into shape and joined to the torso.

8 Scrunch or wrap newspaper around the foam or wire armature to bulk it out and create body parts as desired (for example torso, horn, tail or foot). Tape neatly with masking tape.

9 Keep a small section of foam at the neck free from decoration. This is where the head will join to the torso.

10 Once the torso and limbs are complete, join them together to make the body. Coat with a layer of tissue, as you did for the head. Add fur, felt, and so on to the body shape to make it look real.

11 Make a hole in the foam so the head and wire neck can be pushed into the body. Glue the head into position.

12 To complete the display, create a title, for example, Narnia using an online lettering resource.

Resources

- *The Lion, the Witch and the Wardrobe* by C.S. Lewis
- 1.6 mm, 2 mm and 3 mm aluminium modelling wire
- PVA glue, containers and hogs-hair brushes
- Buttons and beads in a variety of shapes and colours
- Scrap fabrics, felt, fake fur and wool
- Foam pipe insulation of various sizes
- Newspaper
- Sticky tape, brown parcel tape, masking tape
- Tissue papers (PVA coated)
- Polystyrene balls of various diameters (up to 15 cm)
- Glue guns and glue sticks
- Scissors
- Fishing wire and small hooks for displaying characters

Further ideas

A scaled-down version of this project can be explored with younger children. To make characters from their favourite stories, cut and glue half a polystyrene ball to an A4 cardboard base. Add the nose, ears, eyebrows and mouth, using smaller sections of polystyrene balls. Or instead of polystrene use 2 mm modelling wire for facial features and add buttons, beads, tissue paper and fur fabrics for detail.

⚠ **Pupils must be supervised when using wire. Safety glasses may also be required. The use of glue guns should always be supervised by an adult.**

Cross-curricular links

Design and Technology: create a process journal for all the stages of the 3D character production. Children can use this to make other characters from their favourite stories.

Geography: create your own map of Narnia with a key to explain the main features.

History: *The Lion, the Witch and the Wardrobe* was written during World War 2. Write a diary entry from the point of view of a child sent away from their city to the safety of the countryside.

Literacy: encourage children to write a guide to the creatures of Narnia including a special fact file about their own character. Invent new Narnia characters.

Worlds of wonder

Lewis Carroll's *Alice in Wonderland* appeals to people of all ages because it engages their imagination with its strange and curious creatures. Even Carroll's strangest creatures are treated with respect. Show children how to create amazing creatures of their own, basing them on both familiar and unfamiliar animals.

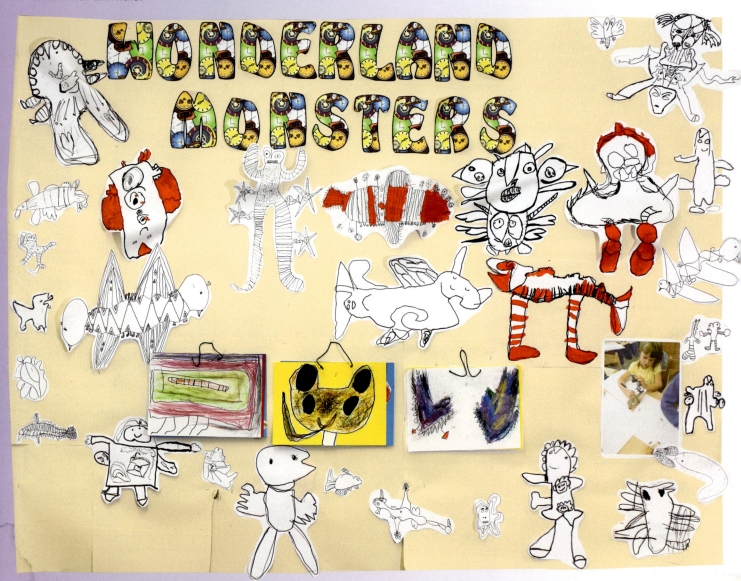

Strange creatures in art

Approach

1   Read a couple of sections from *Alice in Wonderland*, discussing Lewis Carroll's strange animals. Look at the retelling by Emma Chichester Clark, and focus on her illustrations of the characters, especially the weird and wonderful creatures. Give children A3 paper and demonstrate how to fold into eight sections. Using marker pens, tell them to draw an idea for a head, body, tail, legs, claws, and so on in each section. Remind children they are only drawing the monster parts, not whole monsters. Provide children with a range of animal models as stimulus.

Resources

- Marker pens
- A3 and A4 paper
- Animal collection
- Hole punch (adult use only) and string for threading
- Oil pastels
- A4 white card
- PVA glue
- Ready-mix paint and brushes
- *Alice in Wonderland* by Lewis Carroll
- Emma Chichester Clark's retelling of *Alice in Wonderland*

2 Next give the children A4 paper. Working in groups of three, discuss who will design the monster's head, body, or legs in each group. Demonstrate the importance of making the drawings fill the A4 paper.

3 Colour the monster parts using oil pastels then glue them onto A4 card. These can then be used to play mixed-up monster games.

4 Ask children to experiment on A4 paper, then get them to create a new monster on A3 paper with marker pens. The finished design can be painted using ready-mix paint.

5 Use all stages of the children's artwork as well as the final pictures. Cut out the small-scale drawings and add to the edges of the display board. Hole-punch the mixed-up monster card heads, bodies, and legs, and thread with string. Hang them low enough on the display for children to access.

Cross-curricular links

Literacy: imagine that Alice went back to sleep and had another dream, in which she met a set of extraordinary characters from the present day. Write a story or a play to show what happens.

Science: investigate mini-beasts. Look at some of the weird and wonderful features insects have.

Can You Believe It?

Satisfying sequences

It is important for children to learn about patterns and how to predict what comes next in a sequence. This project helps to develop this essential skill by encouraging children to recreate their favourite traditional tales.

The Enormous Turnip

The little old man pulled.

The little old woman pulled.

The boy pulled.

THUD!

The girl pulled.

The dog pulled.

BUMP!

The cat pulled.

The tiny mouse pulled.

Out of the ground came the enormous turnip.

3D display

Approach

1   Read traditional stories that follow a predictable sequence, for example *The Little Red Hen, The Gingerbread Man*. Spend time retelling and re-enacting these stories to reinforce the concept of a story sequence.

2   Choose a favourite tale to create as a classroom display. These ideas pictured were inspired by *The Enormous Turnip* but could easily be applied to other stories. For older children, choose appropriate stories and apply more complex creative techniques.

3   To create the background, pad the board with scrunched-up newspaper before putting the background paper on top. This will give the display a 3D effect.

4   Discuss with children how to make the background more realistic, for example for *The Enormous Turnip* create a turnip field from a mixture of brown paint, PVA glue and wood chippings spread over black paper. Also introduce extra techniques, such as combing thick paint into furrows.

5   Encourage children to create story objects and characters using collage and paint techniques, for example sponging shades of paint onto tissue paper and adding collage clothes to the painted characters. Add extra details to make the overall display more effective.

6   Create captions based on the class's learning objectives. Select and repeat words that emphasise the sequence of the story. Capitalise words for effect where appropriate, for example *THUD! BUMP!* Write or print out the words on paper and mount them onto card. Attach them to paper coils to give them a 3D effect. Create the title and add to the display.

THUD!

The boy pulled.

Resources

- The tale of *The Enormous Turnip* or other traditional stories that include a sequence
- Backing paper, newspaper, paint and PVA glue
- A range of collage materials, including fabrics
- Accessories related to the chosen story, for example real turnips, tiny characters, gravel tray, compost, string

7   Create a border for the display. For example, for *The Enormous Turnip*, cut turnip shapes out of card and sponge-print in shades of purple, yellow and green. Attach a thin border roll around the display and stick the cut-outs to the border.

Cross-curricular links

Literacy: encourage children to use connectors in their writing to sequence stories clearly.

Maths: investigate number sequences and patterns.

PE: Using *The Enormous Turnip* story, invite eight children to represent the turnip and select individual children to be the characters. Ask the 'turnip' children to sit in a row holding a rope in a 'tug of war' fashion. Invite the characters to try to pull up the turnip one by one, following the correct sequence until the turnip is 'uprooted'. If the characters fail, invite other children to help.

Science: grow a variety of plants in a school plot or individual pots. Encourage children to experiment with different conditions, (with/without regular watering, direct sunshine and rich compost). Speculate on ideal conditions to grow an enormous turnip.

Exciting journeys

Encourage children to follow the journey that takes place in a particular story, predicting and discovering where the narrative will take them. Explore novel ways of retelling these journeys.

Journey display

Approach

1   Read some traditional stories that follow a journey, for example *Jack and the Beanstalk*, *Little Red Riding Hood*. Explore these stories through role-play.

2   Choose a favourite tale to create as a classroom display. The images here relate to *Chicken Licken* but can easily be applied to other 'journey' stories. Older children can discuss more complex journeys and perhaps explore a range of possible new endings.

3   Discuss the journey within the story. For example, in *Chicken Licken*, establish where he was going, why, and what he might see along the way. Invite small groups of children to draw simple story maps of the journey.

4   Work together on a large pictorial map incorporating the children's ideas. Roughly staple scrunched newspaper to the board to make the route appear 3D. Cover this in green and blue paper to show the land and sky. Add sticky notes to plan the location of main features, such as Ducky Lucky's pond.

5   Encourage groups of children to use a range of techniques to create environmental features, for example fields, woods and water. For *Chicken Licken*, children could make the house, the fox's den and the castle. Attach these to the display.

Resources
- Tale of *Chicken Licken*
- Traditional stories that follow a journey
- Backing paper
- Paint and PVA glue
- A range of collage materials including fabrics
- Accessories for the chosen story, for example artificial leaves, stick puppets

6   Create a path using strips of card and add texture with PVA glue and sawdust. Attach the path to the display, marking out the route of the journey, for example, Chicken Licken's route from the house to the castle via the fox's den.

7   Ask children to paint the story characters and collage extra details appropriate to the story.

8   Sponge brightly coloured paint over empty spaces, taking care not to overcrowd the display.

9   Add characters' names and key phrases from the story printed as captions (or single words, depending on the ability of the class). Mount the words and attach them to the display board.

10 Create a border for the display using cut-outs, leaves, and so on.

11 Create a stick puppet of the main character so that children can retell the story by moving it along the route of the journey.

12 Encourage children to retell the story in the correct order and from left to right, and consider how they might represent their own journeys pictorially.

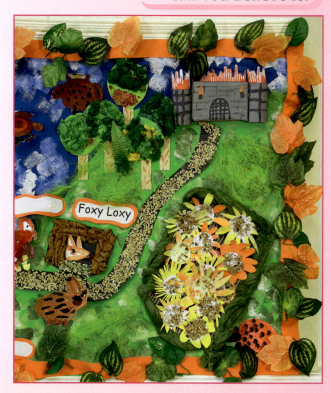

Cross-curricular links

Literacy: using the story of *Chicken Licken*, develop dramatic interaction by creating a fox's den with a pop-up tent draped in camouflage netting. Weave leaves and branches through the netting and put leaves and twigs on the floor. Use soft toys and make masks and tabards for the story characters. Add extras, such as salt dough bones in the den (see page 33). Use the den to role-play other stories, such as *We're Going on a Bear Hunt* (see page 30).

Maths: look at timetables of journeys on public transport. Use calculation skills to solve word problems related to journeys and timetables.

Science: investigate migratory journeys made by birds and animals.

Rhyme and repetition

A good way to teach young children about rhyme and repetition is to use a favourite story. This project, through the process of making the display encourages the reinforcement of key words and phrases. To adapt this project for older children, explore poetry that uses rhyme and other language features and encourage children to write their own stories for younger children.

3D display

Approach

1 Read stories to the children that contain alliteration, rhyme and patterned language. Encourage children to join in, for example *Hairy Maclary from Donaldson's Dairy* (Lynley Dodd), *The Gruffalo* (Julia Donaldson). Have fun making rhyme-chains from the given words, and invent your own rhyme-chains together.

2 Choose a favourite story to recreate as a classroom display. These images relate to *We're Going on a Bear Hunt* but the project could easily be adapted for other stories, ages and abilities.

3 Read the story *We're Going on a Bear Hunt* and make up chains of satisfying phrases inspired by the book, for example, using *We're Going on a Bear Hunt*, a rhyme-chain might be *Swishy-swashy, wishy-washy, bishy-boshy*. Talk about how effective the sounds are. For example, repeat the *We're Going on a Bear Hunt* chant together, showing how the whole context changes if you alter only a few words.

4 Create a large pictorial map as for the previous activity (page 28), but instead of paper, use fabric for the background. Add sticky notes to plan the position of the main features.

5 Ask groups of children to decide how to create key features directly onto the board, for example, a deep cold river with flowing water made from blue crêpe streamers, or a narrow gloomy cave made from painted, scrunched-up newspaper.

6 Encourage children to create the story characters and attach them to the display, positioning each one differently to show the journey path.

Resources
- *We're Going on a Bear Hunt* by Michael Rosen or other favourite stories with examples of rhyme, patterning and alliteration
- Backing fabric
- Tissue paper, newspaper
- Paint and brushes
- PVA glue
- Collage materials

7 Add captions indicating features and introduce patterned 'sound' words, for example *Squelch, squerch!* above the mud. Mount these captions on coloured paper (for example blue for water), and attach so they have a 3D effect.

8 Create a border for the display using different coloured tissue for each section. Add details relating to the story, for example draw a bear paw print, make copies and arrange them to show the bear hunt. Attach a colourful title.

9 Stand in front of the finished display chanting the sounds and miming the actions. Ask children to retell the story in the correct order, using language clues from the display.

Cross-curricular links

Art and Design: invite children to create linked small world environments using boxes covered in fabric and collage materials. Encourage them to add accessories and introduce tiny characters into each one. They could then chant their dialogue and make sound effects based on the story's language.

PSHE: using the story *We're Going on a Bear Hunt* transform the den described on page 29 by draping it in black and attaching two large luminous eyes inside. Re-enact the story together, building up a response as you approach the bear's cave. Pause to discuss how the children feel. Extend this by talking sensitively about things or situations that frighten them.

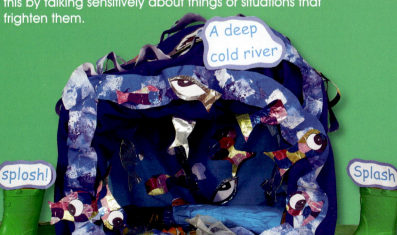

Laugh out loud

This section explores how fantasy stories can be recreated in displays to encourage children to use humour in their language, writing and drawing.

Resources
- *funnybones* by Janet and Allan Ahlberg or other popular stories with an amusing content
- Black fabric, white paint and paper, newspaper and PVA glue
- Additional collage materials, for example dog's lead, skeleton's hat, and so on.

3D display

Approach

1 Read children fantasy stories that will amuse them, for example *Duck in the Truck* (Jez Alborough), *Aliens Love Underpants* (Claire Freedman).

2 Choose a funny story to recreate as a classroom display. The ideas below relate to *funnybones* (Janet and Allan Ahlberg), but can easily be applied to other humorous stories.

3 Read *funnybones* and talk about why some people find skeletons frightening. Decide why these skeletons are funny rather than scary.

4 Create a display based on the front cover of the book, making sure that the skeletons look funny rather than frightening.

5 Create the background using scrunched-up newspaper covered with black fabric to create an undulating effect.

6 Encourage groups of children to draw skeleton outlines on white paper and ask them to glue individual bones made from scrunched-up newspaper firmly onto the outlines. Refer to images of skeletons and the book as a guide. Once dry, paint the skeletons white, making sure that gaps are filled with paint. Discuss how to create features that make the skeletons amusing such as googly eyes, smiling mouths and strange teeth, not forgetting the big skeleton's hat!

7 Attach the skeletons to the display so that their arms and legs stand out and make them look humorous.

8 Sponge stars with white paint into the empty spaces.

9 Ask children to choose words spoken by the skeletons. Print these onto speech bubbles and attach to the display as captions. They can invent words to make the display more amusing if they wish, but it should be a group decision.

10 Create a border by cutting out bone shapes from white paper and attaching them to black strips of paper. Fasten them around the display.

11 The finished display should provide lots of amusement and encourage children to retell the story along with their own 'scary skeleton' anecdotes. It can also be used as an introduction to other funny stories and related visual imagery.

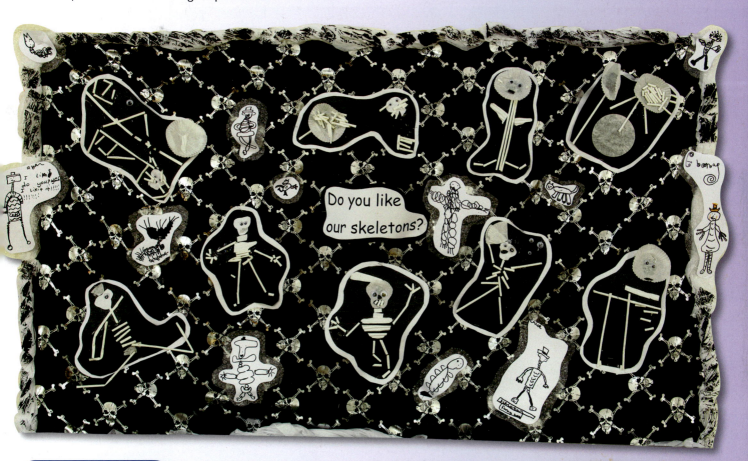

Cross-curricular links

Maths: using images, invite children to create bones from salt dough. Cook these and paint them white. Bury them in sand for children to find and make comparisons of sizes using appropriate mathematical language. Use the bones in sorting, matching and counting activities. They can also be used in the fox's den for the *Chicken Licken* role-play (see page 29).

Science/Art: explore X-rays and images of bones and discuss how bones are connected to form a support frame for the body. Invite children to use these images to help them create drawings of skeletons of people and animals. Use white art straws, paper and collage items stuck to black paper backgrounds, to make 3D skeletons. Mount the children's work and display the X-rays and images of skeletons together ensuring that everything is suitably captioned and labelled.

Illustrating characters

The Bad-Tempered Ladybird is a perfect starting point for encouraging creative pupil responses at KS1. The bold, cut-out illustrations, textured backgrounds and the variety of scales encourage children to explore a range of techniques within this project. Try comparing the work of other illustrators such as Lois Ehlert or Maurice Sendak, or introduce children to the work of Julia Ogden for additional inspiration.

Colourful cut-outs

Approach

1. Show children images of characters from *The Bad-Tempered Ladybird* and ask them to choose one. They should practise sketching the character before drawing it on a large scale on thick paper or card. Explain that the legs, antennae, and so on shouldn't be too narrow otherwise they will be difficult to paint and cut out.

2. Cut around the outside of the image.

3. Explain how to use a dry brush to cover the cut-out thinly with acrylic paint (a pale colour works best initially).

 If using acrylic paints, protect children's clothing. Tip: wash paint-splashed clothes in cold water prior to an ordinary warm wash.

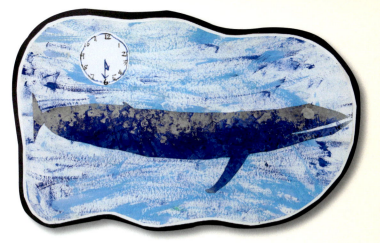

4   Leave the cut-out to dry for five minutes and then experiment with overprinting, using scraps, stencils and block-printing materials on top of the painted cut-out. Point out to children the patterns and textures on their chosen creatures' bodies and encourage them to imitate these. Children can also make cut-out leaves and trees, and so on to add to the display.

5   Use thick paper to create a background. Mix a limited (initially pale) colour palette and create a textured painted effect with acrylics. Large brushstrokes (once dried) can be dragged over with brighter colours, using the end of a brush dipped in paint to create scratch-like marks. You can sponge sections, or over-draw with oil pastels to create a layered effect.

6   Spread an even layer of PVA over the back of the cut-out character and stick on the prepared background, which should be cut into a shape. Stick onto the display.

7   To make 3D ladybirds, teachers should use a bradawl to make holes on either side of a cork and at one end. Put aluminium wire into the holes to build wings and a head. Paint the wire with PVA glue and cover the wings with red tissue paper. Cover the head and body in black tissue. When dry, draw spots onto the wings with a black pen. Attach to the display with blue tack.

8   Print red and black 'spots' with times on them and add to the display together with a title.

Resources

- *The Bad-Tempered Ladybird* by Eric Carle
- A3 white card
- Large, medium and small hogs-hair brushes (round and flat tips)
- Acrylic paints, extender medium, disposable palettes
- Oil pastels
- Scraps, some cut into small pieces for printing, stencilling and mark-making: bubble wrap, cotton reels, corks, sponges, cotton wool buds, matchsticks, leaves, feathers, and so on.
- Scissors and PVA glue
- Corks
- 1.6 mm aluminium wire
- Red and black tissue paper
- Waterproof black pen
- Bradawl

Cross-curricular links

Literacy: Rewrite the story using a different creature. How does the structure of the story need to change?

Maths: use clock times from the story to set a range of questions related both to the story and to children's own daily routine.

PSHE: discuss why manners matter.

Science: study and draw a diagram showing the life cycle of a ladybird.

Further ideas

To extend this project to older children, discuss the story of *Doctor Dolittle* and his many animal friends. Using the book by Hugh Lofting or the *Doctor Dolittle* film as inspiration, create a two-colour paper collage background and print mini-beasts onto the paper using coloured ink and a range of circular objects as stamps. Whilst the ink is still wet, scratch the leg shapes out from the body. Add other patterns using bubble wrap, doyleys and so on to give texture to the image.

Beside the seaside

This project could be used following a class visit to the seaside, where children explore rock pools, take photographs and play on the sand. Before the visit, a selection of storybooks about the seaside including *Tiddler* by Julia Donaldson would set the scene for the trip.

Resources

- *Tiddler* by Julia Donaldson
- A3 and A4 paper
- Graphic materials: marker pens, graphite sticks and wax crayons
- Photographs of water, rocks and seagulls
- Coloured drawing ink (blues and greens)
- Oil pastels
- Water pots and brushes
- Magnifying glasses
- Fresh fish: mackerel, trout or prawns
- Rock-pool collage
- PVA glue
- black and white photocopies of sea and rock pictures
- A4 mark-making sheets inspired by water
- Computer, printer

Seaside collage and costume

Approach

1 Organise a trip to the seaside, or if this is not possible, research images of the seaside, and bring in sea shells, and so on to show the children. Read *Tiddler* by Julia Donaldson.

2 Make a class mind map about the seaside, encouraging the children to recall any details about visits to the seaside. You might include water, rocks, fish, seagulls, and so on. Print out photos from their visit.

3 Give children A4 paper and a selection of graphic materials to explore making marks to show: water, waves, ripples, splashes, swirls and related sounds like 'plop!'. These words should be printed out in an interesting font and will form an important part of the display.

4 Children should work in pairs to create a rock-pool collage. Give out a selection of photocopied sea and rock pictures together with their A4 mark-making experiments showing water. Tear these up and glue onto a sheet of A3 paper, leaving white spaces. Children should draw onto the collage, adding more rocks and water marks in the spaces.

5 Use the collages as the background for the display.

6   Set up an observation drawing activity with a fresh fish. Provide magnifying glasses to look at the scales and the gills. Do fish have teeth?

7   Talk about how children can make their drawings fill up their A3 paper.

8   Cut out the fish drawings and add to the display.

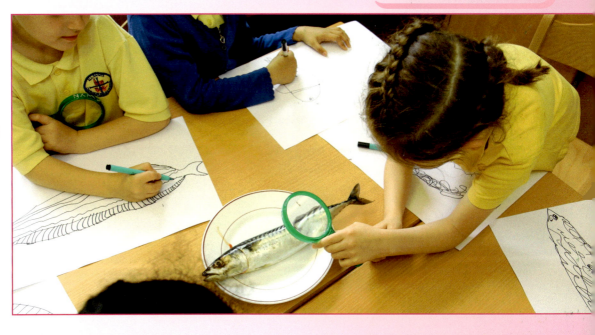

9   Show children images of seagulls and encourage them to draw their own, adding colour with oil pastels. Cut them out and add to the display, together with a title.

10 To make a recycled sea cloak, add lots of fish drawings and sea creatures made from recycled materials to a black plastic bin bag.

Further ideas

Fishing can be used for simple counting games. Cut out a fish shape from thick paper and use this as a template to make several more identical cut-outs. Laminate and glue pairs of fish together with a paperclip sandwiched in between, sticking slightly out. Fix a horseshoe magnet to a piece of string and tie the other end to a cane or stick. Write numbers on the back of each fish and begin fishing!

Cross-curricular links

Literacy: use the display to prompt children to talk about the seaside.

Write sea poems based on the sounds you can hear at the seaside.

Science: research the life cycle of a fish.

To extend this project to older children, have them read *The Voyage of the Dawn Treader* by C.S. Lewis or *Treasure Island* by R.L. Stevenson and ask them to write their own sea adventure.

Imaginary lives

In his picture book, *The Queen's Knickers*, Nicholas Allan tells the story of a little girl awaiting a visit from the Queen. She ponders what knickers the Queen will be wearing. Does she have knickers for various occasions? Do they match her shoes? Read the story with the children and enjoy the humour before designing the Queen some more knickers.

Knickers designs

Approach

1 Brainstorm what the Queen does, her likes and dislikes, for example corgis, flowers, horses, presents, royal weddings, banquets. Discuss her role as head of state, i.e. flags, symbols of the four nations of the UK, the Church of England, British landscapes, famous landmarks, the importance of the navy, the Commonwealth.

2 Imagine what knickers the Queen would wear to various functions or when visiting places.

3 Ask children to draw designs onto the A4 knickers template. These can be coloured in or left as a pencil sketch.

4 Draw and cut out large knickers-shaped templates from A2 sugar paper. Younger children may need support here.

5 Ask the children to select their favourite designs. Use collage materials and PVA glue to build layers of texture and colour on the template.

6 Add finer details with marker pens when dry.

Resources
- *The Queen's Knickers* by Nicholas Allan
- Knickers-shaped template on A4 paper
- A4 white sugar paper
- A2 and A4 coloured sugar paper
- Chalk pastels
- Pencils, rubbers, marker pens
- Photos of Queen Elizabeth II
- PVA glue
- Scissors
- Assorted collage materials: coloured wrapping paper, gummed paper shapes, tissue, fabric off-cuts, ribbon, lace
- Pastels

Drawing portraits

Approach

1 On A4 sugar paper draw the Queen's face looking happy while wearing her newly designed knickers – look at photos of the Queen for familiarisation.

2 Explain how to draw a face using the grid method for placing features.

3 Draw an oval; draw a line down the centre of the oval from top to bottom and across the centre of the oval from side to side. This should be drawn lightly as these lines need to be rubbed out after placing the facial features.

4 Place eyes just above centre line one on either side of the face.

5 Halfway between eyes and chin place the nose.

6 Halfway between nose and chin place the mouth.

7 Add the ears and hair, then colour them in using pastels or other preferred media.

Cross-curricular links

Geography: investigate climates in different countries and consider how this affects the clothes people living there wear.

History: look at clothes from the past. Design some knickers inspired by history. How has the Queen's role changed from the role of Kings and Queens of the past?

Literacy: write a story about a visit the Queen makes to your school.

PSHE: find out about the role of the Queen. Why do we have a Queen? What work does she do? Who are her family? Where does she live?

Further ideas

To extend this project, children could think about what their favourite celebrity/sportsperson/ hero might be wearing underneath instead.

To extend this project to older children, ask them to look at selected passages of Terry Pratchett's comic fantasy series, *Discworld*. Ask them to write about an imaginary world inspired by the series.

Faraway Lands

Animal surprise

This project explores pattern and colour. It is inspired by the picture book *Handa's Surprise*, which tells the story of a little girl's surprise present for her friend, and seven very greedy animals. The children in these photos sent a letter to the author, Eileen Browne, who wrote back saying that she had a large collection of animal photos from her travels and could the children make her some photo frames? This provided the focus for an exploration of colour and geometric, natural and cultural patterns.

Resources

- *Handa's Surprise* by Eileen Browne
- Model animals
- Pattern collection, including fabrics, images, and so on
- Black marker pens
- Oil pastels and chalk pastels
- Sketchbooks or clipboards
- A4 paper
- A5 coloured card for the photo frame
- A5 coloured card for the photo backing
- Paint
- Paintbrushes
- Water pots
- PVA glue and masking tape
- Collage materials including feathers
- Computer, printer

Further ideas

To extend this project to older children, explore stories from countries such as India and South America, like *The Jungle Books* by Rudyard Kipling.

Animal patterns

Approach

1   Talk with children about pattern. Ask children to look for patterns of lines in the classroom. Once they have identified a pattern, children should record the pattern using black marker pens to draw it, either in their sketchbooks, or on A4 paper using clipboards.

2   Repeat this for colour and shape patterns, using oil pastels or soft chalk pastels to provide colour. Remind children not to draw the whole object, only the repeating pattern.

3   Collect patterns in the playground. Talk about the patterns the children have collected. Set up a pattern table, with books, photographs, fabric samples and model animals. Ask children to bring in something patterned from home, for example wrapping paper, food packaging.

4   Read *Handa's Surprise*. Talk about the children's favourite parts of the story. Ask children to choose animals with conspicuous patterned coats for an investigation.

5   Encourage children to explore the vibrant animal patterns of spots, stripes, zigzags, patches, shapes and dots using paint.

6   On a display board backed in white, arrange the children's work, together with a printout display title, such as Animal Patterns. Encourage children to add their own patterns in oil pastels directly onto the display.

7   Prepare A5 card templates of the photo frame. Show children how to collage their frames using torn-up pieces of their explorations in colour, and their pattern collection, as well as feathers. Stick the material down with PVA glue.

8   When the frames are dry, tape each child's photo (postcard size) in place behind their frame. Add an A5 piece of card to the back of the frame and glue in place.

Cross-curricular links

Geography: draw a map of Africa showing where different animals live.

ICT: make a short video of the retelling, using the animal patterns as a backdrop.

Literacy: make *Handa's Surprise* word cards to help children retell the story.

Music: make repeating patterns in music.

African tales

East African art, specifically pattern, is the focus of this project and includes working with a variety of textile techniques that can be adapted for use with younger children. The picture book *Bringing the Rain from Kapiti Plain* by Verna Aardema is a good way to introduce young children to East Africa and the Masai nomadic lifestyle, where so much depends on a successful rainy season.

Patterns and printing

Approach

1   Using a presentation researched from the internet, show the scale of Africa and the huge plains of Kenya and Tanzania where the Masai live. Start a resource collection of art and textiles, and so on from East Africa.

2   Give children A4 paper and ask them to divide it into four sections. Encourage children to focus on parts of patterns from the resource collection and using marker pens, make their own patterns, colouring them in with oil pastels.

3   Provide class groups with a length of white fabric. Use chalk to divide the fabric into six or eight sections about one metre square, depending on the numbers in each group. Cover tables with protective plastic, stretch the lengths of fabric along the tables and secure with masking tape. Demonstrate to each group how to paint their paper patterns onto the fabric using fabric paint. Allow the fabric to dry then draw another layer of patterns using fabric crayons (dye sticks).

4   Use giraffe models to make observational drawings. Cut out the giraffe drawings and use them as templates for drawing onto foam sheets. Cut out the foam giraffe outlines, peel off the backing paper and stick onto cardboard. Trim away the excess cardboard and use the scraps to make a handle for the back of the block. Use the blocks to print onto the fabric. The grass effect used here is made by dipping card strips into black fabric paint and pressing randomly onto the fabric picture.

5   Arrange children's giraffe fabric and drawings on a display board, together with paintings inspired by the African plains. Print and cut out the title, Kapiti Plains, from an online alphabet template.

Resources

- *Bringing the Rain from Kapiti Plain* by Verna Aardema
- Presentation on Africa
- East African resource collection: books, photographs, paintings, printed patterns and artefacts
- A4 paper
- Marker pens
- Oil pastels
- White fabric
- Fabric paint, fabric crayons (dye sticks) and fabric printing inks
- Brushes
- Sheets of sticky-backed foam
- Flour paste
- Measuring jug
- Plastic squeezy bottles
- Masking tape
- Computer, printer

Further ideas

Encourage children to explore their African patterns further and make individual two-colour block prints on squares of fabric. Display the class prints as a colourful patchwork of African textiles.

Flour paste-resist bunting is a child-safe substitute technique for batik, which avoids using hot wax. To make the flour paste, mix flour with water in a measuring jug to the consistency of yogurt. Pour into plastic squeezy bottles (washing-up liquid bottles are ideal). Squeezing the bottle of flour mixture, draw patterns onto triangular pieces of white fabric. Allow to dry, and paint with fabric paint. When the paint is dry, scrape off the flour paste to reveal white patterns. Hang up your bunting!

Cross-curricular links

Geography: research nomadic peoples, discovering how their lives have changed today.

Literacy: write a step-by-step account of making a fabric print, and the decisions involved.

Outback adventures

Stories from the Billabong is a collection of Aboriginal Australian legends by James Vance Marshall and Francis Firebrace. The colourful illustrations and symbols are a useful stimulus for this project which explores fabric printing and pattern. This project could also be adapted for younger children by researching some suitable Aboriginal legends or 'dreaming stories' on the internet. Children can then create dot finger-paintings inspired by these stories.

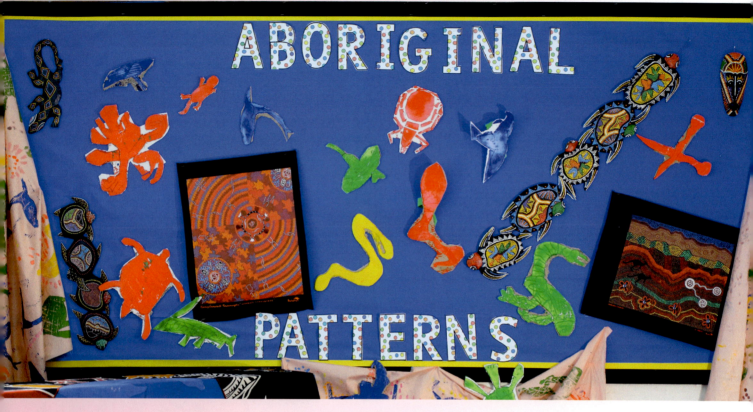

Fabric printing

Approach

1   Make a collection of Aboriginal patterns and artefacts. Use books from the school library, research online images and ask parents and staff for items they can lend for the project. Talk about the distinctive features about Aboriginal art and patterns. What colours are used? Are dots always used?

2   Photocopy as much material as possible, so children can choose images to stick into their sketchbooks. Aboriginal online resources are available from The Pitt Rivers Museum website which is an excellent source of cultural patterns.

3   Encourage children to use the photocopies to make small-scale patterns.

4   Demonstrate how to select a favourite part or shape from their small-scale patterns and enlarge to fill a new A3 page of their sketchbooks. Add colour using colour pencils or oil pastels.

5   Divide the children into groups to create group pictures on fabric. Ask the children to select a piece of polyboard for their design. Use sharp pencils to transfer their chosen pattern to the polyboard tile, then glue their tile design onto a thick card base. Cut around the design to remove the excess card. (See page 7, step 8 for use with younger children.) Use the excess card to make a handle for back of the block.

6   Remind children how to print onto fabric. The process is the same as printing onto paper but requires fabric printing ink.

7   Explain to the children that they need to choose a colour and roll some fabric ink onto the plastic tray. Hold the block using the card handle, with the design facing upwards. Roll the ink across the design, then press the block firmly onto the fabric. Lift the block to reveal your print. Before children start, make sure they know where they are going to put the wet print.

8   Arrange all the stages of the children's work on the display. The title, Aboriginal Patterns, is created using an online alphabet.

Cross-curricular links

Geography: investigate how people live in a very dry climate.

History: research the history of migration to Australia from early times.

ICT: develop patterns inspired by Aboriginal designs on the computer.

Literacy: write an account of a journey across Australia.

Science: research Australian animals. What is special about them?

Resources
- A3 sketchbooks
- Drawing media
- Aboriginal patterns
- Photocopier
- Magnifying glasses
- Fabric: 1 m square is ideal for group printing
- Fabric printing inks
- Protective clothing and protection for work surfaces
- Polyboard tiles in a selection of sizes no smaller than A5
- Rollers
- Trays
- Computer, printer

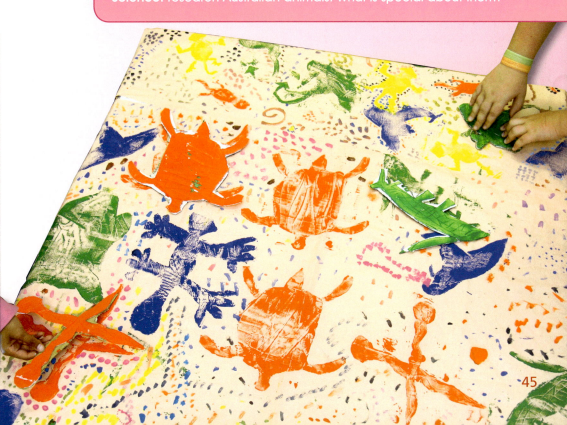

Once Upon a Time ...

As you wish

The *Aladdin* story is part of a collection called *One Thousand and One Nights* (sometimes known as *Arabian Nights*) which includes *Ali Baba and the Forty Thieves* and *Sinbad the Sailor*. Although it is one of the *Arabian Nights* stories, *Aladdin* actually takes place in China.

Suitcases

Approach

1 Read the *Aladdin* story. Look at a globe and ask children, *If a genie popped up and said he could take you anywhere in the world, where would you go, and why? What would you need to take with you?*

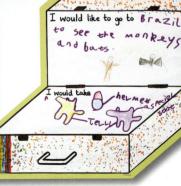

2 Develop an interactive geography display. Give each child a pre-cut cardboard suitcase and encourage them to decorate the outside with felt-tips and crayons. Ask them to write in the lid of the suitcase where they want to go and why they want to go there. In the bottom of the suitcase get them to draw items they would take on their trip. This is a good opportunity to discuss packing requirements such as clothing to suit the climate, or special equipment, such as goggles or snorkels. They can also design a postcard to send from their destination.

3   To make the Earth, start by creating the oceans using blue, purple and green marbling inks on white paper. Cut the paper into small squares to make a mosaic effect. To reproduce the main land masses accurately use an online mapping program projected onto a whiteboard. The countries can then be traced onto paper attached to the board.

4   Draw a genie coming out of a lamp and encourage children to paint it. Each child can add shapes cut from coloured or shiny paper to make the genie's clothes.

5   Provide a globe and a suitcase with clothes for different climates for children to act out different 'journeys'.

Resources

- The tale of *Aladdin*
- Display paper
- Pre-cut suitcases
- Felt-tips and/or crayons
- Marbling inks, paper and paints
- Whiteboard and projector
- Scissors and coloured or shiny paper
- Globe
- Suitcase filled with different clothing

Further ideas

Watch the animated film *Aladdin*. In the film there is a magic carpet.

What other differences are there between the film and the story?

Make a cardboard box display of flying magic carpets. Cut a fringe onto the ends of coloured card rectangles. To make a symmetrical pattern, paint patterns on one half of the card and then fold over while still wet. Attach a pipe-cleaner person to each flying carpet and mount on strings in the box scene.

To extend this project to older children, stories such as E Nesbit's *The Phoenix and the Carpet*, Jenny Nimmo's Charlie Bone series, *The Children of the Red King* or the other tales in *One Thousand and One Arabian Nights* retold by Geraldine McCaughrean are good for inspiration.

Cross-curricular links

Design and Technology: make some simple *Aladdin* board games to play. Provide children with a 100-square with numbers from the bottom left to the top right like 'Snakes and Ladders'. They need to add genies to go up and slides to come down. Make a noughts and crosses game by asking children to design genie-and-lamp counters to place on a large grid.

Geography: Look on the internet and at travel brochures and ask children to create a tourist leaflet for their chosen country.

Literacy: create cinquain poems about the genie using this pattern: Line 1: a noun, Line 2: two adjectives, Line 3: three 'ing' words, Line 4: a four-word phrase, Line 5: a word referring back to the initial noun, e.g:

> Genie
> Mysterious, wonderful
> Hovering, shimmering, gliding
> Granter of many wishes
> Magical

Land of giants

Read or watch *The Selfish Giant* by Oscar Wilde, retold by Michael Foreman. This is a story showing it's never too late to be sorry for what you've done. Make a 3D display comparing the giant's garden before and after he realised how selfish he'd been.

Resources

- *The Selfish Giant* retold by Michael Foreman
- White, green, silver and blue display paper
- Brown paper
- Glue and scissors
- Chalk pastels and plastic mirrors
- Cotton wool and pink tissue paper
- Pencil crayons and/or felt-tips
- Paints
- Plain A4 paper, card and PVA glue

Winter and spring gardens

Approach

1 Read *The Selfish Giant*. Discuss how the children felt when the giant stopped them playing in the garden. *How did they feel when they saw the giant once they'd sneaked back in? What about when they realised that he wanted them to play in his garden again? What might they have said?* Make speech bubbles from the children's suggestions to include in the display.

2 Create a display board with one half in blue and green, and the other half in silver and white, to show spring and winter. Using extra paper extend the display over a table.

3 To make winter trees, roll a sheet of brown paper into a tube so that the tube is several layers thick. Glue down the loose edge. Make 6–8 cm-long snips at one end of the tube to make flaps. Bend down the flaps to make branches and crease again to make the branches point in different directions. Brown, grey or black felt-tips can be used to mark bark on the trunks. Glue cotton wool to the branches.

4   To make spring trees glue on twists of pink tissue paper for blossoms.

5   Glue trees to display paper by making smaller snips 1–2 cm long at the other end of the tube. Fold these out to form a base.

6   Give children plastic mirrors, chalk pastels and paper and ask them to draw their own faces. Add to the display on the wall with their speech bubbles.

7   Provide the children with thin card. Ask them what games they would play in a large garden and encourage them to draw themselves playing these games. Cut these out with a flap at the bottom to glue to the base paper.

8   Cut out the giant's face and hands and encourage children to paint them.

9   Show children how to make snowflakes by folding a circle of paper in half, and then half again. Snip shapes from the edges, then open out to reveal the snowflake.

Further ideas

Read *The Smartest Giant in Town*, by Julia Donaldson. How is this giant different from the selfish giant? Make salt-dough models of the characters, as well as clothing and include a small hole for string to go through using a plastic straw. (**Salt dough:** ½ cup salt, ½ cup water and 1 cup plain flour.). Place models on greaseproof paper and leave to air-dry for a day or two. Turn them halfway through to ensure both sides dry evenly and once dry, paint and 'varnish' them with a mixture of PVA glue and water. Hang from a mobile made from two coat hangers taped together and covered with ribbon.

Older children may like to try reading Oscar Wilde's original *Fairy Stories* as a starting point for related projects.

Cross-curricular links

PE: play Giant's Footsteps (a variation of Grandma's Footsteps). Children sneak up on the giant and every time he/she turns round, they have to freeze. Whoever the giant sees moving is sent back to the start. Scatter plastic fruit or flowers on the floor and challenge the children to collect one object en route to the giant. Alternatively, play 'What's the Time, Mr Wolf?' but substitute a giant for Mr Wolf.

PSHE: ask the children to write about a time when they behaved in an unselfish way.

Science: use this story to talk about the differences between the seasons. Encourage children to record the differences in pictures and words using a circle split into quarters. In spring set up a bird table in the school grounds and observe the birds that visit.

49

Parties and princesses

There are many versions of the *Cinderella* story all over the world. It is a tale that shows that anyone can triumph, whatever the odds. Involve children in a *Cinderella*-inspired party-time display.

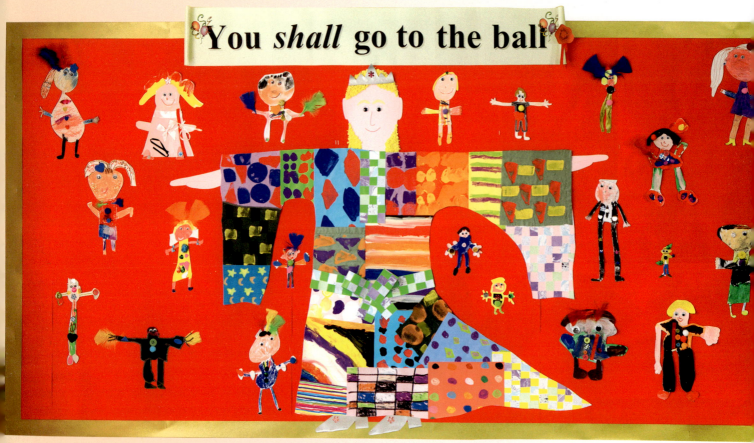

You *shall* go to the ball

Designing party outfits

Approach

1   Read the *Cinderella* story. Talk about how Cinderella felt at different times during the story.

2   Discuss what sort of clothes children wear on special occasions. Ask them to draw themselves in a special outfit that they could wear to a ball/party. Use a variety of media: felt-tips, pastels, paints, a computer paint package, and so on. These can be embellished with sequins, stars, buttons, ribbons, googly eyes, and so on. Cut out and mount on the display.

3   Look at examples of fabrics, trying to spot the repeating patterns. Ask each child to come up with a design for some fabric for Cinderella's ball dress. Suggest different media – sponge printing, painting, using a computer paint package, oil pastels, and so on. Print on plain paper or fabric. Use the children's designs as patches to make Cinderella's dress. Use scrunched-up pieces of tissue paper for her hair and silver paper for her tiara and slippers.

4   Make a banner of the title using a computer, curling the ends of the banner to make it look like a scroll. Add a seal at one end.

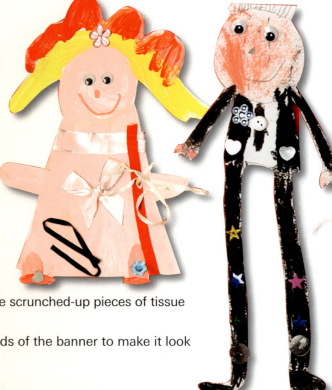

Resources

- The tale of *Cinderella*
- Backing paper
- Silver paper
- Tissue paper
- Computer paint package and printer
- Cartridge paper and fabric squares
- Felt pens, pencils, paints, sponges, pastels and crayons
- Sequins, stars, buttons, ribbons, googly eyes, and so on.

Further ideas

Look at examples of invitations and what details are required. Ask the children to write and decorate invitations from the prince asking everyone to his ball.

Look at examples of menus for important functions. Talk about what sorts of food the prince might provide. Ask the children to create illustrated menus for the prince's ball.

Hold a class party. Involve the children in planning the food, music, decorations and entertainment. Give each team a budget to work within, and price lists for different items. Bake fairy cakes with the children to eat at the ball allowing the children to choose which decorations to add, for example, chocolate buttons, sprinkles, and so on. Write to the head teacher inviting him/her to the ball.

To extend this project to older children, inspire them with stories such as *The Barefoot Book of Princesses* by Caitlin Matthews or the original stories of *The Wild Swans*, *The Snow Queen* and *The Little Mermaid* by Hans Christian Andersen.

Cross-curricular links

Design and Technology: discuss different designs for Cinderella's carriage. The fairy might have used a strawberry or a banana instead of a pumpkin. Encourage children to build their own carriages. Use a computer paint package with a symmetry tool to enable both sides of the carriage to be drawn at once. Print these out onto card. Glue on decorated cardboard wheels and make a tubular body from card. Add lolly sticks as shafts.

Drama: Re-enact *Cinderella* or *Prince Cinders*.

Literacy: ask children to imagine that they are the Ugly Sisters. Have them write lists of chores for Cinderella to do while they are at the ball, using bossy words and time connectives, for example 'First, you must do the washing up and make sure all the plates are sparkly clean. Next, you must dust the house from top to bottom.'

Read *Prince Cinders* by Babette Cole. This is a wacky version of the traditional tale with Prince Cinders being a young man who is bullied by his big, hairy brothers. Draw up a list of similarities and differences between *Cinderella* and *Prince Cinders*.

PE: Explore different types of dance. The children could pair up as the Prince and Cinderella and create their own dance. Alternatively, they could learn some simple dance steps.

Beans and big people

Classic fairytales are great stories and provide good models for drama and children's own writing. Young children will enjoy making a display to show how Jack's resourcefulness and courage help him to triumph.

Role-play area

Approach

1   Read the story and discuss it with the children. Get children to take on the roles of Mum, Jack and the giant while the rest of the class ask them questions. Depending on the age and confidence of the children, this may need modelling by the teacher.

2   Encourage children to re-enact the story, discussing how each of the main characters move, and what they say. Split the children into small teams to include at least one narrator plus extras (for example the person who gives Jack the magic beans). Ask each group to perform to the rest of the class. Allow time for the class to give positive feedback to the group performing.

3   Build a model of Jack's house, the beanstalk and the giant's castle for the role-play area.

4   Cover large cardboard boxes to make buildings with plain kitchen rolls and paint. Sponge-print brickwork all over the boxes and allow to dry. Ask children to draw different windows, cut them out and glue them onto the boxes.

Resources
- *Jack and the Beanstalk*
- Cardboard boxes
- Plain kitchen rolls and wallpaper paste
- Paint and sponges
- Coloured paper
- Green fabric
- Blue display paper
- Card and scissors
- Felt-tips
- White sheet/blanket and newspaper

5   To make the beanstalk, first show children different leaves and ask them to draw them on different shades of green paper. Then add the veins. Cut the leaves out and tape them onto lengths of plaited green fabric. Arrange the beanstalk so it climbs up a table leg, spreads out along the table, and creeps up the wall behind.

6   Use a white sheet or blanket stuffed with scrunched-up newspaper to form a cloud for the giant's castle to sit on.

7   Mount blue display paper on the wall behind the model castle and add painted clouds.

8   Each child can design his/her own Jack on card with finger holes cut out to make finger puppets. (Finger holes are to be cut out by an adult.) Children can re-enact the story using their puppet, with one child as the giant. Provide dress-up clothes for the giant.

Further ideas

Read *Jim and the Beanstalk* by Raymond Briggs. In this story, Jim meets a grumpy giant who can't see very well, has no teeth and is balding. Jim tells the giant about glasses, false teeth and wigs. He measures the giant and fetches the items for him. List the similarities and differences between the two stories.

For further reading, have younger children look at Janet and Alan Ahlberg's *Each Peach Pear Plum*.

To extend this project to older children, have them read *Flat Stanley* by Jeff Brown, *Dodger* by Terry Pratchett or *8 Days of Luke* by Diana Wynne Jones.

Cross-curricular links

Design and Technology: make a large giant's head and shoulders from chicken wire and papier-mâché and ask the children to design the giant some glasses. These could be made from construction sets available in the classroom or made from card. Children should take on the role of Jim and measure the giant's head first to ensure the glasses are the right size.

Literacy: rewrite *Jack and the Beanstalk* in a different setting with different characters, for example a small fish on a coral reef follows a long piece of seaweed and finds a shark's cave.

Science: grow bean plants and keep a bean diary. Whose bean will grow tallest?

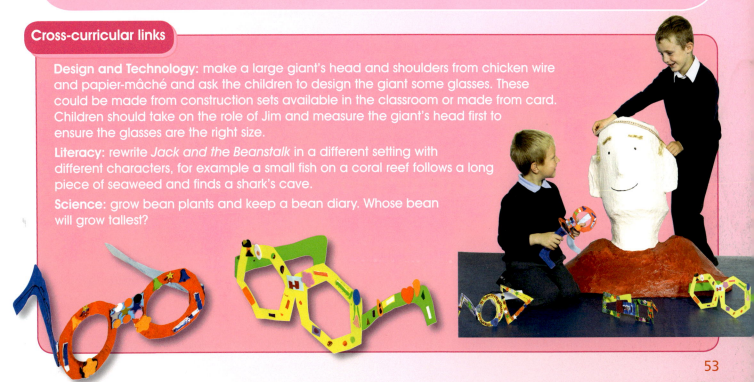

Dragons and Other Beasts

Dragon stories

There are stories about dragons from all over the world, real and imaginary. This project is inspired by *Tell me a Dragon* by Jackie Morris, specifically referring to the following line: 'And in the final gathering of fire, scales and claws you can imagine your own special dragon'. Older children may prefer to read *How to Train Your Dragon* by Cressida Cowell as a starting point for this project.

The display involves investigating patterns, writing and illustrating dragon stories and producing imaginative ink paintings.

Drawing and painting dragons

Approach

1   Using a presentation researched from the internet, show the class different types of scale pattern found on a range of creatures. Give children A4 paper and marker pens to record any ideas, shapes and patterns that they particularly like.

2   Give the children A3 paper and ask them to divide the paper into eight sections. Using their initial ideas sheet, ask children to design eight different patterns of scales.

Resources

- Presentation of animal scales and patterns
- A4 and A3 paper
- Black felt-tip pens
- Photocopier
- Coloured drawing inks
- Scissors
- Masks
- A selection of coloured card and metallic paper
- PVA glue and masking tape
- Six bamboo canes
- Wire

3   On A3 paper, get children to create their own imaginative dragon drawing, making sure it is large enough to fill the paper. Before adding coloured inks, photocopy the children's drawings.

4   Colour the A3 photocopied dragon drawings with drawing inks. Do not use the original drawings because black felt-tip pen will bleed into the wet ink. It also gives children the option of using different media later on, such as oil pastels and chalk pastels, or paint.

5   Demonstrate how to apply the inks. Explain that the inks are very concentrated colours and should be applied to wet paper. Dip a paintbrush into a pot of clean water and gently paint the part of the picture you need to colour with the water only. Dip the brush into coloured ink and paint over the wet part of the picture. Work on different parts of the drawing, making sure not to work on two wet parts next to each other. When the paintings are dry, add pattern details before cutting out the drawings and adding them to the display.

6   To make masks, encourage children to glue down a layer of torn paper on mask moulds. Allow the glue to dry and then paint and decorate.

7   Make a dragon-wing cloak out of recycled materials as part of a school eco-fashion show. The bamboo sticks provide the structure. Fan out six bamboo canes, three on each side. Cut and tape long triangles of paper in between the canes. Glue layers of paper scales onto each of the triangular panels. Tightly wire the bamboo canes together at one end (at the shoulder), and wrap with a strip of fabric for safety.

Cross-curricular links

Geography: research a 'real' dragon such as the Komodo dragon.

Literacy: write a story about a dragon from the dragon's point of view.

Science: research what happens when you add water or dry out different substances.

Beowulf

In *Beowulf*, Michael Morpurgo retells the story of this great Scandinavian hero's epic battles with monsters and dragons. This project develops collaborative working in groups, where children create a 3D scene from the book by building layers similar to a stage set.

3D collage

Approach

1   In class, read *Beowulf*, retold by Michael Morpurgo. Talk about the story and choose a scene to recreate. In the artwork pictured, the class show Beowulf's deadly enemy, the dragon, guarding a hoard of golden treasure deep in the cliffs.

2   Use graphic media to explore lines, marks and textures. Ask children to use one page of their sketchbooks to experiment with each of the three visual elements. Allow plenty of time for children to explore and experiment in preparation for finished artwork.

3   Encourage children to work in groups on larger-scale collaborative mark-making. Colour can be added using chalk and/or oil pastels to mix and make patches of colour. Ask the class to decide which colours each group will use, for example gold or silver for treasure, bright colours for jewels or grey and black for caves. This work will be used later as collage material.

Resources
- Images of dragons, caves, treasure
- Sketchbooks
- Marker pens
- Coloured drawing inks
- Brushes
- Oil pastels and chalk pastels
- A4 and A1 paper and card
- PVA glue
- Scissors
- Masking tape

4   Research images online of treasure, jewels, goblets, and so on and make a presentation. Research images of dragons, especially dragon eyes, teeth, nostrils, tails, claws, scales and wings. Look at images of caves. Use the presentations as stimuli for sketchbook drawing.

5   Encourage each group to create their own version of the scene from *Beowulf*. Each group should share sketchbook drawings; discuss whose dragon design will be used and who will work on the foreground, middle ground and background. Decide on scale. Some groups will want to work small-scale, using A3 card, while others will want to work on A1.

6   Give each group three pieces of card of their chosen size. Ask children to tear up their earlier colour experiments and collage each of the pieces on card.

7   Explain to the children they will need to draw a line 4 cm across the bottom of each of the three layers of card. Fold the card back to allow it to stand up. Begin with the background cave layer and tape the folded card to a separate base piece of cardboard. Do the same for the dragon layer, leaving a 4 cm gap between them. Finally the front treasure layer forms a frame around the whole scene. This step requires children to apply problem-solving skills to find ways of making the scene stand up. One solution is to roll paper to make cylindrical tubes and snip them at the base.

8   Stick the three layers together with masking tape, so they sit forward in a scene. Mount on a display board together with a title.

Cross-curricular links

Geography: look at Scandinavian countries on a map.

History: research the Vikings.

Literacy: research myths and legends of great heroes and heroines.

Write a 'saga' of your own, with a modern hero/heroine.

Dinosaur tales

Dinosaurs, real and imaginary, are always favourite characters. This project covers a range of art processes, including mark-making, drawing and working with clay. This project is introduced by investigating texture through mark-making and taking photographs. *Tyrannosaurus Drip* by Julia Donaldson can inspire a display setting for children's model dinosaurs, including prehistoric trees, both large and small.

Textured dinosaurs

Approach

1   Many schools will not use 'real' clay because they do not own a kiln. It is better to fire the clay, but it isn't necessary. The models in the display are not fired.

2   Make a collection of different textures: feathers, moss, tree bark, bread, wool, metal, twigs and silk fabric. Talk about the textures. Invite children to touch and describe what each of the things in the texture collection feels like and make a list of the words. Words like: rough, smooth, feathery, bumpy, soft, sharp, and so on are often forthcoming. Extend their vocabulary and encourage words like pitted, velvety, jagged, grainy and spongy.

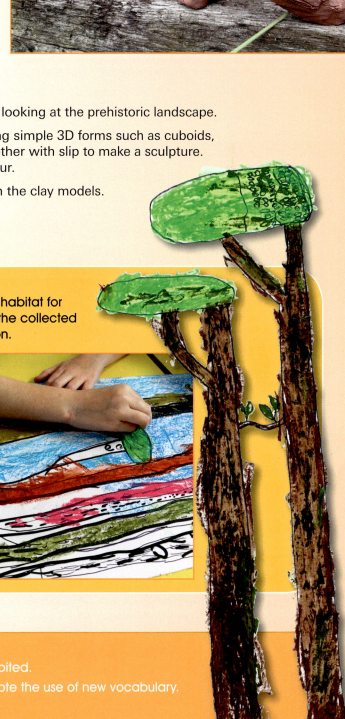

3 Using large A1 sheets and graphic materials, encourage children to experiment making marks related to the texture words. Remind children not to draw pictures but to focus on the textures. For younger children, model the activity first by inviting children to make a mark on a sample sheet of paper, for example a rough mark using a black wax crayon; a rougher mark using a thick black marker pen; a soft mark, and so on. Children can then make their own marks.

4 Ask children to use cameras to take photographs of different textured surfaces around the school.

5 Make mini sketchbooks for collecting textures.

6 Demonstrate how to use a rolling pin to roll out a lump of clay and draw different textures into the surface with a clay modelling tool. Push a pencil through the sampler before the clay dries so that it can be threaded with string and hung up as part of the display.

7 Read and discuss *Tyrannosaurus Drip* by Julia Donaldson, looking at the prehistoric landscape.

8 Ask children to experiment with their ball of clay by making simple 3D forms such as cuboids, cylinders, pyramids, and so on. They can 'glue' these together with slip to make a sculpture. Talk about which 3D forms they can use to make a dinosaur.

9 Assemble all the stages in the investigations together with the clay models. Create the title from an online alphabet template.

Resources

- *Tyrannosaurus Drip* by Julia Donaldson
- Texture collection
- A4 and A1 paper
- Marker pens
- Oil pastels and chalk pastels
- Cameras, computer
- Clay
- **Texture sampler:** a lump of clay per child (about the size of a tennis ball)
- **Dinosaur:** a lump of clay per child (about the size of an apple)
- Clay boards
- Polythene to protect tables,
- Slip (clay and water mix)
- Clay tools

Further ideas

Make a large-scale habitat for the dinosaurs using the collected textures for inspiration.

Cross-curricular links

Geography: look at the different world the dinosaurs inhabited.

Literacy: use the models in small-world situations to promote the use of new vocabulary. Write a short play with the model dinosaurs.

Science: research dinosaurs and fossils.

Dragons and slayers

George and the Dragon by Chris Wormell is a humorous look at a mythical dragon who is scared of mice. Children will love finding out that even mighty dragons have fears and that small creatures can be heroes!

3D dragon

Approach

1 Talk about what makes the dragon so powerful and frightening. Discuss the dragons' size, how they breathe fire and their wings.

2 Use a selection of boxes (reinforced by packing them with scrunched-up newspaper) to create a dragon shape. Glue the boxes together and hold in position with masking tape. Use two kitchen rolls positioned next to one another with a shallow rectangular box underneath to make the dragon's long nose and jaw.

3 Cover the entire dragon's shape with coloured paper and stick down with PVA glue. Do not cover the hollow ends of the dragon's nose.

4 Stuff tights with newspaper and staple to the end of the body to create a tail. Cover in coloured paper.

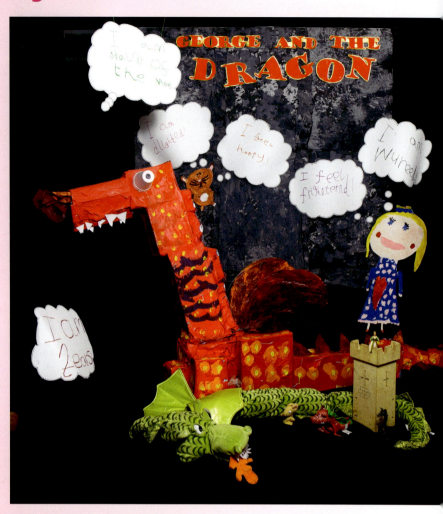

5 In advance, an adult should make two wire hoops by bending a length of wire so the two ends touch and fixing the ends together with tape. Make sure the ends are completely covered. Repeat with a new length of wire. Glue the hoops to layered red and orange paper and allow to dry (see the Shimmering stars method on page 15). Use the off-cuts to make the scales for the dragon's back. Fix the wings to the body by poking the ends of the wire through the cardboard.

6 Paint patterns on the dragon's body and glue the scales to the dragon's back.

7 Use polystyrene balls or cups for the dragon's eyes and add card for the teeth. Stuff red tissue paper into the dragon's nostrils so it looks like it's breathing fire.

8 To create a cave wall, use sponges with grey and white paint on sheets of black paper. Staple these to the wall with some black cloth.

9 Draw large pictures on card of the princess and George and paint with watercolours.

10 Provide dress-ups for the children to role-play the story. Ask the children to 'hot seat' the characters. For example, *how did the dragon feel when he saw the mouse?*

11 Use the ideas from the 'hot seat' to create thought bubbles to add to the display. Ask children to use their phonics to sound out and spell the words.

Resources
- *George and the Dragon* by Chris Wormell
- Boxes
- Tubes
- PVA glue
- Newspaper
- Tights
- Stapler
- Masking tape
- Coloured paper
- Paint
- Tissue paper
- Polystyrene cup
- Two lengths of wire, each around 80 cm long
- Wire cutters
- Card

Gaudi dragons

Approach

1   Use small world dragons and lizards as a basis for drawings using pencil and pen.

2   Show the children pictures of the mosaic used to decorate Gaudi's lizard at Park Güell and ask them to think about pattern for their dragons.

3   Create a 'wash' background on cartridge paper using ink, water and sponges. Allow these to dry. Ask the children to draw a larger version of their dragon on top of their wash. This can be done by looking or by projecting the image onto the background using an overhead projector or visualiser. Go over the pencil outline using a permanent fine marker.

4   Use thick powder paint to decorate the dragon with a mosaic effect by dotting paint on with a fine brush. Highlight areas of the dragon using oil pastels.

5   Spray the background with water. Use a dry paintbrush to sprinkle powdered ink onto the water.

6   Create a dragon's tail on the display board using tissue paper, cellophane and paint. Display the children's dragons on top.

Resources

- Images from Park Güell
- Dragon and lizard small world figures
- Cartridge paper
- Pens and pencils
- Ink
- Water
- Sponges

- Permanent fine marker
- Powder or ready-mix paint
- Oil pastels
- Powdered ink
- Brushes
- Tissue paper and cellophane for tail

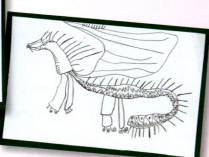

Cross-curricular links

Art: create dragons from clay.

Literacy: write poems or descriptions of dragons.

Music: use percussion instruments to make sound effects linked to dragons, for example symbols for flapping wings, drums for the heavy footsteps, and so on. Create pieces of dragon music using the different sound effects.

PSHE: circle time sessions about things that are worrying. What are people scared of? What can people do when they are scared?

Enchanted lands

There are many magical texts that can encourage children to think about fairies and enchanted lands. Books such as *Jethro Byrde Fairy Child* by Bob Graham provide a stimulus for discussions about friendships, picnics and fairy transport. *Imagine You're a Fairy* by Meg Clibbon and Lucy Clibbon offers lots of possible lines of development, for example make your own fairy wishing wells, design your own fairy outfits and accessories, and even write spells to turn your teachers into frogs!

Fairy-travellers' picnic

Approach

1 Read *Jethro Byrde Fairy Child* to the children. Use the book to discuss friendships, imaginary and real, and the idea of children being able to see magical beings that adults cannot.

2 Ask children to go on a fairy picnic. Get them to design a food menu that fairies might like. Organise a cooking session to make some of the foods listed on their menus, for example fairy cakes, cucumber sandwiches and jam sandwiches. Link to ideas on healthy eating. Check dietary requirements and allergies before commencing.

3 Make observational drawings of the real food that the children have made and paint the drawings.

4 Use model-making resources to construct simple vehicles for the fairies to travel to the picnic in. Cover with paper and paste, then paint. Introduce children to axles and how they work. Make simple axles using dowel and milk bottle lids.

5 Add signs to the tops of the vehicles and display parked around the fairy picnic. Wooden props and glass jewels have been used in the photographs.

Resources

- *Jethro Byrde Fairy Child* by Bob Graham
- Powder paint
- Paper
- Box-modelling resources: cardboard boxes, tubes, pipe cleaners, brightly coloured cellophane
- Dowel and plastic milk bottle lids for making wheels
- Glitter
- Shiny paper and tissue paper
- Sticky tape
- PVA glue

Fairyland maps and fairy houses

Approach

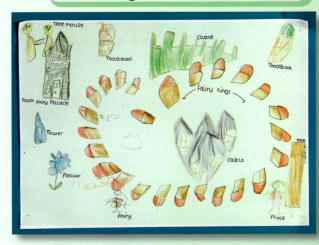

1   Look at maps of the Enchanted Forest and Fairyland in *Imagine You're a Fairy*. Ask children to draw their own maps including places where fairies may live, go to train or sit for wishing. Label the maps and use them to give directions for small-world play.

2   Design houses for fairies. A 'visiting fairy' could leave notes for the children asking for a new home. This gives purpose to the activity and provides letter writing opportunities. Ask children to draw designs on cartridge paper and paint them. Add glitter and stars or collage materials to make the homes sparkle!

3   Use boxes, plastic tubs and cardboard tubes to construct 3D homes for the fairies. Build up basic house shapes, for example tubes make good trunks for tree houses, balloons covered with paper and PVA glue can create pumpkin-shaped homes. When using cardboard boxes, show children how to strengthen them before decorating by stuffing them with old scrunched-up newspaper.

4   Cover with PVA glue and paper. When dry, paint in suitable colours.

5   Add details to the homes using collage materials, for example cellophane windows surrounded by glitter, doors with split-pin handles, chimneys with curled pipe cleaners.

Resources
- *Imagine You're a Fairy* by Meg Clibbon and Lucy Clibbon
- Cartridge paper
- Pencils and colouring pencils
- Model-making equipment
- Newspaper
- Paper and glue
- Powder or ready-mixed paint
- Glitter
- Collage materials, for example split pins, cellophane, pipe cleaners

Cross-curricular links

Literacy: write invitations to the fairy picnic for friends and family.

Younger readers may also wish to do some further reading on enchanted lands. *The Tiara Club* by Vivian French is a good story to start with.

This project could also be extended to older children by asking them to read *The Colour of Magic* by Terry Pratchett or Diana Wynne Jones's *Cart and Cwidder* and *The Crown of Dalemark*.

Maths: set the children maths problems relating to party planning and give them pretend money and props to work with. How many guests will you invite and how much food will you need? How much will you spend on food for the party at the shop?

The Golden Age of Greece

Monsters and mazes

The myth of *Theseus and the Minotaur* can be fascinating to children as the story involves an impossible labyrinth, a monster, a powerful king, a brave son and a daring girl. Labyrinths and mazes have been drawn and made throughout history and provide the inspiration for the following project. Would you have been able to find your way out of the labyrinth in the Cretan palace of Knossos? Show children images of the Greek ruins archaeologists now believe were the site of the labyrinth and ask them to create their own impossible mazes.

Resources

- A suitable version of *Theseus and the Minotaur*
- White backing paper
- Red paper and scissors
- Children's drawings of mazes photocopied onto acetate
- Images of Theseus, Ariadne and the Minotaur
- Coloured thread
- White paper and drawing and painting materials
- Blue tack

Collective labyrinth

Approach

1. Tell the story of *Theseus and the Minotaur* and discuss a display with children.

2. Back your display with white paper. On red paper, ask children to draw the outline of a labyrinth big enough to fill the display board. Cut out and stick onto the display.

3. Photocopy the children's pictures of mazes (see page opposite) onto acetate.

4. Fix the acetate pictures side by side onto the main display so that they cover the entire board. The red labyrinth should be easily seen through the acetate pictures.

5. Finally, show images of Greek figures and encourage groups of children to draw the Minotaur, Theseus and Ariadne about 10 cm high. Cut out and stick these figures onto the display with blue tack, so they can be moved around as children retell the story. Use a length of thread to move around the display with Theseus.

Children's mazes

Show the children pictures and prints by Escher. Look at the way he uses optical illusions to create impossible ideas. Also look at the different mazes and labyrinths that occur in art, literature and in places such as Hampton Court Palace.

Use these ideas as inspiration for creating an impossible drawing of a maze or labyrinth.

Resources

- White paper (20 cm × 20 cm)
- Pencils
- Acetate
- Escher pictures

Approach

1 Study images of a range of mazes and labyrinths throughout history. In particular, look at the work of Escher.

2 Encourage children to create their own mazes and labyrinths with pencil and paper.

3 Photocopy the drawings in high contrast to make them black and white.

4 Photocopy drawings onto acetate for use in the main display.

Further ideas

Write play scripts inspired by *Theseus and the Minotaur* and act out the plays. Encourage younger children to retell the story with moving figures. Greek poets were famous for their use of adjectives. Describe the Minotaur's labyrinth from Theseus's point of view.

Cross-curricular links

History: discuss written and archaeological evidence to decide whether the Theseus myth is based on fact. Investigate any local legends to see if they were based on truth. Similar mazes have been found in Cornish cave paintings, on Roman coins and in Native American drawings – where did they get these similar ideas from?

Maths: explore formulae for completing mazes. The Cretan labyrinth has the simple formula of A to B as there is only one way in. Some are more complex. You can turn a maze into a 'network' by making a diagram of the decision points (nodes) of the maze. Compare the level sequences of the Cretan and Jericho mazes using a network.

Hopes and fears

The Greek myth of *Pandora's Box* explores what happened when Pandora disobeyed the gods and how all the evil in the world was unleashed. However, as long as there is hope, all can be well.

This myth has many themes woven throughout it; power, creation, curiosity, disobedience, punishment, despair, terror and finally hope. The story is ideal for interpreting as a play by getting the children to first discuss the story, then encouraging them to write and then act out their own scripts, using modern dialogue.

Resources

- A suitable version of *Pandora's Box*
- Photocopied playscripts
- Modroc 'evils'
- Strong, flexible wire (about 8 m in total)
- Cardboard box
- Brown and gold paper
- Clay figures

Pandora's Box

Approach

1   Photocopy playscripts children have written large enough to be read at a distance. Cover the background of your display with the enlarged text.

2   Show children how to make cuboids from 3D nets. Decide together on the shape of Pandora's Box and make a 3D net out of strong card, about 30 cm × 20 cm. Cover with brown paper and add a clasp and studs using gold or silver paper.

3   Fix four strong, flexible wires to the bottom of the box, hooking them through the bottom. Have three wires on the left of your display and one on the right. Place a few rocks in the bottom of the box to weigh it down. Slide the plaster 'evils' (see page opposite) onto three of the wires. Twist the 'evils' away from the background and attach the wires at the top of the display. Fix 'hope' onto the right-hand wire at the top in the same way.

4   Surround the box with clay figures of Pandora.

Clay figures

Approach

1 In the myth, humans and Pandora are made from the Earth. Show children images of ancient Greek pottery figures and contrast these with clay figures by contemporary artist, Anthony Gormley.

2 Using air-drying clay, encourage children to imagine their clay figures of Pandora are being moulded out of the Earth.

3 Arrange the figures around the main display.

Resources
- Images of clay figures
- Air-drying clay

The evils and hope

Approach

Resources
- Wire mesh
- Modroc
- Paint
- Newspaper
- PVA glue
- Strips of material

1 Discuss with children why we might want to explain the bad things in our world. Why is hope so important? Encourage children to put a face and a character to the abstract evils using plaster strips, which is light enough to be supported on wire. This will make the figures look as if they are flying out of Pandora's box.

2 Bend wire mesh into a shape which resembles an abstract person.

3 Cut the Modroc into 20 cm lengths. Dip in water, wring out and mould around the wire mesh. Only use two layers of plaster strips on each shape to keep the models light. Make holes at the top and bottom of the models, before they dry.

4 When dry, cut out letters from a newspaper and attach to the models to spell out the words of the 'evils', such as 'fear' and 'war'. Then paint in dark colours, leaving the words showing. Leave 'Hope' white.

5 Glue thin strips of material to the models to create the impression of movement. Attach to the main display by sliding the models onto the wires.

Cross-curricular links

Literacy: read creation stories from different cultures.

Maths: explore 3D nets for cube, cylinder and regular pyramids.

PSHE: discuss with children what makes them feel hopeful.

Flying high

The myth of *Daedalus and Icarus* explains how Daedalus invented a set of wings for flying but rashly, his son Icarus flew too close to the sun, where his wings disintegrated and he crashed to earth. In this project, the myth is used to spark children's imagination as they storyboard and make their own concertina-style book or group big book.

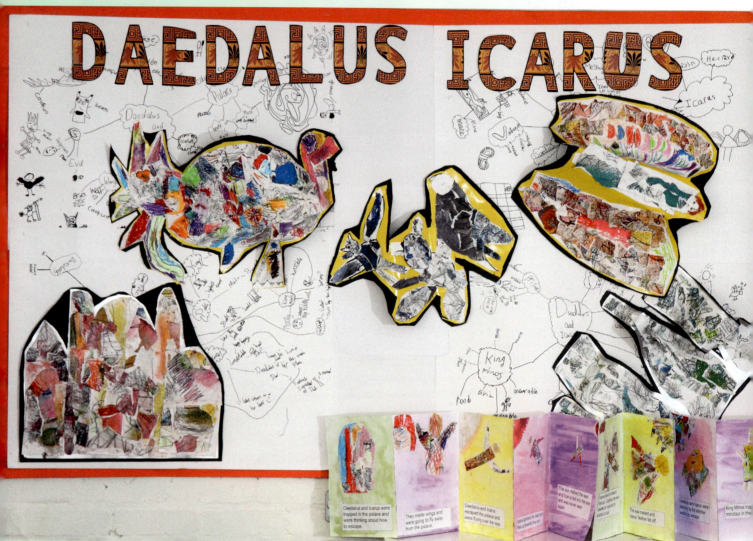

Collage creatures

Approach

1 Read *The Orchard Book of Greek Myths* retold by Geraldine McCaughrean. Discuss the story of Icarus with the children. Ask them whether they would like to have wings. Give them A3 paper to make mind maps of the story. The mind maps will show what the children remember and enjoy about the story and will be helpful in the next activity.

2 Working in five groups, ask children to make a display about the Icarus myth. Each group will make one artwork focusing on a key element of the story. Children can use their mind maps to select an event.

3 Each group should select a colour theme for their artwork. Then, using oil pastels and chalk pastels, give each group an A1 piece of paper to experiment with colour mixing. These colour-mixing explorations will be used to create their collage.

Resources

- *The Orchard Book of Greek Myths* retold by Geraldine McCaughrean
- A4, A3 and A1 paper
- Black marker pens
- Oil pastels and chalk pastels
- Coloured drawing inks and brushes
- Scissors
- A1 coloured card
- A4 white card
- Glue and sticky tape

4   Give each group a second A1 sheet of paper to draw the outline of their picture. Using torn-up pieces from the colour-mixing sheet and PVA glue, ask them to collage the picture. Cut around the collage and glue onto coloured card. The children could add a sentence explaining what is happening in the Icarus story at this point.

5   Make an A4 concertina book. Each child should create an individual collage illustration on A4 paper from the Icarus story and print or write out a sentence explaining what is happening in the scene. The collage technique is described in the previous activity. Put the individual collages aside.

6   Discuss Emma Chichester Clark's illustrations for the Icarus story in *The Orchard Book of Greek Myths*. Give each child an A4 piece of paper and demonstrate how to use ink wash. Dip a paint brush in a pot of clean water and gently 'paint' the part of the picture you want to colour with water. Next, dip the brush into coloured ink and paint over the wet part. Work on different parts of the picture, making sure not to work on two adjacent parts, otherwise the ink will 'bleed'. Allow the paint washes to dry.

7   Cut out the collage pictures and glue to the ink-washed paper. Add the written or printed text. Join the individual pages together with tape to create a concertina book. If you glue thin white card behind each page, the book will stand up.

One day they wanted to escape from the palace so they made themselves some wings to fly away with feathers glued on with wax.

Cross-curricular links

ICT: create a photo story presentation and record the children reading their page.

Literacy: a myth is usually based on a true event. Write a modern myth inspired by a national or local news story or write a modern-day drama inspired by the Icarus story.

Music: make and record compositions and add to the photo story.

Hercules the hero

Greek myths often feature heroic deeds and magical beasts. One such myth is the story of Hercules who was told to spend 12 years serving a horrible king in order to redeem himself from his wrongs. Hercules achieved all the seemingly impossible tasks the king gave him and became a great hero.

Cartoon strip

Approach

1 Read children a suitable version of *The Labours of Hercules* – various versions are available online.

2 Introduce children to pop artist Roy Lichtenstein. Discuss his use of colour, graphics and space and explain that he was heavily influenced by comic books.

3 Discuss the idea of linking the story of Hercules with producing a comic strip. Show the children comic books, modern graphic novels and if possible watch an old Batman TV show focusing on the inserted graphics.

4 In sketchbooks develop impact words with shaped lettering. Place the words inside callouts and colour with marker pens or paints using a limited palette.

Resources

- A suitable version of *The Labours of Hercules*
- Examples of work by Roy Lichtenstein
- Comics, graphic novels and Batman TV show
- Sketchbooks and A3 paper
- Pencils, marker pens, felt-tipped pens and paint
- Thick card and scissors
- Sticky pads

5 Divide the labours of Hercules between 12 groups of children.

6 Working in pairs, ask children to think about Hercules' stance when fighting the monsters. Get one child in each pair to pose while their partner draws them as a stick person in their sketchbook capturing the action movements. Swap roles and repeat the process.

7 Ask children to develop their designs to turn their stick figures into Hercules. This can be done by making the sticks in their drawings into varied oval or sausage shapes and smoothing out the lines to create a figurative form.

8 Ask children to add a monster based on the labours. To add a pop art feel, discourage children from drawing a background.

9   Transfer drawings to A3 sheets and paint in bright colours using a limited palette. Add outlines and features with black marker pen.

10 As a class, select one impact word from the children's sketchbooks for each A3 image.

11 Use tracing paper to transfer the design to thick card. Colour using marker or felt-tipped pens.

12 Trim large pictures to create interesting shapes. Use sticky pads to add callouts to the artwork to create shadows.

13 Arrange the finished artworks in order of the labours on suitable bright background paper. Arrange dividing strips on top to create the impression of a comic strip.

Myths in Greek theatre

Approach

1   The Ancient Greeks were the inventors of theatre and in Greek society plays were often put on to appease or glorify the gods or tell of victories and heroes. Select a favourite Greek myth and draw up a story-telling map with the class focusing on the different characters, settings and events. Create masks for a performance.

2   In pairs, draw oval shapes for the outline of the faces onto a large piece of cardboard.

3   Use scrunched-up newspaper to create 3D shapes for the hair, cheeks, eyebrows, eyes, nose and mouth. Use masking tape to hold features in place.

4   Use heavy-duty scissors or a craft knife to define the chin and shape the face (adult supervision necessary).

5   Apply one layer of Modroc over the moulded side of the mask and leave to dry.

6   Paint with ready-mix paints. Tragic and comic masks look best in single pastel colours.

7   Low-light masks by using a dry brush on the areas of the face where you would expect to see shadows.

Resources

- Cardboard sheets
- Marker pens
- Newspaper
- Masking tape
- Scissors or craft knives (adult supervision required)
- Modroc
- Ready-mix paint

Cross-curricular links

Design and Technology: investigate why a limited range of colours are used in the production of comic books.

History: create masks for Roman, Viking, Egyptian or other myths.

ICT: scan the Hercules images onto a computer to produce the comic-strip style illustrations. Add text and sound to accompany the story.

Heroic characters

Ask children to apply to become a Greek hero, such as Hercules. Some previous teaching about the Greek societies of Athens and Sparta will help here, for example using *The Orchard Book of Greek Myths* retold by Geraldine McCaughrean.

Hero applications

Approach

1   Split children into mixed ability groups and create a list of the qualities of a Greek hero to present to the class.

2   Discuss what sorts of things a hero might do to demonstrate the heroic abilities chosen and explain how these opportunities might occur in Ancient Greek society.

3   Show the class a teacher-prepared job advertisement for a hero. Ask children to think about the content of the advertisement and to use this to write a letter of application for the job. (Remind children how to structure a letter.) Revise and edit as necessary.

4   Age pieces of A4 paper to look like vellum by dipping them into cold tea or using a very weak ink powder solution in brown or ochre. Leave to dry.

5   Show children Greek key patterns (images available online). Decorate the borders of aged sheets with Greek key patterns using ink or black pen.

6   Write out the letters neatly using handwriting pens.

7   As a class, read the applications and shortlist applicants. Interview them and decide on a hero.

8   Refer to images of Greek soldiers and their costumes to create the body of a hero using art papers.

9   Take a photo of the successful applicant to form the hero's face. Display letters around the body of the hero.

Resources

- A4 paper
- Cold tea or ink powders in brown or ochre and brushes
- Images of Greek key patterns
- Ink or fine black felt-tipped pens
- Handwriting pens
- Images of Greek soldiers and costumes
- Art papers

Cross-curricular links

Drama: produce a playlet with the hero fulfilling their role based on a Greek myth such as Jason of the Argonauts, Hercules or Theseus.